15-19

D1083787

DIVIDED MINDS

ALSO BY CAROL POLSGROVE

It Wasn't Pretty, Folks, But Didn't We Have Fun? Esquire *in the Sixties*

DIVIDED MINDS

Intellectuals
and the
Civil Rights
Movement

Carol Polsgrove

W. W. NORTON & COMPANY   NEW YORK   LONDON

Permission to quote from "Liberalism and the Negro: A Round-Table Discussion: James
    Baldwin, Nathan Glazer, Sidney Hook, Gunnar Myrdal," *Commentary*, March 1964:
    Commentary.
Where needed, permission to quote from unpublished papers has been granted by the following:
For Harold R. Isaacs' interview with John Hope Franklin: John Hope Franklin.
For Harold R. Isaacs' interview with James Baldwin: Gloria E. K. Smart.
For Harold R. Isaacs' interview with Kenneth B. Clark: Kenneth Clark.
For Hoyt W. Fuller: Archives and Special Collections, Robert W. Woodruff Library, Atlanta
    University Center.
For Harold R. Isaacs: Institute Archives and Special Collections, Massachusetts Institute of
    Technology.
For Pauli Murray: the Charlotte Sheedy Literary Agency.
For Jean Stein's interview of Kenneth B. Clark: Jean Stein.
For C. Vann Woodward: Yale University Library.
For Howard Zinn: Howard Zinn.

For information about permission to reproduce selections from this book, write to Permissions,
W. W. Norton & Company, Inc., 500 Fifth Avenue, New York, NY 10110

The text of this book is composed in Bell with the display set in Bell and Univers Condensed
Light
Composition by Gina Webster
Manufacturing by The Courier Companies, Inc.
Book design by Dana Sloan
Production manager: Andrew Marasia
Manuscript editor: Otto Sonntag

Library of Congress Cataloging-in-Publication Data

Polsgrove, Carol.
    Divided minds : intellectuals and the civil rights movement / Carol Polsgrove.
        p. cm.
    Includes bibliographical references (p.) and index.
    ISBN 0-393-02013-4
        1. Afro-Americans—Civil rights—History—20th century. 2. Civil rights movements—
United States—History—20th century. 3. Intellectuals—United States—Political activity—
History—20th century. 4. Intellectuals—New York (State)—New York—Political
activity—Hisotry—20th century. 5. United States—Race relations. 6. United States—
Intellectual life—20th century. 7. New York (N.Y.)—Intellectual life—20th century. I. Title.

E185.61 .P67 2001
323.1'196073—dc21   00-053308

W. W. Norton & Company, Inc., 500 Fifth Avenue, New York, N.Y. 10110
www.wwnorton.com

W. W. Norton & Company Ltd., 10 Coptic Street, London WC1A 1PU

1 2 3 4 5 6 7 8 9 0

To my mother, Emma Osborne Claxon, and the memory of my father, William Neville Claxon

CONTENTS

ACKNOWLEDGMENTS

This book rests largely on records from the time, but I have also had the help of several men and women who were there. I had several long talks with historians John Hope Franklin and C. Vann Woodward. Despite his ill health, Kenneth B. Clark graciously welcomed me to his home in Hastings-on-Hudson, and his associate Russia Hughes supplied me with useful information and sources. His editor, friend, and co-worker Jeannette Hopkins also shared her memories and correspondence.

Herbert Hill, former labor secretary of the NAACP, editor of two literary anthologies of writing by African American authors, Evjue-Bascom Professor of African American Studies and professor of industrial relations at the University of Wisconsin at Madison, generously shared his memories of several key figures in this story—James Baldwin, Ralph Ellison, Richard Wright, Lawrence Reddick. Himself a man of the left, Hill knew the political and the literary scenes of these years well, and in countless ways, large and small, helped me to understand it.

Through Hill, I reached June Shagaloff Alexander, who served as NAACP education secretary and worked with Kenneth B. Clark on a proposal for how *Brown v. Board of Education* should be implemented. She also became a close friend of James Baldwin. She, like Hill, talked with me often, offering me insights into Baldwin's role and the role played by intellectuals in general. Both Hill and Alexander read and commented on the manuscript.

I talked with historians Howard Zinn and Staughton Lynd, who both read the manuscript. I talked with August Meier, who participated in the movement and has done so much as a historian to document it. Bennett H. Wall, an eyewitness of several episodes I've described, talked with me. Lillian Ross recalled for me *New Yorker* editor William

Shawn's response to the essay that Shawn called "Letter from a Region in My Mind," and published first in his magazine, before it became the centerpiece of *The Fire Next Time*. James Baldwin's old friend and editor Sol Stein recalled Baldwin's early celebrity days. Others graciously replied to written queries: Gloria Karefa-Smart, Baldwin's sister and guardian of his literary estate; Sam Allen, who gave me insight into the American Society of African Culture; Don Blackmer, emeritus professor, Massachusetts Institute of Technology, who supplied useful information about Harold Isaacs.

I felt closest to the movement when I traveled south to visit archives and southern scenes of action. In Montgomery, Alabama, retired Alabama State professor Norman Walton sat with me on a back bench of Dexter Avenue Baptist Church and shared his memories of the bus boycott and student sit-ins. In Selma, Alabama, lawyer J. L. Chestnut Jr. brought back James Baldwin's visits there. In Tuskegee, Alabama, Mrs. Amelia Boynton described Bloody Sunday, as clear in her memory as if it had happened yesterday.

I owe special acknowledgment to my friend Carolyn Toll Oppenheim, who helped me to understand the impact that the anti-communist movement had on American political life and on the movement in particular. I owe much to my brother, William Neville Claxon Jr., a professor at the University of South Carolina at Aiken, for his sharp editorial eye. He read the manuscript several times, at several stages.

My Indiana University colleague A. B. Assensoh made me aware of Lawrence Reddick's significant role; former colleagues Jane Rhodes and Lynn Hudson suggested I take a close look at Pauli Murray. Several colleagues and friends read portions of the manuscript in draft: John A. Mccluskey Jr., Eileen Julien, Tyrone Simpson, Keith Woods, Linda Lawson, David Nord, Larry Friedman, Marcia Debnam, David Boeyink, Gerald Coomer, Becky O'Malley, Cliff Hawkins. Others helped on particular points: Chana Kai Lee, Dan Wakefield, Ursula Davis.

I thank the fine professional staff at libraries whose archives proved so valuable, and I thank the libraries for permitting me to quote from their collections. Diana Lachatanere, curator for the Schomburg Center for Research in Black Culture, deserves special mention for locating documents on Reddick's departure from the Schomburg.

Indiana University provided research fellowships, travel grants, time, and a fine library. I thank student researchers Ryan Vertner and Chuck Coulter for assistance.

My daughter, my mother, and my father gave me unfailing personal support.

I was honored by my colleague Wil Counts, who took my photograph for this book's jacket; his enduring photographs from Little Rock have brought that crisis home to several generations of Americans.

I thank my agent, Doe Coover, for her support, and, at W. W. Norton, Gerry Howard, for getting me off to a good start before he left, and to Tom Bissell, Amy Cherry, and Nomi Victor for so capably seeing the manuscript to completion.

Finally, I recall with gratitude Robert Hayden, a good poet and a kind man, who guided me through a thesis on Ralph Ellison's *Invisible Man* many years ago.

PROLOGUE

D rinking with a companion after he heard that the United States had bombed Hiroshima, Horace Cayton, Negro co-author of *Black Metropolis,* raised a toast: "To our country, the United States of America, which, by its superior white strength and Aryan intelligence, killed seventy-eight thousand Japanese—pardon me, little yellow bastards—to make the world safe for democracy." In the days to come, Cayton found his public persona unraveling. He was no longer able to negotiate the distance between what he felt and what he could say to white people. One evening he was to speak to an interracial group that had built a community center for Negroes in a small Wisconsin city. Writing later about what happened to him there, he would say,

> *They had wanted some important Negro leader to tell them what a splendid thing they were doing, but instead I found myself talking about the fear and hate that Negroes felt toward whites and the guilt and hate that whites in turn felt toward Negroes. I ended by pointing out that I had not seen one Negro in a responsible position in their city, not even as a store clerk. The chairman of the meeting, the wife of a local banker, sank lower and lower in her seat as I destroyed her dream of brotherhood; when I arrived back in Chicago the next morning I canceled the balance of my speaking engagements.*

Cayton found himself face to face with the question "How could I any longer talk to comfortable, complacent white people about racial good will . . . ?" His ability to speak to whites through clenched teeth had vanished.[1]

Disconnecting himself from the man he had been, troubled by

events in his personal life, he fell into such depths that he was not sure he would ever climb out. But he did, struggling back to the surface, living in New York and still managing to write his column for the *Pittsburgh Courier*. On a May morning in 1954, nearly ten years after the bomb fell on Hiroshima, he read the news that the Supreme Court, ruling in *Brown v. Board of Education*, had declared school segregation unconstitutional. He had been on his way from his apartment in Greenwich Village up to Harlem to get his hair cut. It was a long way to go for a haircut, and he did not like having to do it, particularly on a day when he might be missing something newsworthy at the United Nations, but as a Negro he did not feel he had a choice; if he wanted to find a barber willing to give him a haircut, he would have to go to Harlem.

Then he opened the *New York Times*.

"The magnitude of the decision shocked me," he would write; "a large hole had opened in the dike of segregation, and through it would soon pour a torrent." Cayton had known that the United States could not long hold on to segregation in a world demanding freedom. Here, now, the country had come to a decisive turn in the road. What, then, was he doing on a subway to Harlem to get his hair cut? At Grand Central Terminal he got off and stepped into the station barbershop. The barber there cut his hair, and Cayton made a new, personal beginning. "[F]or the first time I felt free to go any place, providing I had money to pay the bill."[2] For Horace Cayton, a new era had begun.

Four years after the Supreme Court decision, Robert Coles, a white northern psychiatrist who was to become one of the country's leading public intellectuals, was bicycling near a beach outside Biloxi, Mississippi, when he heard sounds of conflict. He soon grasped the situation: a Negro woman wanted to swim at the beach; a group of whites blocked her way. The woman's protest brought him up short. "For a few seconds, I suppose, my lifetime—and I don't think only mine—was recapitulated: its innocence, its indifference, its ignorance, its sheltered quiet, its half-and-half mixture of moral inertia and well-intentioned effort." After that, Coles sought out newspaper stories about the integration of schools—stories he would have passed over earlier. He wondered how he "could have lived so long under a clearly oppressive social, political, and economic system, only to have been so blithely, so innocently unaware of its nature."[3]

Robert Coles was an educated man. He was acquainted with Reinhold Niebuhr and Anna Freud. He had studied at Harvard. Yet he had never given much thought, he would later say, to the fact of American life that had burst astonishingly upon him.

Not all white intellectuals were so slow to confront the meaning of America's racial divide and the difference that *Brown v. Board of Education* could make to it. But the decision that had "opened a dike" for Horace Cayton barely brushed the thoughts of a surprising number of other intellectuals—men and women who had made it their business to understand the culture. In the years after the Supreme Court opened the door to change, white intellectuals, in the North and the South, milled about outside the door, debating among themselves how fast America ought to go through it.

When Swedish sociologist Gunnar Myrdal visited the American North and South in the late 1930s, he had found among whites an ignorance of Negro life so profound that it could not be accidental. Wrong ideas, derived from a "distortion of knowledge," justified the status quo. When Myrdal traveled through the North, he found there, too, "astonishing ignorance," though it derived less from denial than from indifference. Many northerners, he observed, knew more about conditions in foreign countries than about the conditions of Negro life in America. In his landmark book *An American Dilemma*, Myrdal concluded, optimistically, that the majority of Americans outside the South would "give the Negro a substantially better deal" if they understood more about Negro life. The difficulty, he acknowledged, was the wall whites had thrown up to protect themselves from knowing.[4]

White intellectuals had played their part in maintaining that wall. Speaking to the American Society of African Culture in 1959, Harold R. Isaacs, a white researcher from the Massachusetts Institute of Technology, brought in a justified verdict: "Most Negro scholars and writers of the last two or three generations have had all their energies quite fully engaged in the enormous task of lifting the Negro's place in American life and history out of the mire of ignorance, prejudice, and obloquy in which so much white writing and scholarship confined it in the past."[5] Having helped for so long to keep Negroes apart and below, when white intellectuals were faced with the challenge of racial equality, they hesitated—fearful, cautious, distracted, or simply indifferent. Ambivalent whites—novelists William Faulkner and Robert Penn Warren, most notably—held the stage, empowered by editors more interested in southern whites' response to the Negro challenge than in what Negroes had to say. White Georgia writer Lillian Smith felt herself shut out altogether, her support for desegregation too strong for editors' tastes. Historian C. Vann Woodward posed a historical argument for change in *The Strange Career of Jim Crow*, yet still walked a center line.

In the early days after the *Brown* decision, white intellectuals could imagine that southern whites might go along if they were left alone to make change their way. Negro social psychologist Kenneth B. Clark thought differently: to make this turn, the nation required strong, forceful leadership. President Dwight Eisenhower did not provide that leadership. When school districts across the South refused to desegregate the schools, when white demonstrators spat on Negro children, when the governor of Arkansas defied the government of the United States—when all these things happened while white liberals stood by, the hopes raised among Negro intellectuals plummeted. Some went into exile; others considered it. Some remained committed to what Myrdal called "the American creed"; others found more hope in Castro's Cuba and the new nations of Africa.

The Cold War nearly silenced the voices of some Negro writers. The great intellectual W. E. B. Du Bois was sidelined, his work for peace interpreted as sedition. While white magazine and book editors did invite the work of other Negro intellectuals, they also controlled and limited it. Editors (some closely tied to the U.S. intelligence and foreign policy establishment) trimmed the sails of discourse. Knowing the ideological limits of what could be said, Negro intellectuals said what they could or kept silent. Writers associated with communism in the past—Langston Hughes, Richard Wright, Ralph Ellison—spoke carefully or not at all.

When the Cuban missile crisis brought the country to the brink of war, playwright Lorraine Hansberry, at a rally opposing the House Un-American Activities Committee, said that the committee's true goal had never been protecting national security. Its true goal had been intimidation. "We were ceaselessly told, after all, to be everything which mutilates youth: to be silent, to be ignorant, to be without unsanctioned opinions, to be compliant and, above all else, obedient to all the ideas which are in fact the dregs of an age."[6]

Throughout the 1950s, the dialogue on race that intellectuals conducted in public—in magazines and books intended for readers outside academia—seemed muffled, repressed. Whether black or white, from the South or the North, intellectuals who spoke to the hour—individuals allowed by editors to speak to the hour—spoke with restraint. Behind the bland talk lay whole forbidden realms of ideas. Southerners who made plain their support for desegregation were asking for trouble. In the midst of the sit-in movement of 1960, historian Lawrence Reddick, a Negro professor at Alabama State College in Montgomery and author of an early biography of Martin Luther King Jr., found himself under investigation by the state police and attacked by the governor; he was summarily fired. What white historian James Silver called "the closed society" guarded itself from racial change. The Cold War offered both an argument for racial change and a strategy for opposing it: those who argued for desegregation were routinely labeled "communists." Even in the North, advocating racial change could provoke Red-baiting—allegations that support for desegregation was communist inspired. As in a ritual to ward off such charges, those who spoke for desegregation invoked the Cold War: How could the United States win the propaganda war with the Soviet Union if it did not treat its own citizens fairly? Outside a few left-wing journals, intellectuals and their editors alike contained the discussion safely within faith in capitalist democracy. The very name that would be given the movement under way—the "civil rights movement" (not, for instance, "the movement for racial equality")—thus contained it.

Then, in 1962, an eloquent writer named James Baldwin broke through the blur, publishing in *The New Yorker* an essay that became known as *The Fire Next Time.* Seizing the moment, Baldwin expressed the despair and contempt for whites that other Negro intellectuals were feeling. Indeed, he took on all of Western civilization, questioning its righteousness in view of its unrighteous record. Impelled by a sense of mission, he angered not only white liberals but some civil rights leaders as well. His move to center stage forms the heart of this narrative, which continues with Freedom Summer and the work of several intellectuals involved at ground level in the Mississippi movement: historians James Silver, Howard Zinn, and Staughton Lynd and psychiatrist Robert Coles—all white men who, for a time, stepped into the line of fire. Not known as public intellectuals before the movement, they were transformed by their experience in it.

Inevitably, readers may wonder what this story says about intellectuals in general, and their relationship to political life. I am reluctant to make grand pronouncements on the basis of this small slice of time, but I emerged from the libraries shaken. Growing up in the 1950s, coming of age in the 1960s, I saw intellectuals as heroes and wanted to be one of them. All these years later, I have had enough experience with academic intellectuals to understand how small and partial is our vision, how limited our thoughts, and how much of what we do is motivated by the selfish needs of our institutions and our own lives, but I had not taken in fully what I saw around me. Only as I worked my way through this powerful story did I begin to see more clearly how fully intellectuals can fail the test of history.

Some readers may feel that political engagement is not the job of intellectuals—that intellectuals must stay in the ivory tower or lose the integrity required to do their work. The idea that intellectuals can disengage themselves from political life is no more than a fantasy. By failing to respond to the racial challenge, white and even some Negro intellectuals lent support to the status quo. Intellectuals are not only producers of ideas and art (an unattractive industrial model of intellectual life that has taken hold in our universities). They are inevitably players in the political community. The Supreme Court had opened a window of opportunity: here was a chance to affirm the need for change. At moments when social action is called for, intellectuals' silence is itself a political act.

Yet tempting as self-righteousness is, it would be a mistake to heap too much blame on these intellectuals as individuals. The intellectuals who stood by while history happened all around them were themselves captives of their social world, prisoners of a closed society. In arguing that some intellectuals failed the challenge of their time, I do not wish to place more blame on them than they ought to bear. I am describing here a social system of which they were a part. Seeing the limits of their closed society, we may better understand the limits of our own.

PART ONE

Brown v. Board of Education

and the White Resistance

1954–1957

CHAPTER 1

"GO SLOW"

On a waning afternoon in late January 1953, some five hundred writers, editors, reviewers, reporters, literary agents, and booksellers seated themselves in rows of chairs in a Manhattan hotel. It was time for *Harper's* editor Frederick Lewis Allen to introduce the winners of the 1952 National Book Awards—among them, Ralph Ellison's first novel, *Invisible Man*. Not since Richard Wright's *Native Son* had a novel by a Negro writer so captured the interest of the white publishing world. Reviewers fixed their attention on Ellison's unflattering treatment of the Communist Party, although they noted, too, his unconventional narrative approach. Accepting the ten-carat gold medal at the awards ceremony, Ellison, a formal man on such public occasions, himself touched on his experimental approach, and the political point he had hoped to make with it: "I was to dream of a prose which was flexible, and swift as American change is swift, confronting the inequalities and brutalities of our society forthrightly. . . ."[1]

As Ellison spoke, the Supreme Court had before it a set of appeals that did confront the very inequalities most on Ellison's mind: the inequalities of race. One of the Supreme Court justices considering the appeals in *Brown v. Board of Education*, William O. Douglas, followed Ellison as the main speaker at the awards program. Ellison's allotted five minutes over, Douglas delivered a twenty-minute speech on the need for unity in Asia to withstand the power of the Soviet Union. After that, as *The New Yorker* lightly noted in its account of the occasion, "the audience applauded, and in a trice the chairs we had been sitting on were whisked away, two bars were going like blast furnaces on either side of the room, and what is known in literary circles as a reception was under way." In the milling about that followed, Ralph Ellison got lost in the crowd. There were so many more celebrated to attend to, including Justice Douglas himself, who told his listeners how much easier it was to write accounts of his travels than Supreme Court decisions. He described a Malayan shadow play he had come across: "There's this puppet, you see, and a light behind the screen. . . ." The "lion of the afternoon," *The New Yorker* said, was the great southern writer William Faulkner, "who, very small and very handsome, with a voice that never rose above a whisper, stood with his back to the wall and gamely took on all comers."

No southern novelist had done more to shape literate Americans' impression of the South than William Faulkner. Since the 1920s, from his home in Oxford, Mississippi, Faulkner had poured out a stream of narrative—novels differently titled but all of a piece: the patch of South that Faulkner called Yoknapatawpha County. "If you want to know something about the dynamics of the South," Ellison himself once said, "of interpersonal relationships in the South from, roughly, 1874 until today, you don't go to historians; not even to Negro historians. You go to William Faulkner and Robert Penn Warren."[2]

Both Warren and Ellison had abandoned the South, departing for the more cosmopolitan North. Faulkner stayed on, living at the edge of Oxford in an antebellum house, too small and plainly built to be rightly called a mansion, although it could pass for one at a distance. Faulkner called the house Rowan Oak, after a mythical tree, but lanky cedars actually lined the narrow drive up to his door. The house's first owner had hired a landscaper to lay out hedges in formal, concentric circles in the front yard. The place must have had grandeur then, but it had something else in the 1950s: a lived-in quality so worn that

Faulkner felt free to write out the chronology of his newest novel, *A Fable*, on the walls of his study.

Faulkner imagined Mississippi in his novels with more passion than most places have bestowed upon them. His Mississippi had a supernal glow, like a paradise lit by the fires of hell. Slavery loomed large as the region's original sin. Again and again, Faulkner raised the question of race. His novels were, however, convoluted and hard to read, although *Intruder in the Dust* was straightforward enough even for Hollywood, which made it into a movie filmed on Oxford's own streets. Outside of fiction Faulkner put Mississippi's flaws down even more plainly, telling readers of *Holiday* magazine (speaking of himself in the third person), "But most of all he hated the intolerance and injustice: the lynching of Negroes not for the crimes they committed but because their skins were black. . . ; the inequality: the poor schools they had then when they had any, the hovels they had to live in unless they wanted to live outdoors. . . ."[3]

If this comment was more direct than white southerners were accustomed to, so were the letters Faulkner wrote to the nearest big-city newspaper, the *Memphis Commercial Appeal*, in the spring of 1955, the year after the Supreme Court ruled school desegregation unconstitutional. As white officials in Mississippi struggled for ways to evade the ruling, Faulkner wrote that Mississippi schools were "not even good enough for white people." Why, then, did Mississippians imagine they could afford *two* school systems good enough for whites and Negroes?[4]

So unexpected was Faulkner's stand that it traveled all the way to New York. The *New Leader,* a New York magazine on the right wing of the Socialist Party, reprinted it, while *Masses & Mainstream*—a communist magazine—ran an account of it that had been sent in from Memphis:

> *That William Faulkner has shown willingness to carry on this verbal battle in the public forum of as influential a paper as the Memphis Commercial Appeal is noteworthy in itself—that he has taken a stronger position each week and has been able to win adher-*

ents amongst white Mississippians is outstanding. A few years ago no one would have dared to come to his defense. That the Commercial Appeal has been willing to print as many letters on the subject is also newsworthy and indicates a significant change.

The writer expressed surprise at the lack of Red-baiting in the letters. Had the *Brown* decision made advocating desegregation respectable? "The South's most famous author, William Faulkner, has taken a step forward in the fight for humanity. The rest of our American intellectuals could well follow in his path."[5]

What a strange phrase that would seem in later years—"our American intellectuals." Their ranks included novelists, literary critics, even academic historians—all writing for readers outside the academy and beyond the narrow circles of the avant-garde. They held forums and conferences; they published books through commercial presses. Their names might not be quite household words, but they appeared in household magazines—in *Life, Look, Time*—as well as little intellectual and political magazines like *Partisan Review* and *Commentary.* They constituted a leadership class, not known to everyone but known widely enough to make their opinions felt. How would they respond to the challenge the Supreme Court had thrown down to the country?

As one of the first to respond, William Faulkner soon learned the price of courage. After his letters to the Memphis newspaper, anonymous phone calls and critical letters, signed and unsigned, flooded in to Rowan Oak. "Since none of us agreed with Bill's views," Faulkner's brother later observed, "we said, 'It serves him right.' "[6] Life became so difficult that before Faulkner left on a trip to Japan, he worried he might have to abandon Mississippi for good.[7]

In Japan, Faulkner was freed for a while from confronting Mississippi's racial problem close at hand. Another problem pressed harder: the challenge of getting through all the appearances scheduled for him. An intensely private man, Faulkner found public speaking difficult. Only a few years earlier, most of his books were out of print and there was no demand for them, but winning the Nobel Prize in 1950 had made of him a public figure, internationally known and traveling abroad as a representative of his country. Like the jazz bands that the State Department sent around to show that Negroes did have a place in American culture, Faulkner was sent around to show that all white southerners were not bigoted; some could even write.[8]

He did not wear the statesman's robes comfortably. At this point in his life—he was in his late fifties—the South's most famous novelist was an unabashed alcoholic. He could barely set foot in a crowded room without alcohol to hold him up. Even then he sometimes collapsed, pulled down by that which was meant to support him. His Japanese tour was almost cut short near the start: he was drinking so hard that the U.S. ambassador was ready to ship him home. His State Department managers, unwilling to give up so easily, took him in hand, and Faulkner, seeing the difficulties he was causing them, drew himself up and performed honorably and well.

Still, the racial problem remained on his mind. It reemerged in late-night talks with the State Department official accompanying him. He talked of it as they sat on the balcony of their hotel listening to water drip in the garden. Meeting with a group of Japanese professors, he read to them a manuscript, "On Fear," from a book he had begun on the American Dream. Economic fear underlay resistance to the Supreme Court's ruling, he said—fear that the Negro would "take the white man's economy away from him." Explaining that fear, he did not justify it: Americans had to practice freedom if they were going to talk about it to everybody else. Outside of the United States, traveling under the auspices of the U.S. government, Faulkner had become a spokesman not for Mississippi but for his entire country.

On his way home from Japan, another opportunity for public statement opened up. On a stop in Rome, United Press International asked him to comment on a terrible event that had occurred in Mississippi. The body of Emmett Till, a Negro teenager from Chicago who had engaged in a trivial exchange with a white woman at a country store, had been pulled from the Tallahatchie River. Although most southern white brutality passed unremarked by the world, this particular murder did not. Asked by the press to comment, Faulkner wrote out a 400-word statement that would reach a broader audience. U.S. Information Service staff in Rome looked it over; then Faulkner gave the statement to the press.[9]

Fresh from his visit to an Asian country, Faulkner pointed out, practically, the minority status of whites in the world. "The white man can no longer afford, he simply does not dare, to commit acts which the other three-fourths of the human race can challenge him for." Calling up the devastation the Japanese had wreaked on Pearl Harbor only fifteen years earlier, he raised the specter of a prospect even more dire, if all the peoples of color joined with "peoples with ideologies different from ours"—that is, with the communists. America would survive only if Americans presented to the world a united front.

> *Perhaps the purpose of this sorry and tragic error committed in my native Mississippi by two white adults on an afflicted Negro child is to prove to us whether or not we deserve to survive. Because if we in America have reached that point in our desperate culture when we must murder children, no matter for what reason or what color, we don't deserve to survive, and probably won't.*

Masses & Mainstream, so pleased by Faulkner's earlier letters to the *Memphis Commercial Appeal*, liked his Emmett Till statement, too, and reprinted it in full.[10]

In the longer span of his life, Faulkner's political statements of the mid-1950s would appear to some of his biographers an aberration, and in a sense they were. He had not made a practice of public comment, although from time to time he did write letters to the editor, including letters on racial problems. But if it had not been for these journeys abroad under the auspices of the State Department, Faulkner's comments on Mississippi's racial scene might have stayed within the borders of his own state. They might also not have taken on the Cold War tinge they did—the hint of apocalypse: the undercurrent of final struggle between the democratic countries and the communist world.

If the United States wanted to survive its battle with the communists, it needed the world's people of color on its side.

According to Faulkner's Oxford friend Jim Silver, a lanky history professor at the University of Mississippi, Faulkner was a "non-Marxist egalitarian" who had picked up the "Cold War rhetoric" around him on his journeys. Making his "patriotic pilgrimages," Silver said, Faulkner "became alarmed at the powerful influence of racism in the propaganda of the Cold War."[11] Putting himself at the service of the federal government in the international arena, speaking to foreign audiences and the foreign press, Faulkner offered at least a small measure of evidence to the critical world that one white southerner favored racial desegregation. At a time when so many white southerners considered the federal government the enemy, Faulkner's partnership with the federal government was an interesting alliance, and not one that would last.

Memphis, Tennessee, a biracial river city, was just up the road from Oxford, Mississippi. Despite the ease of getting there, Faulkner had not been especially eager to speak to historians gathered at the venerable Peabody Hotel for the annual meeting of the Southern Historical Association (SHA) in the fall of 1955. The spring before the meeting, with the hope of getting Faulkner to speak, Jim Silver had paid frequent visits to Rowan Oak to persuade Faulkner to come. The two men had talked in the side yard while Faulkner worked on a sailboat he had bought, and Silver tried to wrest a commitment from him. "He wouldn't say yes and he didn't say no, so in late summer I placed his name on the program that had a printer's deadline," Silver recalled. "It seemed a good bet that he would appear, not so much out of friendship but because he had something to say to the South and Nation."

In the end, Faulkner came, and the timing of his appearance could hardly have been better. White Citizens Councils formed to oppose desegregation were springing up across the South. They had originated in Mississippi but were spreading as fast as kudzu vines. Forswearing violence, the councils meant to strangle Negroes' efforts to enroll their children in white schools by retaliating economically. Parents who tried to act on the promise of *Brown* lost their jobs, their credit, their homes. Meanwhile, white southern liberals had proved disappointing, their support fading the moment resistance appeared. Washington had done little more. President Dwight Eisenhower, preferring to let the states work things out for themselves, had refused to throw the weight of his office and personal popularity behind the Supreme Court ruling. Congress, caught in the grip of powerful southern Democrats, predictably did no better. With so little support from other quarters, encouraging words from the South's leading novelist would be welcome. But given his eccentricity and his drinking, could he be depended on?

Anticipation had run so high that Faulkner's session had been switched from the afternoon to the dinner meeting, and Faulkner arrived early. Bennett Wall, secretary treasurer of the association, invited the great man up to his hotel room and sat with him most of the day, doling out bourbon in small amounts in the hope of keeping him sober enough to speak.[12] The change to the dinner meeting presented another difficulty. The SHA had trouble talking the hotel management into seating Faulkner's fellow speaker Benjamin E. Mays, president of Morehouse College and a Negro, at the head table in the main ballroom. The management was so worried about how racial mixing might affect the hotel's reputation that it kept photographers out of the ballroom, lest they pick up images of Mays or the thirty other Negroes present. Instead, the press met Faulkner beforehand on the balconied mezzanine above the grand lobby.

As it turned out, William Faulkner was nearly a sideshow. Long a forthright leader in racial affairs, Benjamin Mays could be expected to rise to the occasion, and he did, speaking so eloquently that the audience broke in several times with applause.[13] Addressing "the moral aspects of segregation," Mays did not mince words. Segregation was "a great evil," and if Americans did not follow the Supreme Court's lead and abolish it, then they might as well confess to the world that they did not believe the promises of the Declaration of Independence and the Constitution. In fact, Mays said, ratcheting up his argument, they might as well confess that they did not believe that the Old and New Testaments were meant for peoples of color. They might as well resign themselves to losing their "moral leadership in the world." Would the South "accept the challenge of the Supreme Court" and "make America and the South safe for democracy"? Mays believed so. The stakes were high in the Cold War world. "If we lose this battle for freedom for 15 million Negroes we will lose it for 145 million whites and eventually we will lose it for the world. This is indeed a time for greatness."[14] The five hundred historians rose to their feet in thunderous applause. It was the first standing ovation Jim Silver had ever seen them give.

Faulkner's "slight remarks," by contrast, were a letdown. Recycling his essay "On Fear," he, too, mounted his argument on the Cold War platform. If white people wanted to remain free, they could no longer deny equality to Negroes. He whispered his remarks so softly that Silver, sitting only a few feet away, could barely hear him. Historian C. Vann Woodward wrote a friend that Mays's remarks were better than Faulkner's. Faulkner's comments were, however, the ones featured by the *New York Times* from an Associated Press dispatch. In a one-paragraph article, the *Times*, picking up the Cold War theme, reported that "William Faulkner said last night that continued racial segregation was as great a threat to world peace as communism."[15]

The *Memphis Commercial Appeal* ran Faulkner's speech in full, and the governing council of the SHA voted to publish the three speeches from the session—Faulkner's, Mays's, and a third by Nashville lawyer Cecil Sims. Emory professor Bell Wiley, president of the SHA that year, contributed the introduction. This pamphlet, he said, would show that there *was* a "liberal South": "soft-spoken and restrained, but articulate and powerful—that is earnestly pledged to moderation and reason."[16]

"Moderation and reason"—this became the mantra of liberals, North and South. They wanted to speak out for desegregation without stirring up too much opposition. But even such a moderate and reasonable effort as the little pamphlet of speeches stirred opposition within the ranks of the SHA. Two members of the council, worried about the response from the association's more conservative members, vigorously opposed publication. In the end, the speeches did *not* appear under the SHA imprint, and the book's introduction noted carefully that they did *not* represent the association's official views.

The pamphlet came out instead under the name of the Southern Regional Council (SRC), a moderate interracial organization formed in the 1940s and based in Atlanta. The SRC had been slow to speak out against segregation in its earlier days. Like most southerners, those who ran the SRC would speak out for racial justice but not against segregation outright. With its moderate, southern past, the SRC was a safe publisher for the Memphis talks. A northern organization, the Ford Foundation's Fund for the Republic, covered the cost. The fund's support was kept quiet because Faulkner feared, apparently, that if white southerners knew that northerners had paid for the pamphlet, they might pay less attention to it.[17] Here, writ small, was the state of free speech in the South: on the racial issue, there was not much of it.

Given the difficulty of opposing segregation in white southern publications, all the more important, then, was whatever might be said in the national magazines. Only in *Life* were most white southerners likely to hear support for desegregation. But when Faulkner asked his agent, Harold Ober, to place his essay "On Fear" in a magazine, Faulkner said he would rather it *not* appear in the "slick mags," since southerners assumed their reports on segregation were biased, and "doubt as propaganda anything they print." He particularly did not want *Life* to have the piece. Against his wishes, *Life* had published a long feature on him that had delved into his private affairs. Anything in *Life* would seem to him "automatically befouled and not credible." The *Saturday Evening Post* might have it, if the *Post* would present it "simply and without fanfare or headlines, pictures, etc. as an editorial." Faulkner wanted "On Fear" to be taken seriously. He hoped it would help the South "in a dilemma whose seriousness the rest of the country seems incapable not only of understanding but even of believing that to us it is serious."[18]

Not a man who had made a career out of political punditry, or a man who needed to write essays to enhance his career, Faulkner sought publication out of that rarest of motivations: he had something to say that he wanted to be heard. At his suggestion, the piece went to *Harper's*, where he had published before, and *Harper's*, a magazine for a more intellectual and smaller audience than *Life's*, accepted it.[19] But *Harper's*, a monthly, had a lead time of several months. Before the issue carrying "On Fear" appeared on the stands in June 1956, Faulkner's public position on race had begun to cloud over.

In public arenas, Faulkner had couched his plea for racial equality in the political terms of the Cold War. Privately, writing to Mississippians, Faulkner cut his cloth differently, to fit his correspondent. "Since there is so much pressure today from outside our country to advance the Negro," he wrote to the president of the Lions Club in Glendora, "let us here give the Negro a chance to prove whether he is or is not competent for educational and economic and political equality, before the Federal Government crams it down ours and the Negro's throat too."[20]

Faulkner took an even cruder line to a white segregationist named W. C. Neill, who was corresponding with Faulkner in the hope that the great man ("the prime literary figure of our generation") might swing over to his side. "If you will excuse the symbolism," Faulkner wrote Neill on January 23, 1956, "we are like the man whose bed was infested. He has three choices: 1. Burn the bed (i.e., kill the bugs) 2. Move away. 3. Draw their teeth. We can't kill them: against the law. We can't move: we live here. We can draw the teeth: give them such schools that they wont [*sic*] want to enter ours."[21] It was an ugly argument.

The ambivalence that underlay Faulkner's support for desegregation spilled into his public statements when a series of violent events at the start of 1956 touched off his fear that things were moving too fast for white southerners to adapt. The *Brown* decision itself had left the speed of change open to question; so had the implementation decision that followed a year later. The Supreme Court ordered the South to desegregate its schools with "deliberate speed," which might have meant anything, especially as interpreted by white southern judges. When Negro parents began filing suits and judges actually ruled in their favor, resistance erupted.[22] In Montgomery, Alabama, bus boycott leaders' homes were bombed. At the University of Alabama campus in Tuscaloosa, a riot blocked the entry of Negro student Autherine Lucy. Preventing racial violence had long served as an excuse for the race barrier. Remove it, South Carolina attorney John W. Davis had said in argument before the Supreme Court, and reap an outcome "one cannot contemplate with any equanimity."[23] That prediction appeared to be coming unpleasantly true.

For so many years, the white South had trailed behind it the guilt of slavery. William Faulkner had hoped for an end to that awful legacy, a new day in race relations. Now, instead of progress, he saw the possibility of a great leap backward. After the university expelled Lucy, Faulkner feared that the NAACP would try to force her return. Then she would be killed, and the white South would have her death on its conscience.[24] Violence would breed more violence; there could be a new civil war, and more years of guilt.

At this point, in the spring of 1956, Faulkner wobbled badly. In the wake of the storm at the University of Alabama, he was seized by a conviction of crisis. He wrote out an appeal to the NAACP and all others who sought "immediate and unconditional integration" through the courts: "Go slow now. Stop for a time, a moment." Let the South catch its breath, he said. Dropping any pretense of speaking as an American, dropping his Cold War talk of democracy, he spoke as a southerner speaking to northerners. He had opposed those who wanted to keep things as they were in the South, he said. Now he denounced those outside forces that would compel the South "to eradicate that evil overnight." Pushed too hard by the North, recalcitrant white southerners would push back with "fierce unanimity" and "against any odds." Faulkner and others occupying the middle ground would "have to vacate it in order to keep from being trampled."[25]

He asked his agent to get his call for caution into print as quickly as possible, and on the radio even faster: he wanted to reach a large audience. This time, he accepted publication in *Life*, under the title "A Letter to the North." *Life* had run a sympathetic six-page photo spread on Autherine Lucy's ordeal, but it had already begun to pull back before the force of resistance, falling behind the "moderate" line.

Describing the NAACP's suit to force the university to readmit Lucy, *Life* said, "However legal their claim, this was a new provocation by an organization which inflames the Negroes' most bitter enemies. And it alienated some who had deplored the earlier violence."[26]

Before Faulkner's essay could appear in the March 5 issue of *Life*, a federal court ordered Lucy reinstated. Fearing the consequences and believing that what he would say might affect the outcome of events, Faulkner cast about for an immediate forum. He found one through Jean Stein, a young woman with whom he had formed an intimate relationship. The daughter of Jules Stein, founder of the Music Corporation of America, Stein used her connections to get him on a radio interview show. There he said that separate schools would be acceptable if Negroes had good schools—with full integration possible in a hundred years. The show went out to radio stations in the East, and NBC news picked up his comments for nationwide broadcast. Meanwhile, by now drinking heavily, as he did under pressure, Faulkner agreed to be interviewed by Russell Warren Howe for the *Sunday Times* of London.[27]

Faulkner's fear poured out in the interview. "If that girl goes back to Tuscaloosa she will die. Then the top will blow off. The government will send its troops and we'll be back at 1860. They must stop pushing these people. The trouble is the North doesn't know that country. They don't know the South will go to war." Then, according to Howe, Faulkner spoke the words that would cause him no end of trouble and undercut the stand he had taken in more sober moments: "As long as there's a middle road, all right, I'll be on it. But if it came to fighting I'd fight for Mississippi against the United States even if it meant going out into the street and shooting Negroes." He urged Negroes to "go slow," and let southern whites feel they were changing their own minds, not having change forced upon them. Howe recycled his London *Times* interview in an account for an American magazine, the *Reporter*.[28]

At this volatile time, Faulkner's comments about shooting Negroes were like a declaration of war. They were picked up by the *New York Times*, which headed its story, "Faulkner Believes South

Would Fight." The *Times* article was short and inconspicuously displayed, but *Time* magazine picked up Faulkner's remarks, too, spreading them at home and abroad. Faulkner would never be able to live them down, though he tried. A month after its first report, *Time* ran a statement he had released to the press, saying these were opinions he had "never held and, for that reason, never expressed." It would be "foolish" and "dangerous" to choose a state over the nation and shoot a human being in the process. *Time* had quoted "statements which no sober man could make and, it seems to me, no sane man believe."[29] Had he said things, drunk, that he would not have said sober? Or did he not really say them?

Several years later, Negro sociologist St. Clair Drake, talking about a different article by Russell Warren Howe, the reporter who interviewed Faulkner with such unfortunate results, raised questions about Howe's accuracy as a reporter.[30] Editors at the *Reporter* also found "some rather alarming discrepancies" between Howe's facts in a 1963 manuscript on South Africa and research by the *Reporter*'s fact checker.[31] But fact checkers are sometimes less right than reporters, and as for Drake's criticism—well, the editors had changed the piece Drake was talking about so much that Howe himself hardly recognized it.[32] Howe's published interview with Faulkner does have the feel of truth, Faulkner's protests notwithstanding. Published as a Q. and A. and presumably taped, the interview sounds like Faulkner from start to finish. Except for that hyperbolic remark about shooting Negroes, the positions he takes in it are consistent with his remarks at other times. Ralph Ellison, for one—an admirer of Faulkner's work but not of Faulkner's current remarks—believed that Faulkner said what Howe said he said. "Faulkner wrote a letter to TIME denying that crap he dropped on the world," Ellison wrote his friend Albert Murray, "but the reporter stuck to his guns and insisted that he reported true. Which I believe he did."[33]

Even without the incendiary interview with Howe, Faulkner set off fireworks with "Letter to the North" in *Life* (its reach expanded with republication in *Reader's Digest*). In response, descendants of former slaves called him to account. One *Life* reader observed that the moment Faulkner asked for "has now lasted more than 90 years." In the new pacifist magazine *Liberation*, Montgomery boycott leader Martin Luther King Jr. commented dryly, "It is hardly a moral act to encourage others patiently to accept injustice which he himself does not endure." *Masses & Mainstream*, hitherto so approving of Faulkner's statements, took him to task. Why should Negroes be stopped by the fear of violence when they had faced violence for so many years? On a radio program in Oakland, California, the eminent Negro intellectual W. E. B. Du Bois challenged Faulkner to a debate at the courthouse where Emmett Till's murderers were tried and released.[34]

Faulkner received a more sympathetic reading from Walker Percy, a white Alabama-born essayist living in New Orleans and newly committed to the Catholic faith. Percy had not yet made his name as a novelist; *The Moviegoer* was still several years away from publication. In fact, Percy was barely a published writer at all when he confronted the South's moral crisis in *Commonweal*, a Catholic magazine. There, in "Stoicism in the South," Percy portrayed Faulkner as the upper-class white southerner who could no longer live a Stoic's life based on hierarchy, with honor, courtesy, and dignity as its highest values. In such a society—though Percy did not put it quite this way—everyone politely knew his place. That era was over. The genteel white southerner had fallen silent. "The day has been lost and lost for good. . . . [T]he white man has lost his *oblige*, the black man has lost his manners, and insolence prevails."[35]

Other critics were less elegiac. The *Nation* parodied Faulkner, and in a lead editorial in the same issue, its editor Carey McWilliams attacked the whole rhetoric of gradualism. No New York editor was firmer in his support for the civil rights movement and civil liberties than Carey McWilliams, a lawyer. "The middle position has become so crowded that standing room only signs have been posted," McWilliams wrote. "The words 'gradual' and 'moderate' have acquired magical properties."[36]

In *Partisan Review*, a little magazine at the heart of New York intellectual life, a young James Baldwin struck the note of moral indignation that McWilliams asked for. "After more than two hundred years in slavery and ninety years of quasi-freedom, it is hard to think very highly of William Faulkner's advice to 'go slow,' " he wrote. "[T]he time Faulkner asks for does not exist—and he is not the only Southerner who knows it. There is never time in the future in which we will work out our salvation. The challenge is in the moment, the time is always now."[37]

Faulkner weathered the storm over his remarks in the *Reporter* and his piece in *Life*. He even tried to explain himself in an essay for *Ebony*, a glossy magazine for middle-class Negroes, where he reiterated what he had said in *Time*—that these were not the words of a sane, sober man. He tried, too, to put his *Life* plea to "go slow" in more attractive terms. If he were a Negro, he said, he would want Negro leaders to keep on pushing for equality but flexibly, adapting their methods to local conditions. They should send each day a Negro student—"fresh and cleanly dressed, courteous, without threat or violence, to seek admission" to a white school. When that student was refused, another, the following day, should take his place, "until at last the white man himself must recognize that there will be no peace for him until he himself has solved the dilemma." That, he said, "was Gandhi's way."[38]

Faulkner told his agent he assumed he would be paid for the *Ebony* essay, if only a token. "But the money will not matter. I would rather have it in the Negro journal, even at no price, if they will print it intact, unedited."[39] He told Allan Morrison at *Ebony* that the other editors and publisher might not like the article (it *was* paternalistic and condescending), but he assumed Morrison shared with him the belief that "our dilemma and problem can be solved only by men of good will regardless of race, stating their honest ideas to one another that the erroneous ones can be corrected."[40] In its graceful ineptness, its wrongness for the audience and the moment, the piece Faulkner titled "A Letter to the Leaders in the Negro Race" (and *Ebony* changed to "If I Were a Negro)" betrayed Faulkner's distance from those he advised. Yet his interest in appearing in *Ebony* was as remarkable as *Ebony's* interest in having him.

Speaking out as he did, Faulkner made himself a lightning rod, drawing fire from those in the North who saw him as a spokesman for southern intransigence and from those in the South who saw him as a traitor. There was no particular reason he had to keep putting his ideas up for view, except that he was worried and felt that as a public man he was obliged to do what he could. He had not done as well by the race issue as he might have; his caution and his drinking had hobbled his best intentions. If he failed in his attempt to lead his region to enlightenment, at least he had seen his duty and had tried to do it.

Faulkner's political energy soon waned (he was busy planning a move to the University of Virginia and was, besides, not in the best of health and only a few years from death), but for a while he kept on trying. He and Jim Silver joined with an editor named P. D. East in putting out one issue of a satiric newspaper. East edited a suburban Mississippi weekly, the *Petal Paper*, and he had used it to launch his own crusade against segregation. Discovering in the White Citizens Councils a suitable object of satire, East had so angered his local subscribers by the summer of 1956 that he had only a couple dozen left. He had been called a "nigger-loving, Jew-loving, Communist son-of-a-bitch." A man in Hattiesburg had offered to mop up the street with him. East felt fairly sorry for himself but did not cave in. He published the story of a young Negro boy's brutal beating under the headline, "A New Organization in Business—The Bigger and Better Bigots Bureau?"[41]

On an unusually hot day in June, East drove with Jim Silver to pay a call on William Faulkner at Rowan Oak. They parked, and Faulkner strolled out from behind the house. His blue shirt was faded, his khaki pants torn. He wore a sailor cap. They all exchanged a few words—Faulkner's voice was quiet and made East feel he ought to be quiet himself. They drove out to a reservoir and sailed without wind for a couple of hours. Faulkner, silent, sat knee to knee with East in the stern of the boat. Eventually, Faulkner spoke: "Well, East, anybody put any dead cats on your porch lately?"

After that, they got along fine. The sailing over, Faulkner offered East a Coke back at a country store, and East paid for Cokes all round.

Over dinner they talked about putting together a "Mississippi Moderates" group but gave up on the idea. They would just spend all their time defending themselves. Instead, inspired by "The Nigble Papers" published by students at Ole Miss, they planned a satiric venture, the *Southern Reposure.*

East and Faulkner thought they'd better not put their own names on the first issue. If people knew they had a hand in it, the whole thing might be dismissed as the work of two cranks. So East invented a publisher, Nathan Bedford Cooclose. In the debut issue, Cooclose explained the purpose of the *Southern Reposure*: to maintain segregation of an obnoxious group of people who threatened "our way of life," the Scotch-Irish (the ethnic group from which most white Mississippians derived). Stories included a report on a speech "The Botch Made by the Scotch." The satire was as sophomoric as its origins, but the paper was meant for college students. Faulkner contributed the streamer that ran over the name plate and featured Mississippi's number one racist, Senator James Eastland: "Eastland Elected by NAACP as Outstanding Man of Year." East not only banged the copy together; he paid most of the printer's bill. Some eight thousand copies went out to college campuses, where the paper had some effect: East heard copies were actually selling for a dollar apiece at a college that tried to suppress it.

Faulkner worried that the paper's originators might be targets of violence if their identity became known. Silver feared his job at the University of Mississippi might be in jeopardy. To protect himself, Silver got rid of East's letters to him and asked East to destroy the letters Silver had written him. To protect Silver's identity further, East renamed Silver "Josh Brass" in his 1960 memoir. None of them felt prepared to push their luck with another issue—this one had cost too much and taken too much effort, mostly East's. Some checks came in, probably solicited by Silver. As for Faulkner: "Hell," East remarked, "he didn't even buy the Cokes. But it was good to know he was on the same side as I."[42]

Despite his involvement in this attack on racism and his earlier days as something akin to a standard-bearer, Faulkner would move farther and farther to the rear. In February 1958, teaching at the University of Virginia, he delivered a speech in which he entertained the idea that Negroes might not be capable of first-class citizenship. In remarks picked up by the Associated Press, Faulkner said that whites needed to teach Negroes how to bear "the responsibilities of equality"—to learn "self-restraint, honesty, dependability, purity." Speaking in the wake of the crisis at Little Rock, where for a time whites prevented a little band of Negro students from entering Central High School to further their education, Faulkner appeared unaware that he was saying anything absurd.[43]

From her mountain home in north Georgia, white novelist Lillian Smith heard what Faulkner was saying and was disturbed by it. Faulkner was painting the South worse than it was, writing as if southerners were "all Snopeses," the opportunistic rednecks of Faulkner's Yoknapatawpha County. "Profoundly shocked" by his essay in *Life*, Smith had cabled the magazine offering to reply. She was turned down. She told all this to Dorothy Canfield Fisher, a white Vermont writer and Quaker who had volunteered to help in this "great moral crisis of our country's history." Would Fisher talk editors of the mass-circulation magazines into letting Smith "speak quietly" to readers in the North and South? "I can't be heard in southern newspapers," Smith wrote bitterly, "certainly not in the Georgia ones. But through *Look* or *Life* or *Colliers* I could be heard by southerners and northerners."[44]

It is not hard to see why *Life* and the other magazines put their pages at Faulkner's disposal. He was, after all, a Nobel Prize winner, highly respected by the literary establishment. At the same time, Lillian Smith, too, had a right to be heard. Not as gifted a novelist as Faulkner, she had nevertheless written two best-selling books about race in the South: *Strange Fruit*, a novel about interracial love, and *Killers of the Dream*, a memoir that psychoanalyzed the South. The books were only part of her long campaign against segregation. With her close friend Paula Snelling, she had published a magazine, spoken from countless platforms, corresponded with Negro leaders and whites interested in racial change, and hosted informal sessions at her mountain camp for girls. It would be difficult to overestimate Lillian Smith's importance as a southerner who had given courageous, unstinting support to the work of racial change. Yet after the *Brown* decision, Smith was distressed to find that Faulkner could be heard in the big national magazines while she could not.

Time and *Newsweek* had not even reviewed her latest books, she wrote a friend bitterly. *Saturday Review* and the *New York Times* had assigned *Now Is the Time*, her most recent call for racial equality, to newspaper editors Hodding Carter Jr. and Ralph McGill—"two southerners who are gradualists and who are known to be extremely hostile to me. The northern magazines do this not because they have anything against me personally; indeed, many of their editors call themselves my 'friends' when they speak of me; they do this in order not 'to antagonize the South.' If you ask them 'What South' they grow vague and cannot reply. Fear of offending white people is in the North as well as in the South. This is the new state of mind we have to deal with, now."[45]

Clear about her own support for desegregation, Smith watched while McGill and Carter published their cautious views in magazines with circulations in the millions. Before the *Brown* decision, neither McGill, editor of the *Atlanta Constitution,* nor Carter, editor of a smaller paper in Greenville, Mississippi, had favored desegregation outright. They had spoken against segregation's worst abuses, but not against segregation itself. Now, since change must come, they spoke for change, but in good time. They, cautious and cautioning, and not Lillian Smith, were speaking for the white South in *Life, Reader's Digest,* and the *Saturday Evening Post.*

Smith's feeling of being shut out of the racial dialogue surfaced again and again in her correspondence. *Now Is the Time* had sold 100,000 copies in paperback, yet she suspected Dell Books of then suppressing it by failing to fill orders. She imagined pressure not only from southern bookstores and people of power but also from Jews in publishing who were not interested in "the color problem" and feared that the Negro movement might lead to a backlash against Jews. She even asked the American Civil Liberties Union to investigate Dell, and the ACLU did, inconclusively.[46]

However inconclusive the evidence for suppression of *Now Is the Time*, Smith was not imagining her exclusion from the public dialogue on race. Around the time of the *Brown* decision, a southern editor at *Holiday* magazine turned down a piece white novelist Carson McCullers wrote on Georgia because, as McCullers's biographer Virginia Spencer Carr has reported, "she put too much of Lillian Smith and Miss Smith's social consciousness into an article that was meant to publicize Georgia."[47] Howard University professor Rayford Logan recorded in his diary another time when Smith was clearly excluded because of the strength of her views. The occasion was a 1957 meeting to plan a symposium on desegregation; the men involved thought it would be good to include a woman or two, and Smith's name came up, along with Eleanor Roosevelt's. Neither passed muster. According to Logan, two of his fellow planners—C. A. McKnight, the white editor of the *Charlotte News*, and Lambert Davis, the white director of the University of North Carolina Press—saw them as "anathema to the white South."[48]

At least once, however, Smith was offered an invitation that she turned down, with good enough reason. Not long after the *Brown* decision, the *Antioch Review* ran a piece by a New York–born white Alabama professor that was little more than an exercise in contempt. "[M]ost Alabama Negroes," Norman A. Brittin said, "live in crowded huts and shanties, they are ignorant, they are dirty, they are frequently drunken and immoral, their reading matter is trashy or nonexistent, their speech is an ungrammatical *patois.*" The article went downhill from there: "By and large, Alabama Negroes are still primitives." Smith, one of the southerners invited to respond to these views in the same issue, was appalled. This was the stuff of demagoguery. Publishing it only encouraged it. Refusing the invitation, she asked the editors, "What has happened to the intellectual life of Antioch?"[49]

Whatever had happened to the *Antioch Review* had happened elsewhere as well. The gradualism of Carter, McGill, and Faulkner paled beside the extreme views offered up by some of the national magazines. In January 1956, *Harper's*, generally a liberal magazine, ran an article in which a South Carolina newspaper editor attributed an array of faults to Negroes—venereal disease, illegitimacy, crime, intellectual backwardness. *Harper's* prefaced the article with a disclaimer: Thomas R. Waring's point of view was "far removed from the editors," who published it in the interest of "dialogue."[50]

In a 1962 book, *The Cold Rebellion: The South's Oligarchy in Revolt*, Negro journalist Lewis W. Jones would cite Waring's article as an example of the many such articles that placed Negroes "in an unfavorable light" at this bend of the road. At least, he said, *Harper's* editors "had taken pains to point out the author's errors of fact and logic. Most editors do not undertake to comment on the half-truths and innuendo with which these articles are often crowded."[51] At a time when national magazines ought to have been leading the way to change, they had opened their pages to those who resisted it.

After Lillian Smith asked Dorothy Canfield Fisher to help her get into the big magazines to counter the tide of resistance, Fisher, a woman of some influence, did try. She wrote to the *Saturday Review of Literature*, the *Yale Review*, and *Reader's Digest*. Then Smith changed her mind and called off the letter campaign on her behalf—it hurt her pride. She asked that Fisher and her fellow Quakers lend support instead to the Montgomery bus boycott led by Dr. Martin Luther King Jr.[52] For her part, Smith said, she would go on speaking to small groups on college campuses and elsewhere. She was grateful for Fisher's efforts, and sorry that the rest of the country was not getting the true story of what was happening in the South. But she saw "many white southerners who are risking and sacrificing for the cause of human dignity," and she believed that risk would bear fruit: "Gradually, the North will learn to risk, too. It hasn't had to risk anything, really, in the name of integration. But it will have to and it will, later. In the meantime, I believe the South is going to keep changing and growing. It won't be the Faulkners who make it change and grow."[53]

With Lillian Smith marginalized, only two southern intellectuals, both white and both male, rivaled Faulkner on center stage: C. Vann Woodward, historian, and Robert Penn Warren, poet and novelist. The care with which they positioned themselves in their public comments suggests the delicacy of the hour.

Born in Kentucky, a slaveholding state that never left the Union, Robert Penn Warren had been taught never to say "nigger." "When I was a boy," he recalled when he was nearly eighty, "I used the word 'nigger' once at home. My father said, 'If you go on living under this roof, you're never to use that word again in my presence.' "[54] The instruction did not wholly take. The word was to fall casually from the lips of characters in *All the King's Men*, the novel for which Warren won the Pulitzer Prize, and in *Brother to Dragons*, a long poem about Thomas Jefferson's nephews' murder of a slave. Indeed, throughout his work Robert Penn Warren had circled the issue of race without coming firmly to land on it. From his first book *(John Brown)* to his latest novel *(Band of Angels)*, slavery and its legacy had preoccupied him. Yet there was something abstract about his approach to the subject, as if he could not quite get hold of it.

He had come a long way since his contribution on Negroes in *I'll Take My Stand*, the Nashville Fugitives' 1930 defense of agrarian life. There he had questioned neither the rightness nor the inevitability of segregation. Yet as recently as 1951 a professor in the Southern Historical Association suggested inviting Warren to speak at the annual conference in order "to try to make him wrestle with the problem of the Negro which he has so far successfully dodged until now in all his books."[55] Thus, when Warren traveled through the South toward the end of 1955 to report on developments there for *Life* magazine, he went as a man who had himself not yet confronted the South's racial realities head-on.

As a reporter, Warren did passably well. He was a likable man, unpretentious and easy to talk to. Called "Red" by his friends, he would remind Negro writer Albert Murray, who met him later, of Telegraph Road Red, the fellow who ran the Texaco station back home.[56] When Warren wrote up his travels through the South, he put on the casual air of a man strolling across the courthouse square, chatting with those he encountered along the way. Yet despite his Kentucky lilt and easy ways, he found folks edgy, unsure whether they could trust this Kentuckian who had moved north and was teaching at Yale.

Warren did find his way past the caution of many whites, who thought things out in front of him while, in a small notebook he could hold in one hand, he took careful notes. "But like I was saying," one white man told him, "the point is there's just two races, black and white, and the rest of them is a kind of mixing. You always get a mess when the mixing starts. Take India. They are a pure white people like you and me, and they had a pretty good civilization too. Till they got to shipping on a little Negro blood." Not all whites Warren met clung so tightly to their bigotry. A superintendent in southern Kentucky, where the high schools were about to desegregate, told him, "I'm a Rebel myself, and I don't deny it, but I'm an American and a law-abiding citizen. A man can hate an idea but know it's right, and it takes a lot of thinking and praying to bring yourself around."

Judging from the report Warren wrote for *Life*, no Negroes talked to him so frankly, opening up so plainly to what was inside. He had to find words himself for their feelings: *"After all the patience, after all the humility, after learning and living those virtues, do I have to learn magnanimity, too?"*[57] The wall of silence was high, and men and women on both sides helped prop it up.

Warren did not yet know how to breach it. Sympathetic as he might be, he pronounced himself relieved to leave the South, relieved of responsibility as the plane bore him away. He thought "of the new libel laws in Mississippi, of the academic pressures, of academic resignations, of the Negro facing the shotgun blast, of the white man with a nice little, hard-built business being boycotted, of the college boy who said: 'I'll just tell you, everybody is *scairt*.' " In the face of the violence breaking over the South, Warren, writing his piece far removed in the Connecticut countryside, remained calm, almost aloof. In the published piece, appearing in *Life* on July 9, 1956, just a few weeks after Faulkner's, he concluded with a final interview—with himself, coming out cautiously:

> *Q. Are you for desegregation?*
> *A. Yes.*
> *Q. When will it come?*
> *A. Not soon.*
> *Q. When?*
> *A. When enough people in a particular place, a particular county or state, cannot live with themselves any more. Or realize they don't have to. . . .*
> *Q. Are you a gradualist on the matter of segregation?*
> *A. If by gradualist you mean a person who would create delay for the sake of delay, then no. If by gradualist you mean a person who thinks it will take time, not time as such, but time for an educational process, preferably a calculated one, then yes. . . . Gradualism is all you'll get. History, like nature, knows no jumps. Except the jump backward, maybe.*[58]

Warren did not, like Faulkner, ask for gradualism, but he accepted its inevitability.

When his *Life* essay came out in longer form as a book, *Segregation: The Inner Conflict in the South,* white newspapers in North and South gave it a warm reception. They liked his unpolemical approach. They stressed the absence of "theory" or conclusions. "It is not necessary to write a book that is 'pro' or 'anti' Negro segregation," the *Christian Science Monitor* observed. "You can report the state of the American southern mind."[59]

In the *New Republic,* Negro historian Lawrence Dunbar Reddick struck a note of dissent. A native of Florida, Reddick had received his bachelor's and master's degrees from Fisk University. He had earned a Ph.D. in history from the University of Chicago. At the time he reviewed Warren's book, Reddick was chairing the history department at Alabama State College in Montgomery. He had witnessed the boycott there firsthand and could speak with authority on the developing movement. Reviewing *Segregation* for the *New Republic*, Reddick began quietly but ominously. Robert Penn Warren had been teaching at Vanderbilt, he said, when he himself was attending Fisk. Warren had contributed the sole essay on Negroes to a book published by the Nashville Fugitives, *I'll Take My Stand*, and in it had neither questioned segregation nor expected much of Negroes.

"I keep hearing loud echoes from Nashville in his latest book, *Segregation: The Inner Conflict in the South*," Reddick said. Warren had offered up no more than a polite version of the southern picture painted "in cruder colors in the extremist press of the Deep South: The mistakes of the North are emphasized; the weaknesses of the Negro are underscored; and, above all, there is the determination of Southern white folk, they say, that 'nobody's a gonna *make* us. If we let the nigger in . . . we'll do so when we're good and ready!' "

That, he said, was the substance of Warren's last remarks in his interview with himself: that desegregation would come only when the white people themselves decided they couldn't go on living with their divided minds. "This is the way it goes: Countless editors, scholars and men of letters, in and out of the South, who personally might shrink from killing an insect, give their sanction to the intransigence of the racists. Is it too much to say that there is a connection between the essays, editorials and novels of the literary neo-Confederates and the howling mob that blocks the path of little Negro children on the way to school integration?"[60]

More frankly supportive of change than either his friend Robert Penn Warren or William Faulkner appeared to be, C. Vann Woodward, the South's leading white historian and a professor at Johns Hopkins University in Baltimore, nevertheless wended his own way with similar caution through the conversation on racial change in these first years after *Brown*. The care with which he positioned himself is more surprising, for Woodward's own record of support for integration was clear, unambiguous.

A tall, sandy-haired Arkansan, author of books that had reframed the way historians viewed southern history, C. Vann Woodward had traveled in interracial circles in the 1930s as a young man in Atlanta and New York. When he visited Russia and Europe in the summer of 1932, what made the greatest impression on him were the European protests of the Scottsboro Boys' trial back in Alabama. Despite the lack of evidence against them, the young Negro defendants were found guilty of rape. Returning home to Atlanta, Woodward found something like the Scottsboro case developing—a Negro communist named Angelo Herndon was charged with inciting insurrection under an old state law; he helped raise funds for Herndon's defense. Woodward's support for civil liberties continued during World War II, when he came to the aid both of professors sympathetic toward fascism and of Japanese Americans placed in internment camps.[61]

In 1949 Woodward and Negro historian John Hope Franklin, a good friend, integrated the Southern Historical Association. When Woodward proposed the idea, other members of the program committee asked anxiously, "Where will he stay? Where will he eat?" Woodward had replied (as Franklin would tell the story, laughing), "You know, Franklin's very resourceful. He will probably be able to bring his pup tent, his k-rations—I don't think we should worry about that." Franklin stayed with a friend, although with Woodward's encouragement he did apply for a room at the Williamsburg conference hotel (he got no response). The paper reading went well. The old Phi Beta Kappa hall at William and Mary was packed, with people peering in at the windows.

Three years later a Knoxville hotel balked at serving Negroes at the SHA banquet. The historians, bolder now, abandoned the hotel and trekked out to a suburban restaurant instead. There they heard Woodward deliver his memorable presidential address, "The Irony of Southern History," a challenge to the McCarthyism that was closing in. Playing on the title of theologian Reinhold Niebuhr's *The Irony of American History*, Woodward pointed out "the futility of erecting intellectual barricades against unpopular ideas."[62] His speech established him further as a spokesman for civil liberties.

When NAACP Legal Defense Fund lawyers set to work making a historical case against segregated schools, they turned both to Franklin, author of *From Slavery to Freedom,* and to Woodward, author of *Origins of the New South* and *Reunion and Reaction.* Both historians contributed monographs, and Franklin traveled weekly from Washington, D.C., where he taught at Howard University, to the NAACP's headquarters in New York to help coordinate the research effort.[63]

The summer after the *Brown* decision, the ruling fresh on his mind, Woodward began work on guest lectures he was to deliver at the University of Virginia that fall. He had built a new home on a wooded lot, and at the edge of the woods, in an old stone springhouse, he thought out what he would say. He did not immediately come to rest on his theme, but when he did, he knew it would be controversial. At the university founded by that democratic idealist Thomas Jefferson, he would challenge an idea that underlay southern resistance to the *Brown* decision: the belief that "stateways cannot change folkways." Examining the historical evidence, Woodward concluded that laws had indeed helped to fix segregation as a southern habit. The Supreme Court's own 1896 ruling in *Plessy v. Ferguson* had granted constitutional authority to segregation laws. What the Court had helped do, could not its new decision help undo?

That was the argument he made on a hot night in Charlottesville. The audience, he was pleased to see, included both Negroes and whites, and they appeared to accept what he said with good grace. Woodward was not much of a public speaker. He typically mumbled the words that he had written out so elegantly. Still, the response to the lectures seemed cordial.[64] A sympathetic listener sent Woodward a clip of a newspaper story on his final lecture, commenting wryly, "I thought you might be interested in finding out what you emphasized in that last lecture." The report from the Charlottesville newspaper bore the perhaps wishful headline "To Herald Demise of Jim Crow Seen as Premature Just Now."[65]

The next spring, Oxford University Press rushed the lectures out as a slender volume, *The Strange Career of Jim Crow.*[66] Woodward was disappointed to learn he had signed away his rights to royalties as part of the lecture arrangement, an oversight he remedied when he revised the book for a new edition.[67] *Strange Career* would undergo several revisions, repeated printings, and much criticism, as historians picked his analysis apart.[68] Immediately, however, whatever its shortcomings as history, it played a useful political role because in it Woodward argued persuasively for the possibility of change. Traveling in ever-widening circles—reaching seminarians and labor organizers, academics and journalists—*Strange Career* thrust C. Vann Woodward himself into the limelight as an interpreter of developing events.

The magazine to pursue him most persistently was *Commentary*, a leading New York intellectual magazine published by the American Jewish Committee. There, in the June 1956 issue, Woodward turned his attention to the topic "The 'New Reconstruction' in the South." It was an unfortunate phrase: the "New Reconstruction." Woodward had already used it in *The Strange Career of Jim Crow*, and here he brought it out again. It set up an unhelpful frame for the challenge to segregation. This was no New Reconstruction. No civil war had been fought. No soldiers had been sent in to occupy a defeated nation. Whites were not disenfranchised, nor were Negroes politically empowered. Woodward had simply plucked from his historian's brain a handy phrase bound to have an unfortunate effect on white southerners. To white southerners, "the Reconstruction" was a red flag. They hated the first Reconstruction and would hardly welcome a second. Woodward developed the analogy between new and old Reconstructions at length, seeing in both an "effort by the majority to impose its will upon a recalcitrant and unwilling minority region." Resisting that effort, the South had triggered a "constitutional crisis."

"However hollow and antiquated the constitutional arguments may seem to others, they were self-evident truths to a great many people in the South," Woodward wrote. *"It is a real Constitutional crisis that we are facing, not a sham parade in ancestral costume. The law of the land* had been clearly defined by the Supreme Court of the United States, and that definition had been just as clearly rejected by responsible spokesmen of millions of our people."[69]

Negro political leaders would scarcely have applied the word "responsible" to Mississippi Senator Jim Eastland, who like a great poisonous spider was spinning a web of resistance at that very time. Nor would they have applied it to any of the others who had joined Eastland in a manifesto against the Supreme Court that nearly every southern congressman had signed. Nor would they have regarded as "responsible spokesmen" the state politicians who tried to "interpose" state governments between the Supreme Court and the people.

By framing the NAACP's challenge as a New Reconstruction, Woodward lent support to the idea that the North was once more forcing its unpalatable ideals down the South's throat. He bypassed the better explanation of events: that southerners themselves—*Negro* southerners—were demanding change in their own region. While the New York–based NAACP Legal Defense Fund had argued the *Brown* appeals, southern parents were the plaintiffs. Like so many other whites who wrote on desegregation, Woodward fixed his eyes on southern whites, all but ignoring the role southern Negroes played in the history of their region.

At the end of "The 'New Reconstruction,' " Woodward weighed in on the side of gradualism. He did not say he wanted it. But like his friend Robert Penn Warren, Woodward said gradualism was inevitable. "Impatience with the word among people who have already waited nearly a hundred years for promised rights is readily understandable. I use the word here not to propose or define a policy, but to characterize a historic phenomenon. *Undesirable or not, gradualism is an inescapable fact and a basic characteristic of the New Reconstruction.*" Without urging gradualism, Woodward, like Warren (who probably read what Woodward had said), appeared to accept it. In his last paragraph, he went a step further, beyond realism to advocacy, implying that gradualism, after all, might produce more lasting change than demands for quick action. Borrowing a phrase from Francis Thompson's poem *Hound of Heaven*, he said, "However deliberate and halting its speed, the Second Reconstruction would seem to promise more enduring results."[70]

Why was C. Vann Woodward, who had proved such a bold defender of civil liberties in the past, so accepting of gradualism? In Negro political circles, "gradualism" had become such a sensitive word that one of Adlai Stevenson's advisers, John Fischer, editor of *Harper's*, cautioned Stevenson against using it.[71] A candidate for the Democratic presidential nomination in the 1956 election, Stevenson had worried Woodward himself by his temporizing on desegregation. Yet if Woodward did not temporize, he at least exercised caution.

He was *asked* to exercise caution. An editor inviting him to write the entry on segregation for the *Encyclopedia Americana* told him "that most people, even those who strongly favor segregation, will react favorably to a restrained and factual presentation."[72] Woodward inspired trust that he would approach this inflammatory subject without setting off explosions. "What we want to do is to find one or two Southerners who can expound thoughtfully and dispassionately on these matters," a professor wrote him, inviting him to speak at Kenyon College.[73]

An editor at *Current History* even imagined, apparently, that Woodward might put forward white southern views akin to those expressed in the *Atlantic Monthly* by one Herbert Ravenel Sass. In an article that an editorial note identified as "the fundamental case for the white South," Sass maintained that the United States was "overwhelmingly a pure white nation" and ought to stay that way. Desegregation of the schools would inevitably lead to "widespread racial amalgamation." To balance the article, the *Atlantic* ran a second, by white historian Oscar Handlin, who, curiously, accepted the premise of Sass's argument—the undesirability of social mixing—and argued that desegregation of schools would not necessarily lead to it.[74]

When a *Current History* editor hinted the hope that Woodward would write something like Sass's article, Woodward responded in terms that were polite but chill. The *Atlantic* had "performed a service of very dubious value in seeking out the elderly gentleman they chose," he remarked. He did not sympathize with the man's views, nor could he possibly identify himself with them. On the other hand, he *could* present the position Sass represented "in a detached way," along with other positions held by southerners.[75] That was fine with *Current History*, and Woodward wrote the piece. As the editor had asked, he tried to explain the feelings that produced southern white resistance to desegregation. He quoted Robert Penn Warren, who "has argued persuasively that the real conflict in the South over Segregation is an inner conflict, a conflict within the individual mind."[76]

Despite the boldness of his own record, Woodward tiptoed through the discussion of race like a man walking through a minefield. Stepping carefully in his public comments, he stayed well within the bounds of his role as a historian. However strong his opposition to segregation, he felt a professional commitment to detachment. When a Charleston newspaper accused him of using history as propaganda, he worried over the charge, especially when a history professor at Princeton brought it up in conversation. Woodward thought the man was joking, but he wasn't sure and wrote him to ask. "If I have offended the rules of the craft it is your duty as a friend to tell me," he said, "even if it hurts."[77]

If detachment served Woodward's identity as a historian, it also served his identity as a reformer. He wanted to be able to speak to diverse audiences; he did not like the idea of shutting himself off from people who did not agree with him. He explained to another professor at a southern college, "I can still talk to Negro audiences and white audiences in Georgia, as I did this year, and make them listen to what I have to say. And I can talk to integrated audiences in Virginia, too. I do not know how many Southerners there are left who can do that."[78]

He was guided, as well, by a philosophical stance: a belief that history was not straightforward, that motives were tangled, relations between causes and effects difficult to sort out, ironic consequences likely—consequences opposite to those intended. Woodward shared the skeptical spirit that marked much of intellectual life in the 1950s. It was a natural response to the horrors of fascism and the disillusion with communism. Radical social change, imposed by strong governments, had given the world the Holocaust and the Gulag. Like other intellectuals, Woodward had traveled in radical circles in the 1930s, but even then he had not gone all the way. Leading the fund-raising effort for Angelo Herndon, he had disliked the tactics the Communist Party had brought to the effort, and he remained permanently soured on communism. He was a liberal and a civil libertarian; he was not a radical, and he feared what too forceful a push for change might bring about. He could understand why literary scholar Louis Rubin planned to cut out the section on segregation in a speech to the 1956 Southern Historical Association meeting because, Rubin explained, "I am simply not going to say or do *anything* that will give any tacit encouragement to Massive Resistance."[79]

Robert Penn Warren told Woodward in 1958 that he envied his clarity on the racial changes taking place. Commenting years later on what Warren had said, Woodward would say he understood Warren's confusion because he shared it. "He knew violence and he feared it. I can easily see because I share some of those hesitations. Shall we push this as an issue when we know it will cause bloodshed and result in worse conditions in the end? Shall we continue to work for these objectives—and wait for the proper moment? I was willing to take risks for myself but not for the public safety."[80]

He explained himself at the time in a passage added to *The Strange Career of Jim Crow* when it came out again, revised, in 1957. Once the white resistance began,

> *in genuine fear of more explosions in chain reaction, Southern liberals and moderates raised the cry of forbearance, directed toward the North. Further pressure and haste at the moment, they maintained, would leave them no ground on which to stand and would only provoke additional violence that would defeat the purposes of the reformers. The appeal met with wide response among northern liberals, many of whom called for an easing of the pressure and a slowing down of the campaign against segregation.*[81]

Woodward had another reason for caution: he did not want the South to lose its identity. No region was more self-conscious about its special culture, flamboyantly captured by writers from William Faulkner to W. J. Cash, the author of that enduring portrait *The Mind of the South*. Woodward hoped that in the rush for change the South would not lose its sense of itself as a separate region. When he spoke at a conference at Maine's Bowdoin College, the student newspaper found his reflections on "regional distinctiveness" uncomfortably close to views held by "bigoted southern journalists." The proximity shocked the young editors because, "calculating and quite open-minded, he has been widely recognized as one of the leading authorities on the question."[82]

Woodward's preference for the center came through in the report he wrote for *Commentary* on the Civil Rights Act of 1957. He lavished praise on that "presiding genius from Texas," the towering Senator Lyndon Johnson, for finding a compromise that would get the bill through. Like the Supreme Court, Woodward wrote, the Congress had opted for local authority over central power, for compromise over radicalism. The NAACP had nearly opposed passage of the compromise bill, so inadequate did it seem. Woodward gave no hint of reservations on his part. Instead, he implied satisfaction with the moderate course Congress had taken. He warned readers they need not imagine that "the radical alternatives originally proposed have been forever forsworn."[83]

C. Vann Woodward wanted change but, like William Faulkner, did not want change forced on the South. So carefully did he phrase his comments that detecting his own preferences requires some imagination, but now and then he came out of the thicket and showed himself plainly. Reviewing Negro journalist Carl Rowan's *Go South to Sorrow* for *Commentary*, Woodward gave this first major chronicle of the movement an unkind review. Twice he misrepresented what Rowan was saying. What Woodward disliked most about the book was Rowan's call for "passion and zeal," and Rowan's apparent distaste for moderation.[84] Woodward liked to think of himself as a radical, and he really *was* ahead of his time, his friend John Hope Franklin believed, until "the times caught up with him."[85] By the 1950s, Woodward had already shown himself to be an essentially moderate man.

His moderation was more considered, more calculated, more complex than Faulkner's, and not known by such a broad audience. But although he was not reaching millions as Faulkner and Warren did through *Life*, Woodward was steadily building a presence, through articles in smaller magazines and mentions by editorial writers who had read his speeches and articles, and through *The Strange Career of Jim Crow*. His would ultimately be the more lasting influence. An accomplished, esteemed historian by any measure, Woodward brought the weight of his reputation and knowledge to bear on events whose end was not yet in sight. For that, he deserves credit. Not many others stepped forward as he did. Yet for all his good intentions, Woodward, like William Faulkner, had weighed in on the side of "going slow."

In his review of Robert Penn Warren's *Segregation*, Lawrence Reddick had put his finger on a shameful truth. For two years after *Brown*, as the white resistance gained strength, white southern men, ambivalent or worse, had led the commentary on race in the national media. Editors were of course journalists with their ears pricked for conflict, and whites were the ones providing conflict by resisting the Supreme Court. Nevertheless, there was something askew in the national media's fixation on the white South's response to *Brown*. Why, at this bend in the road, were the nation's magazines—still the primary vehicle for serious national political discussion—so much more interested in southern whites' discomfort than in the long-standing injustice suffered by Negroes? Why were they so little interested in what Negroes themselves had to say about what was happening?

Before the *Brown* decision, *Look* magazine did try to get United Nations official Ralph Bunche, formerly a professor at Howard University, to write on segregation in the schools,[86] and after the decision political magazines like the *Nation* did run commentary by Negroes involved in the NAACP and other political organizations. But on the whole, as Lillian Smith had observed, the big-circulation national magazines turned over the stage to southern white gradualists. When the *New Republic* finally let her have her say in 1957, she spoke of the "magnolia curtain" that had dropped down between the South and the North. She mocked the magazines' approach to racial change: "[D]on't let one intelligent white Southerner who opposes segregation speak. Keep them smothered. . . ."[87] As one who felt shunted aside, Smith fixed on the exclusion of desegregationists like herself, but the exclusion of Negroes constituted no less a political act. As Ralph Ellison understood, rendering Negroes invisible was one means of disempowering them.

If whites did not notice the one-sided nature of the dialogue, Negroes certainly did. In *Cold Rebellion*, published in England just a few years later, Lewis W. Jones observed, "Negroes are frequently unhappy in having their case presented by 'moderates' or 'liberals' whom they surely would not identify as being either moderate or liberal." (The fact that Jones could not find an American publisher for his own timely book underlined his point.)[88] A *Reader's Digest* article Hodding Carter contributed on the southern racial situation infuriated Kenneth B. Clark, the social psychologist who had helped the NAACP Legal Defense Fund make its case for *Brown*. In an impassioned two-page letter to the editors, he questioned Carter's good faith and the editors' judgment in selecting him as an authority. "While Mr. Carter might feel competent to speak in the name of 'moderate' white southerners, it is presumptuous, patronizing, and not justified by recent events for him to attempt to speak for Negroes."[89]

Clark himself, like Robert Penn Warren, traveled south on a fact-finding trip at the start of 1956. He found Negro communities unshaken in the face of White Citizens Council reprisals, Negroes' support for desegregation stronger than ever. He met vibrant young leaders, including Martin Luther King Jr. Clark ran into King quite by chance on a train, introduced by a porter who somehow knew that each man would want to meet the other. As Clark and King talked, two Negro porters watched, "ready to participate in any emergency." Clark took their watchfulness as a sign of Negro solidarity.[90]

Clark wrote up his findings in a long report. A couple of magazines showed an interest in it, but, possibly because the Unitarians who had sent him South shied away from the publicity, nothing came of the interest. Although the Unitarian magazine *Christian Register* did publish a summary, the full report was not forthcoming. Toward the end of 1957, almost two years after Clark had made his trip, he was astonished to find that the report had still not been reproduced.[91]

For a time, it looked as if his research might lead to a book. After he gave a talk to a Unitarian group, one of those present, Lawrence Hill, of the new publishing company Hill & Wang, told him, "If you have not already made other commitments, would it be possible for Mr. Wang and me to get together with you to talk over the possibility of a book?"[92] No book materialized. Clark may have been too busy to produce a book. Among other things, he taught at City College and, with his wife, Mamie Phipps, ran a psychiatric clinic for children in Harlem. He was also involved in efforts to end de facto segregation of New York schools.

And, in fact, he did have a commitment, to Beacon Press, which had published his first book, *Prejudice and Your Child*, based on the social science research that he had marshaled for *Brown*. He also had a commitment to Jeannette Hopkins, his former editor at Beacon Press. Hopkins had moved on to another company, but she and Clark maintained ties, and she had entertained the idea of pairing his southern report with Robert Penn Warren's in a single book. When Warren's article appeared as a book on its own, she wrote regretfully to Clark, "He has done exactly the kind of book which I had in mind that you could do—with him or alone—and it saddens me to reflect that this may mean serious difficulties in the way of doing another book somewhat similar. This, as you are discovering, is a competitive business."[93]

It was a revealing remark. There was just so much space in the public sphere, it seemed, and white men had occupied most of it.

CHAPTER 2

NORTHERN RESERVATIONS

Never completed, St. John the Divine, the world's largest Gothic cathedral, stood towerless on Amsterdam Avenue—its front toward Columbia University, its back toward Harlem. On the evening of May 17, 1956, the second anniversary of the *Brown* decision, twelve thousand people gathered in this place so symbolic of America's racial affairs to hear the Reverend Martin Luther King Jr. speak at an interdenominational, interracial service of prayer and thanksgiving. Facing a formidable audience in the very heart of intellectual New York, the slim young preacher from the South took as his text not a peaceable New Testament passage but a violent verse from the Old Testament—Exodus 14:30: "And Israel saw the Egyptians dead upon the seashore." He rolled out before his listeners the great drama of his time: the freedom movements of the world's oppressed people.

> *The great struggle of the Twentieth Century has been between these exploited masses questing for freedom and the colonial powers seeking to maintain their domination.*
>
> *What we are seeing now in this struggle is the gradual victory of the forces of freedom and justice. The Red Sea has opened. . . .*

The message was more stirring than King himself could imagine, one of those present wrote him afterward: "When we rose to sing Ein' Feste Burg, the ancient hymn had greater power and grandeur than ever I have experienced in it before."[1]

Another powerful preacher who had spent much of his working life only a few blocks away was not apparently so moved by King's message, which he may not have heard that day but which he could hardly have escaped altogether. Reinhold Niebuhr, a member of the faculty at Union Theological Seminary, had, through his writing, shored up King's own belief in nonviolence as a strategy for the Negro cause. Other young men by the dozens (and a few women) had passed through Niebuhr's tutelage at Union and gone out to serve the world. No religious intellectual had made a greater impact on the postwar years than Niebuhr, and none better exemplifies the caution that northern white intellectuals, like their southern counterparts, displayed toward desegregation.

When *Time* magazine's Boston bureau came up with a list of leading intellectuals in the spring of 1956, Niebuhr emerged (with literary critics Lionel Trilling and Edmund Wilson) in the top three.[2] In an essay published in a 1956 collection, his friend historian Arthur Schlesinger Jr. proclaimed, "No man has had as much influence as a preacher in this generation; no preacher has had as much influence in the secular world." A stroke had slowed Niebuhr down and set off recurring depression, but he retained his professorial position at Union. Nearly bald, stern of face, Niebuhr was still a celebrity with an unparalleled power to command the spotlight for his tough-minded Christian views.[3]

From *Moral Man and Immoral Society* to *The Irony of American History*, Niebuhr had argued for pragmatic politics and Christian realism. Given the human potential for bad behavior—Nazi Germany and the atomic bomb had suggested how bad that could be—Niebuhr placed no faith in utopian schemes. Human beings might still hope for a just society, but they had better temper their hope with realism. Once a socialist, Niebuhr had by the 1950s become something else: a Cold War liberal. Indeed, Schlesinger portrayed him as very nearly the intellectual architect of Cold War liberalism. Niebuhr had helped "accomplish in a single generation a revolution in the bases of American liberal political thought," Schlesinger wrote. From the ashes of despair Niebuhr had pulled a brand of hope: "that men and women could act more effectively for decency and justice under the banner of a genuine humility than they had under the banner of an illusory perfectibility." Liberalism had triumphed over radicalism.[4]

Like other Cold War liberals, Niebuhr opposed Senator Joseph McCarthy's attacks on communism chiefly because McCarthy was giving anti-communism a bad name. Niebuhr approved of the execution of Julius and Ethel Rosenberg as Soviet spies—although afterwards, considering the outrage in Europe over their deaths, he wished they had been sent to prison for life instead. He and Schlesinger both played leadership roles in the Committee for Cultural Freedom, one of the organizations spawned by the Central Intelligence Agency to support its anti-communist efforts in Europe. Essentially a support group for the European Congress for Cultural Freedom (also created by the CIA), the American committee was part of a complex apparatus designed to build pro-American, anti-communist sentiments in Europe, especially on the left, which the agency feared might otherwise be drawn into the communist orbit.[5] The intellectuals who led and joined the American committee covered a broad political range, with Schlesinger and Niebuhr among the more moderate.

Schlesinger and Niebuhr had also organized the Americans for Democratic Action (ADA), defined by Schlesinger as "a group of pragmatic liberals opposed to all dogmatisms, conservative, socialist, or communist, and dedicated to piecemeal and gradual reform."[6] The ADA became a veritable engine of Cold War liberalism, opposing the Soviet Union abroad and communism at home, favoring progressive causes like civil rights—but favoring them moderately, respectful of circumstances and contending forces, preferring compromise to open conflict. Applying these principles to the *Brown* decision, Niebuhr came out at a place not all that distant from William Faulkner's. He was glad that the Supreme Court gave the southern states time "to adjust themselves."[7] He praised the "statesmanship" of the Court for combining "boldness and concern for the political realities." Given the strength of local mores, it was best to give southern states time to acclimate themselves. Forcing the South to act too quickly would just strengthen white resistance, Niebuhr wrote in *Christianity and Crisis* immediately after the ruling.[8]

Niebuhr saw before him "a great moral crisis in our national history" nearly as great as the crisis of slavery, yet he held back from arguing for an urgent solution. Rather, he cautioned northerners "to be as patient and understanding as possible in viewing the trials through which the South is moving."[9] Regarding the tempting idea that "the total Christian community in America should give some dramatic expression of its concern," he cautioned that such a move would be construed as " 'Yankee' meddling." Better to leave the work of change to southern Christians.[10]

Niebuhr's stance was symptomatic. Despite a chorus of private and public praise for the *Brown* decision, the white northern liberal establishment had scarcely mounted a crusade for equal rights. As late as 1958, philosopher Sidney Hook would remark on what seemed to him a "surprising" absence of a "defense of desegregation" on democratic principles. Whatever defense had been made had followed a different line: the Court has ruled; therefore the Court ought to be obeyed.[11] "From the point of view of a Negro," social psychologist Kenneth B. Clark said in a 1956 speech (before white liberal Hook took his principled stand), "the Northern white liberal appears confused, ambiguous, and often blocked by his own guilt."[12]

Behind some northern liberals' confusion in the face of racial challenge lay a retreat from radicalism.[13] The radical hopes stirred in New York intellectual circles before World War II had faded. The Soviet Union had betrayed the socialist dream, burying it beneath a brutal, oppressive state. The American Communist Party had proved itself a too willing lackey. Examining his generation's disillusion with communism in the novel *The Middle of the Journey*, literary critic Lionel Trilling, a professor at Columbia University, said his own goodbye to all that. Fellow literary critic Irving Howe, still a socialist, blamed Trilling, in fact, for encouraging a whole generation of intellectuals to turn away from politics. Trilling's influential 1950 collection of essays, *The Liberal Imagination*, provided 1950s intellectuals with a rationale for pulling away from engagement, Howe believed. "To a generation that in its youth had been persuaded, even coerced, to believe that action in the public world was a moral necessity, Trilling's critique of 'the liberal imagination' eased a turning away from all politics, whether liberal, radical, or conservative," Howe would write in his 1982 memoir, *A Margin of Hope*. Sociologist David Riesman took essentially the same position as Trilling, Howe thought, but spread it further in his own popular book, *The Lonely Crowd*. "He wanted intellectuals to admit their incapacity for public life and the consequent desirability of adopting a more modest stance. The abominations of McCarthyism, the crudities of the Cold War were jarring to sensitive people: it seemed best to pull away and dig in."[14]

Reinhold Niebuhr, however, did not pull away from politics—only from radical politics. Still an engaged Democrat, he offered advice to Adlai Stevenson during the 1956 Democratic primary campaign. On the racial issue, Niebuhr counseled, Stevenson ought to take the middle way. "The South and the whole nation have made steady progress in racial justice. It would be a calamity if this progress were arrested by heedless action either on the part of those who would enforce the Supreme Court decision by police action, or by those who would defy it." Prohibition had taught the limits of force when communities resisted the law, Niebuhr said. "The Supreme Court has wisely left it to the communities to adjust their practices to the law, and we must do all we can to give these organic processes of persuasion a chance to close the hiatus between the standard of equal justice and the mores of the community."[15]

Several months later, as the primary campaign heated up, Niebuhr wrote *New Leader* editor Sol Levitas a worried letter. Niebuhr was concerned that Stevenson's Democratic opponent Averell Harriman would "go out on a limb on the segregation issue." Niebuhr sent along a cautionary article, which the *New Leader* published. Stevenson's and Harriman's positions on integration appeared similar, Niebuhr wrote. Both said they would carry out the *Brown* decision, yet both had also said they would not use federal force to do so. The two differed in this: southern moderates would accept Stevenson but not Harriman.

"From this difference in temper a very tragic situation could arise," Niebuhr said. If either man failed to hold to their common line—if Harriman, for instance, strengthened his appeal to Negro voters—then the Democratic Party would lose "not only the Southern racists but the Southern moderates" and "might face a split." Worse, pressing too aggressively for desegregation could strengthen southern resistance and "arrest the promising organic growths of racial amity." Niebuhr argued that advocating gradualism was in one sense politically unwise, since it could cost Democrats the Negro vote. But because gradualism would produce the best results, it was the correct moral option. Thus he reinterpreted his own political pragmatism as a moral stance.[16]

Arthur Schlesinger would later explain how Adlai Stevenson could have actually proposed a year-long moratorium on agitation for civil rights; the explanation served for Niebuhr (and Schlesinger himself) as well. "No white leader seemed to understand what was going on in the consciousness of black America: the ebbing away of patience; the mounting bitterness; the spreading demand, all other roads blocked, for direct action."[17]

Cut off from feelings in the Negro community, in late November 1956, writing in the *Reporter*, Niebuhr counseled patience while "the slow erosion of racial prejudice" did its work.[18] A few months later, he wrote to Justice Felix Frankfurter that he and other northern ministers had talked of issuing a statement in support of desegregation but had decided to hold off because "anything from the North would seem like Yankee interference." In another development, he wrote Frankfurter, Martin Luther King had asked him to sign his name to a request that President Eisenhower intervene in the South. "I was advised that such pressure would do more harm than good," Niebuhr said, without explaining who had advised him to turn King down.[19]

In 1963, Niebuhr would express his hope that President Kennedy would complete the job of making "the South conform to the standards of the nation." But in 1957 he was willing to let southerners speak for themselves and Dwight Eisenhower do what he would. If Reinhold Niebuhr was not ready to speak on behalf of the Negro South, what white man was likely to? Here was a man who had spent much of his life introducing moral questions into the political realm, a man much admired by Martin Luther King, a man who served on the board of the Highlander Folk School, a movement training center that had been founded by men who had studied under Niebuhr himself. Yet, when the question was called, he stepped back—counseled restraint, patience, and wondered if the *Brown* decision, provoking resistance, had not made things worse.[20]

Niebuhr's caution did not go unremarked. Irving Howe took Niebuhr to task in *Dissent*, a little magazine he had lately started to give non-communist socialism a voice. For the spring 1956 issue, Howe began work on an essay with the idea of taking up Adlai Stevenson's "shameful twists on the question of integration." But that point scarcely needed making, he decided. Stevenson's record was "so clearly opportunistic, so patently appalling that even his most ardent supporters are now a little apologetic." Howe therefore spread his attention around—to the *New Republic*, for instance, so infatuated with Stevenson, he thought, that it "proposed that the 'emotional race issue' be dropped from the political campaign."

And then there was Reinhold Niebuhr, or, as Howe put it, "Reinhold Niebuhr, a man of God," who, writing in the *New Leader*, had approved of Stevenson's "counsel of patience" as the wisest course. "Surely," Howe observed, "one might expect something a little more forthright—a little more *moral*—from the foremost exponent in the United States of the Protestant 'crisis theology.' " Niebuhr's response to the challenge of civil rights seemed to Howe all too typical of the times. The bus boycott in Montgomery had launched "a major social and political revolution" in the South. Why, then, such "moral bewilderment and opportunism" in the white response? "Everyone, from President Eisenhower to most of the liberal journals, cries 'moderation.' But if you inquire what 'moderation' means in the circumstances, it is impossible to get a precise answer. Is the cry of 'moderation' directed against the North Carolina police who arrested Clarence Mitchell, NAACP leader, for ignoring the segregation 'rules,' or is it directed against Mitchell for insisting that he is a human being?"

To Howe, here was yet more evidence of the gray conformity permeating the culture. "The issue is very simple, and those intellectuals who habitually worry about the dangers of oversimplifying might here trouble themselves about the dangers of undersimplifying. The issue is not whether federal troops are to be sent into the South or any other such irrelevancy. It is simply whether a substantial beginning is to be made toward integration, whether the Supreme Court order is to be obeyed or not, whether the Negroes of the South will be granted their rights or not." In Howe's view justice was a matter "of extraordinary importance to our entire national life."[21] Instead of backing away from the change, he embraced it.

Given the strength of Howe's views, *Dissent*'s own offerings on America's racial problem were less plentiful than they might have been. *Dissent* did publish a report on the Montgomery boycott by L. D. Reddick, the historian who had given Robert Penn Warren a hard time. *Dissent* also ran an excerpt from exiled Negro writer Richard Wright's collection, *White Man, Listen!* Neither of these articles by Negro writers, however, drew as much attention as an essay *Dissent* published in 1957: Norman Mailer's "The White Negro."

Norman Mailer had burst into fame as a young man with his World War II novel *The Naked and the Dead*. He followed that with a political novel, *Barbary Shore*. Calling himself a libertarian socialist, Mailer made his own political way through the 1950s. At a time when other intellectuals and artists were fleeing politics, he held the course.[22] He selected freedom of speech as his own particular issue. Confronting book and magazine editors who shrank from expletives and sexual detail, Mailer had made a point of pushing the limits in his newest novel, *The Deer Park*, which he had difficulty publishing.[23]

That difficulty naturally made him wonder just how free the media were. He took up the question with Lyle Stuart, publisher of a small newspaper called the *Independent*, when Stuart visited him in his Connecticut farmhouse in early 1957. Stuart told Mailer he could publish anything in his own paper. That might be, Mailer conceded. But if he, Mailer, were to write up a half-page statement on school integration, the big newspapers wouldn't touch it. Stuart challenged him to give it a try.[24]

Mailer sat down at his typewriter. In four paragraphs, he argued that whites did not want to integrate their schools, because they knew Negroes were superior sexually. Stuart took the piece and, to give it an extra spin, mailed it to William Faulkner for comment. Faulkner replied, "I have heard this idea expressed several times during the last twenty years, though not before by a man. The others were ladies, northern or middle western ladies, usually around 40 or 45 years of age. I don't know what a psychiatrist would find in this." In an attempt to widen the controversy, Stuart sent Faulkner's and Mailer's comments off to W. E. B. Du Bois, Eleanor Roosevelt, and several others for their responses.

Of those who replied, Du Bois agreed that "sex jealousy between races and classes is to blame for much of their friction" but placed the most blame for the racial problem on "respectable white Southerners" who had done nothing through the years to stop slavery, the Civil War, or lynchings.[25] Former first lady Eleanor Roosevelt responded, "I think Mr. Mailer's statement is horrible and unnecessary." Stuart offered six newspapers in the South the opportunity to pick up the pieces. None did.

Mailer found himself discontented with his own argument. "My statement had been incendiary but unilluminating," he wrote with unusual modesty in *Advertisements for Myself*.[26] He began work on the essay that became one of the best-known and controversial pronouncements on race in the 1950s: "The White Negro: Superficial Reflections on the Hipster." He said that southerners resisting desegregation in the South rightly saw that "the deeper issue is not desegregation but miscegenation." He said that when miscegenation came, it was likely to "be a terror," and that the Negro's movement for equality could usher in "a time of violence, new hysteria, confusion, and rebellion."[27] This was precisely what liberals counseling moderation feared. Mailer had wrapped the argument in a more sensational cover, but the gist was the same: after desegregation, things would fall apart.

Mailer thought "The White Negro" one of the best things he had written. The young writer James Baldwin would speak of it with contempt. Baldwin claimed to like Mailer, seeing him as a rebellious brother under the skin. But Baldwin could not, "with the best will in the world, make any sense out of 'The White Negro.'" He could not imagine how the man who had written *The Naked and the Dead* and *Barbary Shore* could have written this piece. Baldwin did not like the title, he did not like Mailer's attempts to imitate Jack Kerouac "and all the other Suzuki rhythm boys," and he did not like Mailer's main point. In fact, it sent Baldwin into a fury to see "so antique a vision of the blacks . . . stepping off the A train." It seemed to Baldwin's playwright friend Lorraine Hansberry that Mailer had "manufactured absurdity and locked himself in it."[28]

In the light of second thoughts, Howe said later he should not have run "The White Negro" in *Dissent*, at least not with the sentence justifying the murder of a candy-store keeper as an act of self-liberation. ("[O]ne murders not only a weak fifty-year-old man but an institution as well. One violates private property; one enters into a new relation with the police and introduces a dangerous element into one's life.")[29] But Howe often had to rewrite articles for *Dissent* line by line. Here was a flamboyant, provocative piece by one of the country's leading novelists. As Howe explained to one interviewer, "When you put out a little magazine like *Dissent* with a small circulation and you get something which can pass for a scoop—and 'The White Negro' was by our lights a scoop—it's hard to be sufficiently intransigent or principled to send it back."[30] Howe was shortly to have a shot at another scoop—a controversial piece by another celebrated Jewish writer, the brilliant philosopher Hannah Arendt.

Hannah Arendt had never been south and would not go there, she said later, because of her idea of what it was like. She had few southern friends; one she did have, Randall Jarrell, was a poet, and he was more likely to talk with her about poetry than about politics.[31] Although she had met Richard Wright,[32] no Negroes figured in her inner circle of intellectuals, the Jews and gentiles who clustered at *Partisan Review*, *Commentary*, and Schocken Books, where she had worked as an editor. And so in the fall of 1957, confronted with a newspaper photograph from Little Rock, she brought to the image not experience of the South, Negro or white, but her own experience as a German Jew.

Educated as a philosopher, Arendt had fled Germany in 1933 and wound up in New York. What had happened in Germany obsessed her, her friend Alfred Kazin would say. "Hitler's war was the central fact in the dark shadowy Morningside Drive apartment where she and her husband, Heinrich Bluecher, now lived, taking in a boarder to make ends meet. Hannah never stopped thinking. . . . How did *it* happen? How had it all happened? How had this modern age happened?"[33]

After the war ended, she devoted four years to writing *The Origins of Totalitarianism*, a historical analysis of the Nazi years and, more briefly, of Soviet communism. Published in 1951, the year before Niebuhr's *Irony of American History*, the book had made an enormous impact on intellectual New York. *The Origins of Totalitarianism* laid out in Arendt's grand style why fascism rose in Germany, then turned to the Soviet Union to assert the equivalence of the two systems: the Nazis and the communists were two sides of the same totalitarian coin. Since other intellectuals had already said the same thing, and since, besides, her analysis was brilliant and persuasive, her argument was warmly received. It fed the fires of apocalyptic thinking, the idea that Western civilization—democratic, rational—was engaged in a last-ditch struggle with the forces of darkness.

Few had better reason to fear the abyss than Hannah Arendt. Her own world had been upended, its continuity shredded in the Nazi years, not so long past; in the midfifties, the war had been over for only ten years. She and her husband watched the American scene nervously, alert for signs of impending dissolution. In long letters to her German mentor, Karl Jaspers, she intermingled thoughts about philosophy with comments on American politics.

Senator Joseph McCarthy's rise frightened her. She was astonished by the readiness of intellectuals in her circle—including Jewish intellectuals who wrote and edited for *Commentary*—to support the campaign against communism. She had no sympathy for communism, but neither did she have any for the use of state power against communists. "The great danger that the ex-Communists represent at the moment is that they are introducing police methods into normal social life." When McCarthy passed from the scene, she watched, relieved, as the temper of the country changed overnight.[34] Then, in the fall of 1957, came the discomfiting sight of paratroopers in Little Rock.

For three years after *Brown*, President Eisenhower had stood aside from the fray; he did not approve of the Supreme Court decision and said so publicly, and he did not lift a finger to support or enforce it. He made no move to call the South to compliance. Despite his earlier life in the military, the president was not, on the whole, a man of action. In the international arena, he had maintained the Cold War, but he had steadfastly resisted temptations to turn it into a hot war. When the Soviet Union crushed the Hungarian rebellion in 1956, he turned a deaf ear to the Hungarians' call for help.[35] Eisenhower took the same stance at home: he was not eager to risk civil war for the sake of liberty.

But in the back-to-school days of September 1957, Arkansas Governor Orval Faubus, egged on by politicians from other states, so openly defied the law that Eisenhower was forced to act. First Faubus called out the National Guard to keep nine Negro students from entering Little Rock's Central High. Then he withdrew the guard, leaving the inadequate city police force to protect the students from a mob Faubus himself had helped to stir up. General that he was, Eisenhower, deciding finally to act, acted decisively, ordering a thousand soldiers of the integrated 101st Airborne Infantry flown in from Fort Campbell, Kentucky. In the days to come, federal marshals escorted the Negro students past the jeering mobs, through the lines of armed paratroopers, into Central High.

Until the crisis at Little Rock, Hannah Arendt had not shown much interest in America's racial situation, though she had made passing remarks about it in her letters to Jaspers. Later, explaining what started her thinking about Little Rock, she said she was moved by the photograph of an unhappy Negro child, led by a white man, while a mob of white teenagers jeered. If she were a Negro mother, what would she do?

"Under no circumstances would I expose my child to conditions which made it appear as though it wanted to push its way into a group where it was not wanted." That, she believed, was a way to strip the child of personal pride, essential for personal integrity. "If I were a Negro mother in the South, I would feel that the Supreme Court ruling, unwillingly but unavoidably, has put my child into a more humiliating position than it had been in before."[36] She was echoing the position her own mother had taken, bringing up her own daughter in Germany.[37] Arendt saw all the news coming out of Little Rock through the lens of what she had seen in Nazi Germany: a mob, the strong arm of the central state, a child bearing the brunt of adult political zeal. Out of her confrontation with that photograph, a line of thought unwound itself as an essay for *Commentary*.

What she made of events at Little Rock was unsettling. *Commentary* had published some of the more thoughtful observations on the racial situation—essays by C. Vann Woodward and reporting by David Halberstam, as well as James Baldwin's memorable essay "Equal in Paris." *Commentary* already had in hand a strong Little Rock essay by historian Oscar Handlin, who argued that the crisis at Little Rock demonstrated the "failure of moderation": "Moderation works only with moderates. Extremists are ruthless, and moderation (which they identify with weakness) only stimulates them to increase their demands."[38]

Now here was Hannah Arendt, the most famous Jewish intellectual in America, arguing *against* forced desegregation of the schools. She cast her chief objection in the terms of her newest book, *The Human Condition*. Schools belong to the social realm, she argued, where groups may discriminate against other groups, not to the political realm, where, in a free society, they may not. "To force parents to send their children to an integrated school against their will means to deprive them of rights which clearly belong to them in all free societies—the private right over their children and the social right to free association." Furthermore, if children from segregated homes were forced to go to desegregated schools, the conflict between value systems would eliminate "at one stroke both the teachers' and the parents' authority." Was it fair to burden children with a problem that adults had not been able to solve? She thought not.

Addressing the constitutional question, she supported the right of states to make decisions about education. Education was not constitutionally the concern of the federal government, she said. By intruding in state governance of this area, the federal government diminished state power. Since state power formed the foundation of federal power, intervention undermined government at all levels. Intervention was justified, therefore, only in areas where the federal government had a clear obligation to enforce the Constitution.

Opponents of segregation ought to begin, she thought, not with education but with the state laws against intermarriage—laws that violated basic individual rights of association. (As a Jew married to a gentile—a mixed marriage that had been forbidden in Hitler's Germany—she was particularly sensitive to this issue.) On the whole, like others before her, she urged caution. She, too, worried about the race problem's potential for violence. The Negro question, along with other issues of race, could be a catalyst for creating mobs, she warned—a possibility that "may one day even prove more explosive in the big Northern urban centers than in the more tradition-bound South."[39]

Arendt's essay would have been provocative enough on its own merits. The peculiar circumstances prevailing at *Commentary* made its reception even more problematic. Elliot Cohen, the magazine's Alabama-born editor and a contentious man, had made *Commentary* one of the leading intellectual New York magazines. Less literary than *Partisan Review*, less political than the *New Republic* or the *Nation*, more intellectual than the *Reporter*, *Commentary* occupied a special niche. But Cohen, despairing as well as contentious, had suffered an emotional collapse two years earlier. Institutionalized for a while, he now drifted in and out of the office at 34 West Thirty-third Street. His writer-editor friend Sol Stein, who had an office up the street, would recall Cohen's dropping by after work to sit sadly, saying nothing.[40] (Cohen would eventually commit suicide.)

In what amounted to Cohen's absence, the magazine was governed by three editors: Martin Greenberg, Norman Podhoretz, and George Lichtheim. Podhoretz, the youngest editor, an ambitious son of Brooklyn who had studied at Cambridge, liked Arendt's essay for its flash of argument, its originality, and the style with which Arendt made her case.[41] He also liked her sheer audacity—everyone else he knew thought the Little Rock Negroes were right and the whites were wrong. He argued hard for the piece. Greenberg was concerned about its repercussions for *Commentary*'s publisher, the American Jewish Committee, which had allied itself with the NAACP by filing amicus curiae briefs in the Legal Defense Fund's civil rights cases. Worried that the committee might rein in the magazine, Greenberg opposed publication of Arendt's article. The third editor in the troika, Lichtheim, Arendt's editor, was prepared to publish the article because, as he later told Arendt, he thought it would "do the magazine some good." But he suggested stylistic changes, and he wanted to eliminate the passage on states' rights that did not seem to fit in. It would be wise to avoid opening herself to attack by rehearsing constitutional arguments (which he had been told were wrong anyway). He was having enough "trouble here getting the view accepted that something which affronts American Jewish-liberal sentiment in some respects, should nonetheless be published."[42] In fact, the editors proposed that *Commentary* run with her essay a rebuttal by Sidney Hook.

To young Podhoretz, Hook was a logical choice. As a philosopher and author of an influential study of Marxism, Hook was intellectually equipped to meet Arendt on her own ground, yet scornful of metaphysics and unlikely to be seduced from the path of reason. And, Podhoretz recalled, he was "a worthy adversary" because he was not a "ritualistic liberal"—a term Hook had come up with. Hook was, in fact, an anti-Stalinist socialist. But unlike some socialists who disliked the Stalinist brand of communism yet disapproved, too, of McCarthyism,

Hook had written an essay, then a book, justifying the attack on communists' political rights. His argument: communists did not deserve the protection of the First Amendment, because they conspired to destroy the very system of government that guaranteed First Amendment rights.[43] Hook, a professor at New York University, had publicly supported purges of communist teachers on the grounds that, taking their orders from the party, they lacked the free minds essential in education. He was one of the anti-communists for whom Arendt had the greatest contempt. "Our friend Elliot Cohen plays a really disagreeable role and Sidney Hook is simply unbearable," she had written a correspondent when McCarthyism was at its height.[44]

Offended by the idea that her views could not stand on their own, but surely troubled, too, by the editors' choice of Hook as critic of herself, Arendt, not one to suffer editors gladly, hit the ceiling. Drawing herself up to her commanding intellectual height, she replied to *Commentary*,

> [T]he "judgment of natives" is against my judgment: in political matters I am as much of a native as any other American. And since in addition to being an American citizen, I am also a political scientist, my judgment has at least as much weight as the judgment of journalists. . . .
>
> Sorry—and now let us forget this whole affair.[45]

A few days later, after a conversation with Podhoretz, she relented. The article could run with Hook's rebuttal, so long as she could have equal space to respond to it in the next issue. Since she understood that *Commentary* paid between $150 and $300 for articles, she would expect at least $200 for the second article. She sent her terms to Lichtheim, who threw up his hands in dismay. He had hoped he was out of the loop—he thought Podhoretz was handling her now—but Podhoretz was out of the office with an upset stomach, and so Lichtheim replied. She was raising new conditions, he said, and that did not seem at all a good idea. "If I know Martin at all, this is going to throw the whole thing right back into the melting-pot from which I had rescued it—not without some trouble."[46]

By early December, Podhoretz had all but despaired of saving the article for *Commentary* but kept up his efforts at negotiation. In early January, the chair of the magazine's publication committee approved it for publication. Then, encouraged by Greenberg, the chair asked the editors to delay publication so he could show the article to the members of the committee.[47] Having labored to bring the matter this far, Podhoretz nearly resigned (and would in fact resign not long thereafter, when the heat of the moment had passed, though later he would return).

Informed that her article would not appear in the January issue and angered because of what she called "a steady stream of gossip all over town," Arendt again withdrew the piece. Heated letters were exchanged by Arendt and Lichtheim, but the article was really gone, a casualty of unusually acrimonious relations between a writer and editors. The editors, in a bind, had tried to honor both Arendt's intellectual freedom and their own institutional commitment to desegregation. Arendt, in her arrogance, had cared less about putting her position forth than about putting it forth unchallenged. Not one to waste work, Sidney Hook took the forty-page reply he had hammered out on deadline when he was about to fly off to Europe, eliminated the references to Arendt's still unpublished essay, and published it in the *New Leader.*[48]

At *Dissent*, Irving Howe saw an opportunity. The following September, when school integration crises flared again, Howe wrote to Arendt, "You may remember saying that, if and when the Southern school situation became topical once more, you would reconsider printing your piece, the one that didn't appear in 'Commentary' but which we'd like very much to have for *Dissent*."[49] Howe and Arendt were on familiar terms: when she was an editor at Schocken Books after the war, he was her assistant for a time. He had found her "a remarkably attractive person, with her razored gestures, imperial eye, dangling cigarette. 'Szee here,' she would declare with a smile meant both to subdue and to solace, and then she'd race off into one of her improvisations." Although he appreciated her performance, he felt he often missed the point of it. He suspected "she impressed people less through her thought than her style of thinking."[50]

Aware of the need to rethink socialism in America, Howe was determined to "avoid like the plague any party line" in *Dissent*, which he intended to be an alternative to *Commentary* and *Partisan Review*. He also knew that "the one thing a new magazine needs is attention."[51] IIe had already managed that by publishing Norman Mailer's essay "The White Negro." Arendt's piece would give him another "scoop." Howe promised to publish her article "exactly as you want it, without a word changed." He *was* asking a couple of professors for responses to the article, but he assured Arendt that any response "would be within the bounds of political decency." While Howe kept Arendt from bolting, another editor warned Negro novelist Richard Wright, just coming on board as a contributing editor, that the Arendt piece was on its way out and would probably infuriate him.[52]

The article ran in *Dissent*'s winter 1959 issue, along with the critiques Howe had solicited. ("At first one thinks," wrote Melvin Tumin, author of a book on desegregation, "this is a horrible joke.") Sidney Hook sent in remarks for the next issue, correcting the record on several points. Lichtheim, writing from London, could not resist the last word. Dryly, he apologized to Arendt for imagining she had withdrawn her article from publication by *Commentary* because she had known she was wrong. Now, seeing her essay in *Dissent*, he saw how unlikely that interpretation was. "You really do shrink from nothing."[53]

Hannah Arendt utterly missed the point of the *Brown* decision, Herbert Hill, then NAACP labor secretary, would say many years later. The issue was not education—it was segregation. The challenge was less to the schools than to *Plessy*, the ruling that legitimized the notion of "separate but equal." The NAACP had selected education as the battleground because public education was indisputably a state service. The Fourteenth Amendment, guaranteeing equal protection of the law, clearly applied. "She had no understanding of the potential of the law as a force for social change, no notion of the uniqueness of the constitutional system. This was all a world entirely foreign to her."[54]

Naive as her essay appeared to be—abstract, built on the slightest knowledge of the American system of government and southern life (although she did quote William Faulkner twice)—it at least provoked discussion. Up to that point, Podhoretz has recalled, there had been little debate on the subject of integration. It seemed simply right— what more was there to say? Arendt broke the ice. Of her many critics, Arendt's biographer Elisabeth Young-Bruehl has said, she "gave ground to only one—Ralph Ellison."[55] In an interview with novelist Robert Penn Warren several years after Arendt's essay appeared, the author of *Invisible Man* explained why she was wrong. Arendt had failed to understand what motivated the Little Rock parents: "the ideal of sacrifice"—an ideal that Negroes had to embrace because of their situation. The Negro children integrating Central High School were passing through a "rite of initiation" into the reality of their lives.[56]

Reading Ellison's comment in Warren's *Who Speaks for the Negro?*, Arendt was moved to reply humbly, "You are entirely right: it is precisely this 'ideal of sacrifice' which I didn't understand; . . . this failure to understand caused me indeed to go into an entirely wrong direction."[57]

To psychologist Kenneth B. Clark, the crisis at Little Rock was disappointing proof that he had been right all along. Helping the Legal Defense Fund make the argument for prompt, forceful implementation of *Brown*, Clark had maintained that gradualism only gave resistance time to form and made change more difficult.[58] Even before the mob sealed off the high school and the federal troops landed in Little Rock, Clark had seen evidence that token desegregation simply encouraged the opposition. As he wrote to the *Washington Post* and the Louisville *Courier-Journal* when the crisis at Little Rock was still developing, opponents of desegregation interpreted gradualism as "a sign of weakness or vacillation by those in authority."[59]

All along, Clark had called on leaders to lead. They had not. Instead, school boards that did try to come up with plans in good faith found themselves under attack by politicians making political hay out of the issue. In Arkansas, a city government inclined to go along with desegregation found itself under attack by its own state government.

Only a handful of Arkansas whites, among them newspaper editor Harry Ashmore, had stepped forward to support the school board's plan to place a handful of Negro students in white Central High. Not even Senator William Fulbright, a self-styled liberal but segregationist nevertheless, had stood up to be counted. As Lillian Smith wrote in a letter to the editor that neither the *New York Times* nor the *Atlanta Constitution* would publish, Little Rock had shown "how dangerous silence can be."[60]

Visiting Little Rock under the auspices of the Southern Regional Council, Clark found that Little Rock whites, accommodating in the past, had demonstrated a conspicuous "lack of courage."[61] Toward the end of 1958, Ralph Ellison, too, told an interviewer that white liberals who could stand up to pressure were rare indeed. There were some brave ones—Lillian Smith, for instance, but Ellison did not place much faith in moderates like Little Rock editor Harry Ashmore.[62]

Negro intellectuals' disillusion with liberals had not yet reached its height, but it was gathering strength. The hope unleashed by the *Brown* decision was already faltering. Four years later, Kenneth Clark said that Little Rock was the turning point, the place where his own hopes for compliance began to crack. "I'm talking about the apparent victory of moderation, the more overt ambivalence of liberals, the willingness to settle for tokenism, which has eroded the whole business of compliance."[63] The narrative Clark had imagined for America's future had taken a wrong turn. He had imagined—hoped—that white liberals, north and south, would step forward to lead their fellow whites to accept desegregation. They had not, or at least not in enough numbers to turn back the resistance.

Historian C. Vann Woodward's hopes also plummeted with Little Rock. "The power trooper melodrama at Little Rock has just about knocked out what optimism I entertained about the future of desegregation," he wrote one correspondent.[64] Federal intervention was clearly necessary in Little Rock, he held in a letter published in *Commentary*. "The movement for racial justice must not be disbanded by the threat of disorder, frustrated by constitutional pettifoggery, nor intimidated by mobs and demagogues," he said plainly. On the other hand, he also argued for realism. A mere 15 out of the 1,300 school districts in the old Confederacy had been desegregated since the *Brown* decision, and even that desegregation was token, involving just a few students. How to do better? "The answer is not an army jeep full of frightened children under armed escort or school corridors patrolled by troops. If that becomes the image of desegregation in the popular mind or the model of procedure, the cause is surely lost. The American people will abandon it as they abandoned the first experiment in reconstruction." However necessary upholding the Constitution was, Woodward said, lasting change required the cooperation of white southerners of good will, who needed to be "encouraged and protected."[65]

Little Rock had produced scant evidence, however, that these southerners of goodwill would stand up to be counted in sufficient numbers to counter the mob. Reinhold Niebuhr, always opposed to the use of force to carry out *Brown*, took what had occurred at Little Rock as evidence of what he had said all along: the "power of custom at odds with the law."[66]

Bleak as the outlook appeared to many of those who had hoped for the best, the crisis at Little Rock had accomplished what no other event so far had. It had shattered the "tragic illusion"—as labor lawyer Joseph L. Rauh put it in a letter written shortly before the crisis—that "the fight is over at the very time when it is just beginning."[67]

The Little Rock crisis also widened the dialogue. Things were being said that had not been said so openly before. Martin Luther King himself not only called on southern moderates to come out of hiding; he also called on white northern liberals to abandon their "quasi-liberalism"—"so bent on seeing all sides that it fails to become dedicated to any side." The race problem was national: "we are caught in a network of inescapable mutuality." Northern white liberals needed to go beyond approving of desegregation and begin to work for it in their own communities.[68]

Historian John Hope Franklin believed that Negroes savored the international shame Little Rock had brought on the United States. Negroes were glad to see the United States embarrassed, Franklin thought. Little Rock made them more militant.[69]

That November of 1957, as winter closed in, Franklin, Woodward, and other historians gathered at Gettysburg, Pennsylvania, to reconsider the Civil War. The centennial was approaching—the Civil War had begun in 1860. Celebrating its 125th anniversary, Gettysburg College had invited historians to convene near the scene of the war's bloodiest battle. The conference began Sunday, November 17, with a tour of the tragic ground where Abraham Lincoln had presented one of the most revered articulations of American ideals.

Now, nearly a hundred years after the Gettysburg Address, on the third day of the conference, at the Soldiers National Cemetery, John Hope Franklin recited Lincoln's memorable words: "Four score and seven years ago, our forefathers founded on this continent a new nation, conceived in liberty and dedicated to the proposition that all men are created equal. . . ." Franklin was the first Negro ever to play that role in the annual ceremonies, and the *New York Times* marked the occasion with a boldfaced subhead: "Negro Recites the Address."[70]

Woodward spoke, too, on the third day. The North had begun the Civil War with a limited goal, he said: to preserve the Union. To that goal had been added a second—freedom; and to that, a third—equality. The goals of union and freedom were achieved. The goal of equality was not. Guarantees of equality had been written into law, but the guarantees failed. It was easier to abolish slavery, based on property law, than to establish equality. For that, thousands of relationships would have to be transformed. If the North had committed itself to equality everywhere, the goal might have been achieved. But the North had withdrawn its support, and the law failed.

As the centennial of the Civil War approached, the pledge of equality remained unfulfilled. As the Civil War had raised the promise of freedom, so the Cold War and pressure by Negroes themselves had called the debt in. It was a national debt, but, as a century before, it was falling most heavily on the South. Would the South behave more graciously this time around? The signs were not favorable. "We are presently approaching the centennial anniversary of the Civil War. Simultaneously we are approaching the climax of a new sectional crisis. . . . It would be an ironic, a tragic coincidence if the celebration of the anniversary took place in the midst of a crisis reminiscent of the one celebrated."[71]

The *New York Times* reported parts of the speech, and Woodward published the full version in the *American Scholar*. "Equality: America's Deferred Commitment" circulated widely in academic circles. From Chapel Hill, North Carolina, white dramatist Paul Green wrote, "Keep up the good work for the Lord knows we need it."[72]

CHAPTER 3

MISSING
PERSONS

F ar away in Paris, William Faulkner's fellow Mississippian Richard Wright had watched events unfold in his native South and said surprisingly little about them in the American press. Author of *Black Boy* and *Native Son*, best-selling books written out of his own experience of being black in America, Wright wrote now about the international scene, but his agent discouraged him from commenting on American affairs. Novelist Chester Himes was in Paris as well, and though he had written political commentary for magazines during the war, he now wrote crime fiction for French publishers. Novelist William Gardner Smith, once an NAACP officer and commentator in the Negro press, was in Paris, too—and writing fiction and nonpolitical articles for men's magazines. In Rome on a fellowship, Ralph Ellison had thought about what was happening back home and even tried writing about it, but what he wrote was not published. James Baldwin wrestled with the position of race in American identity but focused his comments on his European experience. While William Faulkner and Robert Penn Warren published their views in *Life*, America's best-known Negro novelists had gone into quiet exile.[1]

Why, at this moment of opportunity, did these other writers—all once political men—apparently have so little to say? Why, in these first years after the *Brown* decision, did they stand on the sidelines while white intellectuals talked among themselves about what ought to be done? Were they excluded? Were they afraid to speak? Did they simply have other interests? Why, especially, did Richard Wright and Ralph Ellison—the two who had achieved the greatest measure of fame—stand so far off?

The answer lies nearly twenty years back, when Ellison and Wright met in Harlem and political advocacy was in vogue. Battered by the depression, New York writers, white and black, had turned left-ward. With one-third of the workforce unemployed in the early thir-ties, the American way of life seemed to Malcolm Cowley, a young white editor at the *New Republic*, "about to collapse in the wind like a circus tent."[2] Marx's prediction was coming true: capitalism was going under for the last time. Was not revolution imminent? Even literary intellectuals as vaguely political as Lionel and Diana Trilling had been drawn into the movement. "The lure of Communism," Diana Trilling wrote later, "was everywhere in the city; one had only to be open of mind and generous of heart to accept its promise."[3]

To Negro writers like Ellison and Wright, the Communist Party had offered opportunity and hope. The party sponsored newspapers and magazines and social gatherings, a biracial world of ideas at a time when America's intellectual culture was racially divided. But it was an imperfect world, as Wright learned in Chicago before he moved to New York. Party members squabbled and undermined one another and had little respect for intellectual or artistic independence. Wright hoped things would be better for him in New York, where he went to work for the communist *Daily Worker*. He found more of the same. "He was distrusted not only as an 'intellectual' and thus a potential trai-tor," Ellison later said, "but as a possible 'dark horse' in the race for Harlem party leadership, a 'ringer' who had been sent from Chicago to cause them trouble."[4]

By his own account, Ellison stood aside from the fray, though he wrote and edited for communist publications. Whereas Wright was openly communist, Ellison's affiliation was quieter, but Ellison, too, was a passionate Marxist and probably a member of the party. His let-ters to Wright in the 1940s would surprise a later generation accustomed to thinking of him as a conservative man. Reading Wright's *12 Million Black Voices* in 1941 had made Ellison "a better Marxist," he told Wright. He had wept "tears of impatience and anger. When experience such as ours is organized as you have done it here, there is nothing left for a man to do but fight!"[5]

Through Wright, Ellison met C. L. R. James, the brilliant Caribbean intellectual who belonged to the Socialist Workers Party, a Trotskyist group. At the start of 1945, the last year of the war, James joined with Wright, Ellison, Lawrence Reddick, Horace Cayton, and Cayton's *Black Metropolis* co-author, St. Clair Drake, to plan a collection of essays on the Negro. But the first meeting disintegrated in argument, and the plan died. In his journal Wright observed that they all seemed caught in "morbid fear."[6]

Just a few days after that meeting, Wright returned to this theme, recording news from Ellison that a couple of Negro intellectuals had suddenly gone crazy, breaking down (Wright appeared to believe) when they faced the "full meaning of the Negro problem in America." Ellison was passing through a period of depression himself; he had gone to a psychiatrist, who told him, Wright noted, that he was "thinking too much and too hard. Of course, this was because he was a Negro. Ralph said that he wanted to hit the doctor."[7]

As the war neared its end, Wright described Ellison's anguished efforts to avoid military service in a Jim Crow army that had given his father a dishonorable discharge and swallowed up his brother. Despite a letter on Ellison's behalf from a psychiatrist, Dr. Frederick Wertham, Ellison could not escape. He faced a choice between the draft or the merchant marine. He took the merchant marine. He told Wright he would go to jail before he would fight. On a boat bearing supplies to the Battle of the Bulge, Ellison worked on a prison-camp novel on the experience of Negroes in wartime. He had heard terrible stories of white and Negro sailors arguing on the high seas and naval gun crews called in to restore order. Wright recorded one story that caught the terrible intensity of wartime racial hostility. "The white man told the Negro: I'll grab you about your fucking goddamn neck and leap into the sea with you, you black bastard, though I can't swim a single fucking lick! . . . I'll get a half-nelson on your black neck and won't turn loose till we both reach the bottom of the sea!"[8]

Both Ellison and Wright emerged from the war despairing and disillusioned. Whatever faith they had had in the Communist Party had died. Tacking its sails to the winds from Moscow during the war, the party had used Negroes for its own ends. So long as the nonaggression pact between the Soviet Union and Germany held, the party urged Negroes to oppose the war. Then, after the Soviet Union came in on the side of the Allies, the party urged Negroes to support it. The waffling compounded the party's other faults: its rigidity, its lack of support for individual artistic vision. In 1944 Wright publicly announced his defection in an *Atlantic Monthly* article, disseminated more widely in a book that collected several writers' similar stories, *The God That Failed.*

The year after Wright defected from the party, a high-ranking French communist named Jacques Duclos raked the American Communist Party over the coals for its wartime dalliances with liberal reformers. Duclos accused the party of substituting social reformism for Marxist class politics. The Duclos letter, published in the communist *Daily Worker*, precipitated panic in the American party. In the summer of 1945, confessions of wrong thinking poured through the pages of the *Daily Worker*. In a resolution passed in July, the communists acknowledged their wartime failures on the Negro question. They had been wrong to expect the bourgeois class to continue wartime concessions after the war was over. Henceforth, they would return to a policy of national liberation for Negroes.[9]

Throughout this flap in the party, Ralph Ellison was recuperating from health problems on a farm in Vermont with his wife, Fanny. It was a beautiful, pristine place. They bathed in an icy brook, drank water from a stream, ate blackberries and raspberries growing along the trails through the woods, watched deer bound through the meadows. At night they heard porcupines chewing on the front porch.[10] For Ralph Ellison, a lover of nature, it was paradise. He set up his typewriter in a barn overlooking a field of goldenrod and hay. There, he reflected on Negroes' betrayal by their own leaders, who seemed to him stand-ins for white power.[11]

He was especially bitter over the communists. In a letter to Wright, Ellison unleashed a torrent of criticism of "the most brass confessions I've ever seen anywhere." Mentioning party leaders by name, he let loose a fury that would have shocked many who knew him in later years as a self-contained man. These party leaders were "as dangerous as Nazis," he said. "If they want to play ball with the bourgeoisie they needn't think they can get away with it. If they want to be lice, then by God let them be squashed like lice. Maybe we can't smash the atom, but we can, with a few well chosen, well written words, smash all that crummy filth to hell."[12]

In this state of mind Ellison wrote the first words of his novel: "I am an invisible man."[13] *Invisible Man* would be widely read as a race novel, especially as time went on and the immediate context of its publication dropped away. But it also belonged to the genre that explored his generation's great disillusion with communism: it belonged with Lionel Trilling's *The Middle of the Journey*, Chester Himes's *Lonely Crusade*, Norman Mailer's *Barbary Shore*, Whittaker Chambers's *Witness*, and the collection to which Wright contributed, *The God That Failed*.

Disappointed in the party, neither Ellison nor Wright had abandoned Marxism. Discussing the Duclos confessions, Ellison told Wright the Marxist dream was still "the only possible future." But the Communist Party was not the right vehicle for it. The party was "a broken, swaybacked nag when the times call for a tank coordinated with jet planes." All around, Ellison saw evidence of "the party's corruption." Something had to be done: the explosion of the atomic bomb had upped the ante. "We've got to do something, to offset the C.P. [Communist Party] sell-out of our people; and I mean by this, both Negroes and labor. With such power in the world there is no answer for Negroes certainly except some form of classless society."[14] By 1948, however, Ellison told Wright he was "so disgusted with politics that [he] hardly read the newspapers."[15]

In New York, a remnant of the left remained loyal to Soviet-style communism. Ellison expected criticism from those quarters after *Invisible Man* came out. "The moment that I begin to speak and write like a man they'll use all their energy to jam me off the airways," he told Wright.[16] He was right. John O. Killens, whose own first novel, *Youngblood,* would be published in 1954, contributed a harsh review to actor-singer Paul Robeson's newspaper, *Freedom,* a haven for the Stalinist left wing.

> *Mix a heavy portion of sex and a heavy, heavy portion of violence, a bit of sadism and a dose of redbaiting (Blame the communists for everything bad) and you have the making of a bestseller today.*
>
> *Add to this a decadent mixture of a Negro theme with Negro characters as Uncle Toms, pimps, sex perverts, guilt-ridden traitors—and you have a publisher's dream.*

Communists had earlier chastised Richard Wright for his rough portrayal of Negro life; now Killens criticized Ellison. He concluded, "The Negro people need Ralph Ellison's *Invisible Man* like we need a hole in the head or a stab in the back. It is a vicious distortion of Negro life."[17] The next year, another *Freedom* reviewer, Lorraine Hansberry, not yet the playwright she would become, attacked Wright's new, existentialist novel *The Outsider* on similar grounds. Writer Harold Cruse, himself a former member of the Communist Party, had no doubts that Hansberry attacked Wright "because he was a renegade from Communism."[18]

Alienated from the communist left that had for a while given him a literary base, Ellison found a safer place in the broader community of American writers. Politically disillusioned, he had already arrived at the position he would voice in a 1963 review of LeRoi Jones's *Blues People:* that ideology was a crude instrument for understanding culture. His revolutionary instrument would be literature. In a 1955 *Paris Review* interview, Ellison acknowledged "no dichotomy between art and protest." Critics labeled books by Negro authors protest literature because twentieth-century white authors had avoided "profound moral searching."[19]

This was a subject to which Ellison had given considerable thought. He had written his thoughts out in 1946 in an essay not published until 1953 as "Twentieth-Century Fiction and the Black Mask of Humanity." The great novels of the nineteenth century had been characterized by moral purpose, he said, but in the twentieth century only one distinguished white writer had *not* evaded America's central moral problem, the failure to recognize Negroes' humanity, and that was William Faulkner. The task for all American writers was to recognize literature, however artful, as "an ethical instrument."[20] Returning to that idea in his 1955 interview with *The Paris Review*, Ellison spoke of writing fiction as a high calling. There he placed his own work squarely within the political context of the Cold War. "Our so-called race problem has now lined up with the world problems of colonialism and the struggle of the West to gain the allegiance of the remaining non-white people who have thus far remained outside the Communist sphere; thus its possibilities for art have increased rather than lessened."[21]

Ellison had negotiated the passage from the thirties to the fifties. He had retained a belief in the social relevance of literature while expressing that belief in terms a new age could accept. He had also committed himself to his work as a novelist, finding in that work his contribution to the culture.

His commitment to his art would be tested in the next decade as the question of equality moved, at long last, to the center of American political life. So completely the artist would he come to seem that even people who knew him would not always know what a political man he had been. Herbert Hill, who edited two significant anthologies of Negro literary work in the 1960s, has recalled a story that Oklahoma Negro poet Melvin B. Tolson told him. Tolson had known Ellison in the Communist Party back in the thirties, but when they met again at a party years later, Ellison had turned away from him. Although it is possible that Ellison turned away from some other reason altogether, Tolson, hurt, assumed Ellison was disclaiming the old communist tie between them.

Ellison had seen early the necessity of distancing himself from the

Communist Party—indeed, distancing himself from politics altogeth-er. By the midfifties, as the conflict over desegregation was deepening, he had definitively made the turn. In interviews, he shied away from identifying the Brotherhood in *Invisible Man* with the party. He spoke and wrote of his days in party circles as if he had been a man on the periphery, looking on bemused. He and Wright, once so close, nearly lost touch; the bonds of friendship were loosening. And Ellison had already begun his journey underground. So thoroughly would he erase traces of his radical past that, in coming years, young militants would nearly consider him an Uncle Tom.

In 1948, Ellison had told Wright that Chester Himes had deluded himself into believing his new political novel, *Lonely Crusade*, would be a success. Himes had "misjudged the nature of the red-scair [*sic*]," he said.[22] Ellison did not make that mistake. Catching the drift of the times and disillusioned with the political life, he retreated to the high ground. Awarded a two-year fellowship from the American Academy of Arts and Letters, he spent the midfifties in Rome with his wife. They found life strange in academy quarters on a hill overlooking the city, Fanny Ellison wrote to poet Langston Hughes—more public than they were accustomed to. But the other academy fellows were pleasant, and Ellison was working hard in a studio set into a corner of an ancient wall and looking out over a garden. *Life* magazine took a photograph of him there, adding him to the other Americans featured in a Cold War–tinged issue, "America's World Abroad: Millions of Ambassadors over the Earth."[23]

In the fall of 1956, Ellison renewed an acquaintance with Robert Penn Warren. Visiting Rome, Warren and his wife, writer Eleanor Clark, stayed at the American Academy complex where the Ellisons were living. Nearly thirty years later, Fanny Ellison recalled the din-ner Warren and Eleanor Clark shared in the Ellisons' rooms "when lacking the proper table I spread the cloth on the floor and served the baby lamb in plates which we held on our laps." Strolling around Rome, Ellison and Warren swapped folk tales, talked about literature, writing, history, politics. "He damn near walked my legs off," Ellison would say.[24] Through Warren, Irving Kristol, co-editor of *Encounter*, a magazine published in London by the European Congress for Cultural Freedom and subsidized by the CIA, found out how to contact Ellison to ask him to write an article on segregation.[25] Ellison worked on the article—even, with Warren's encouragement, thought of turning it into a book on desegregation, but neither book nor article appeared until nearly ten years later when the *Nation* published an essay—presumably this essay—that Ellison had begun in Rome.[26]

In his introduction, he said that it began as a response to the southern congressmen's manifesto against the Supreme Court. A friend back home had mentioned the "cracker senators cussing out the Supreme Court" and wondered what Ellison thought. It was not easy to put down what he thought, not easy to *know* what he thought. "The greatest difficulty for a Negro writer," he wrote on another occasion, "was the problem of revealing what he truly felt, rather than serving up what Negroes were supposed to feel, and were encouraged to feel."[27]

The difficulty was especially great at this point in his life, the American past aswirl for him in the many centuries of Rome. Caught up in "barely controlled chaos," he put his thoughts in the form of a dream—a complex allegory, grotesque in its details. He saw Abe Lincoln dead and stripped nearly bare by a crowd, a corpse "twisted in the cordwood postures of Dachau." Awakened from the dream, Ellison wrote, he tried to replay the words of the Gettysburg Address. Although he knew them well, the words would not come. The nightmare had wiped them out. Here was the awful truth of this moment in time: there were no successors to Abraham Lincoln—no leaders, only men who looked like leaders. "No one tried to stop the mob," and he, Ellison, was "but a trapped and impotent observer."

Looking back, novelist William Gardner Smith, another Paris exile, would trace the flight of so many Negro artists and intellectuals to France in the postwar years to three causes: the slow pace of racial change in America, a hedonism derived from nuclear fear (why not live well, if tomorrow we die?)—and McCarthyism. "Through myriad pressures, many of us were threatened with the loss of our jobs, with little prospect of finding another."[28] Anyone who has not lived through these years can only begin to imagine the surreal political scene. While many Americans bounded through a period of unprecedented prosperity, others knew their worlds could turn into nightmares at any minute. All it might take was a call to testify before the proliferating loyalty committees.

As the great lid of McCarthyism settled over postwar America, advocates for racial change were so frequently labeled communist that it is hard not to believe that resistance to racial change accounted for much of the energy behind the domestic assault on communism. In 1951, even before McCarthyism reached its height, journalist William Worthy wrote, "Negroes in government service have found that mere self-respect and expressed dislike of racial barriers in various federal agencies have been equated with 'Communism'. Since 1947, numerous workers, possessed of varying degree of candor and backbone, have been suspended or fired following Kangaroo hearings of the type that any fledgling Hitler might well grant to a Jew for window-dressing purposes."[29]

As the NAACP came under direct attack in southern states as a subversive organization, Rayford Logan went to its defense in the *Christian Century.* The charge that the NAACP was communist was, he said, "of course, groundless. The N.A.A.C.P. and the communists have been fighting each other for at least twenty-five years." Those making the charge were making it for political reasons. "Southern politicians see the handwriting on the wall. They fear the loss of the committee chairmanships which go to them when Democrats have a majority in either or both houses of Congress." Hence the violence, economic reprisals, and accusations of communism leveled at Negroes working for change.[30]

The Cold War gave racist politicians an opening to badger anyone likely to speak up for racial change. The equation of racial change with communism continued to be drawn with relentless regularity. The same Cold War that provided liberals with an argument *for* racial change provided opponents with an argument *against* racial change.

Since the Russians used the American racial situation to smear the United States, were not Americans who advocated racial change behaving suspiciously like Russians? In the minds of many southern whites, the very idea of whole-scale social reform imposed by a central government was a communist idea. Even Robert Penn Warren spoke worriedly, in *Segregation*, about the "power state."

While communism was used to taint the whole desegregation movement with a broad brush, Negro intellectuals in particular felt the sting of the Red chill. The eminent W. E. B. Du Bois was sidelined by a 1951 charge that he and other members of a peace organization had failed to register as foreign agents. A judge dropped the charge, but not before the damage was done; nearly overnight, Du Bois became a pariah.

Unrelenting in his criticism of American capitalism and foreign policy, Du Bois made nearly everyone nervous. As historian Rayford Logan's *Negro in the United States: A Brief History* moved toward publication in 1957, the secretary to the publisher (Van Nostrand Reinhold) posed a question raised by outside readers: Would Logan delete Du Bois and communist historian Herbert Aptheker from his bibliography? "These authors have been linked with communist fronts and their inclusion would automatically cut down our prospective government sales." Logan did not consent to the cuts.[31]

But the following year, seeking approval to invite Du Bois to speak at Howard University, Logan assured Howard's president, Mordecai Johnson, "that we would see to it that Dr. Du Bois would say nothing to embarrass the University." Johnson, to his credit, replied that Du Bois should be allowed to say whatever he wanted to say. Yet Logan spent the afternoon before the speech with two other colleagues (as he confided in his diary) "editing Dr. Du Bois's speech so as to present something of its flavor while omitting the party-line."[32]

With old allies like Rayford Logan wary about his political stands, Du Bois found himself isolated, along with Paul Robeson, in left field. A towering political intellectual—a founder of the NAACP, editor of the *Crisis*, and author of numerous books that laid a foundation for understanding race in America—Du Bois had been nearly erased from mainstream American life by the mid-1950s. He still spoke out at public gatherings and in small left-wing periodicals, but the *New York Times* no longer turned to him for comment. Even the Negro press shunned him. A generation was growing up, he lamented, without hearing his name.[33] It was an incalculable loss to the national conversation on race.

The beloved poet Langston Hughes, like Du Bois, had not escaped to Europe, and he, too, had come under fire. His biographer Arnold Rampersad has documented his long ordeal in compelling detail. His persecution had begun many years earlier, before World War II, when the Special Committee on Un-American Activities heard testimony that he was "a Communist poet." In more recent years, columnists, *Reader's Digest*, and broadcasters had joined J. Edgar Hoover in unremitting efforts to silence him. To some degree they succeeded. Under the force of their Red-baiting, Hughes's lectures were repeatedly canceled, a hard blow to his livelihood and ability to make himself heard.[34]

The climax of Hughes's persecution came in 1953, the year before the *Brown* decision, when Senator Joseph McCarthy's subcommittee called him to testify. McCarthy was investigating the political purity of books appearing on U.S. Information Agency library shelves around the world, and Hughes's writings were among them. Struggling to preserve his ability to publish, Hughes said he no longer held the views he had once held. Although he had never been a member of the Communist Party, he admitted that communism *had* attracted him once, but the Nazi-Soviet pact and Soviet treatment of Jews had undermined that attraction. He expressed surprise that his older writings, outdated now, still appeared in the State Department's libraries overseas.[35] It was a sad position for a writer: renouncing his own work.

There is little question that Langston Hughes, under such intense pressure, reined himself in. At the same time, he pointed out to authors at a New York gathering in 1957 that, as a Negro, he had never been free to publish what he wanted to publish. He had had plays turned down because who, he was asked, would perform a play about Negro life? An editor turned down a story about racial violence because he "did not believe his readers wished to read about such things." To writers worried about the Red chill, Hughes said, "Censorship, the Black List: Negro writers, just by being black, have been on the blacklist all our lives."[36]

The movement for racial equality would eventually open doors that had been shut, and speech would flow more freely, but even in a freer climate, Langston Hughes held back. At a 1962 writers' conference in Uganda, he omitted his early revolutionary poems from a reading, an omission so surprising that African writers asked him for an explanation. The poems were not appropriate for the occasion, Hughes replied. But they *were* appropriate, the African writers pointed out. Had not the conversation at the conference turned to revolution? Were they not talking about black people freeing themselves from Western cultural control? At that, according to American Negro writer J. Saunders Redding, also present, "Langston lapsed into silence."[37]

A story told by white foreign correspondent Theodore White illustrates how the chill affected those who might have otherwise spoken more strongly for change. On their 1953 European trip to cleanse the U.S. Information Agency libraries, Senator McCarthy's legal counsel Roy Cohn and his assistant David Schine located copies of White's *Thunder out of China* on USIA shelves in Berlin and then had them purged and burned. Undefeated, White wrote a book on Europe and returned to America, riding out his appearance in *Counterattack*, a newsletter dedicated to exposing communists, especially in the field of entertainment (friends at CBS let him know he would not be reappearing on that network). Finally, White met his Waterloo, and it came on racial ground.

Going to the defense of an old friend in the State Department, John Paton Davies, White volunteered to testify before the State Department's Security Hearing Board in 1954. He found himself, abruptly, a target. "[A]s they closed the questioning on Davies, and opened the unexpected dossier on White, the first charge hurled at me seemed preposterous—that I had tried to organize the Negro troops on the Burma Road for a revolt during the war."

White groped to remember the time, ten years before, when a friend—a Jewish officer for a Negro battalion of engineers—had asked White to speak to his troops, who, malaria-ridden and demoralized, were cutting their way through the jungle. Already angered by the segregation of soldiers, White had obliged and, he figured later, said something like this: "that the Japanese were the worst racists in the world after the Nazis; and we had to help the Chinese knock off the Japanese; this road would do the job; then after we knocked off the racist Nazis in Europe and the racist Japanese in Asia, we would all go home and knock off racism in the United States." That, apparently, was what got him in trouble with the committee.

White thought he emerged from the questioning without serious damage and, unintimidated, went on in the *Reporter* to defend atomic scientist J. Robert Oppenheimer, who had been denied a security clearance. When White asked to have his passport renewed so he could go to Germany for *Collier's*, his request was denied. He eventually got the passport, but the experience had come too close to undermining his hold on his own profession.

> *[N]o amount of self-reproach will reconcile me, even today, for the self-doubt that followed my clearance. . . . It was not so much that I was afraid; I had stood up when I had to and the fear passed away in time. It was that I would never again be as sure of myself on anything as I had been on the need of our getting out of the path of the Chinese revolution. And unless I was that sure of myself, I would never again want to be a polemicist or an advocate in a national debate.*[38]

A screen of self-restraint had fallen in place. In the intimate diary he kept of his daily life, historian Rayford Logan recorded the Red chill's effect on one Negro intellectual. Long engaged in the movement for racial equality, Logan found himself in the 1950s trying still to fight the fight, but clearly nervous about it. In 1953, the same year that Langston

Hughes was brought before the House Un-American Activities Committee, FBI agents questioned Logan for fifty minutes. He described the session in a letter he mailed to historians across the country. "The inquisition has descended upon Howard," he said. The FBI had so effectively sown seeds of suspicion that political talk could no longer be heard in the men's restroom—an informer might be listening from a stall.[39] In the summer after the *Brown* decision, the FBI approached Logan again. This time he was interviewed for an hour and a half about his former membership in the Council on African Affairs, which the attorney general had put on his list of subversive organizations.[40]

Writing that same year about the conventionality and timidity of Negro intellectuals, the eminent sociologist E. Franklin Frazier, author of *The Black Bourgeoisie*, explained bluntly, "If they show any independence in their thinking they may be hounded by the F.B.I. and find it difficult to make a living."[41] From 1952 to 1955, the years bracketing the *Brown* decision, an array of leading Negro intellectuals underwent some type of investigation: Frazier himself; Langston Hughes; Ralph Bunche, winner of the Nobel Peace Prize for his work at the United Nations; novelist Richard Wright; poet-lawyer Pauli Murray; and historian Rayford Logan.

Regarding these years, historian John Hope Franklin would say,

> *You have to know that the general description of any radical, or even a black who stood up for equality—he was regarded as a communist. I was designated a communist plenty of times. And people would write me these terrible letters. Maybe I had made a sort of innocent speech, but I do favor equality, and then they would write me, "Nigger communism," and that sort of thing, unsigned of course. That's part and parcel—the view that if you were for equality, for civil rights, it must have come out of some sort of terrible radical orientation, like communism.*[42]

In this political climate, Ralph Ellison's old friend Richard Wright was uncomfortably aware of his own vulnerable position. As a defector from the Communist Party, Wright might not only be called up by the House Un-American Activities Committee; he might also lose his passport if he did not cooperate. When American military intelligence questioned him in New York near the end of World War II, Wright had been relieved that he had not been asked about the "real and important Communists" he knew in "confidential government positions."[43] Departing the American scene, Wright had hoped he might avoid the matter entirely.

Wright had left the United States a best-selling author. In exile he quickly lost ground.[44] In the early fifties, an essay in which Wright explained why he chose exile in France over life in America bounced from *Ebony* to the *Atlantic* to the *Paris Review. Ebony's* executive editor Ben Burns ("a white editor in black journalism," as he would describe himself in a memoir, *Nitty Gritty*) had asked Wright for the piece, although Burns had only recently (by his own account) had a tough time getting another Wright article into the magazine over publisher John H. Johnson's objections. Johnson preferred to put the best face he could on American life, and he balked again at this new piece, which compared the United States unfavorably with France. "In the other article, he was just attacking Chicago," Johnson told Burns. "Now he's going after all America. We can't print that."[45]

When *Ebony* delayed publishing "I Choose Exile," Wright acknowledged in a letter of January 23, 1952, that the article might be "a little too strong for your magazine." That was the editors' business, and he would not argue the point. Perhaps, he suggested, the article would be better placed in a white periodical since a white periodical would be less vulnerable to accusations of disloyalty. In a comment that reveals the awful tenor of these years—the fears of retaliation by a government run amuck—Wright explained, "As you well know, my primary aim is to fight the battle of the Negro in the nation's thought, and I do want to try to deal blows where I think they will do the most good. It is therefore advisable, on some occasions, to let white periodicals carry the moral burden of printing articles that might harm Negro publications in the eyes of the Government."[46]

Later that year, an editorial assistant at the *Atlantic Monthly* asked

Wright's agent, Paul R. Reynolds, if Wright would do an article "saying why he chooses to live in France, why the Negro finds life more satisfying and complete there, free of prejudice, free to do as he pleases, etc." Wright sent the piece he had written for *Ebony*, but the *Atlantic*'s interest suddenly cooled. Hearing from the editorial assistant what had transpired, *Paris Review* editor George Plimpton wrote Mrs. Wright, presumably in her role as literary agent, "We are very interested in taking a look at your husband's essay written for *The Atlantic Monthly*, and which, I understand, they did not have the courage to print."[47] Still, the piece went unpublished.

"I Choose Exile" might not have encountered such editorial resistance if Wright, who had married a white woman, had not brought up intermarriage, approved of it, and noted French tolerance for it. On the other hand, simply his criticism of the United States, his favoring France, might in itself have been enough to keep the article out of print in these patriotic times.

Richard Wright had always challenged the boundaries of what could be said in America. "I have made a strange observation in the last several years," Chester Himes told Wright in 1952.

> *As long as you were on the scene and exerted a vital force on the position taken on racial matters by literary criticism and the liberal group, the issues could never be entirely excluded from discussion. You were the only one over whom they could exert no control; and you were the one who had access to the public. But since your departure the boys [by which he apparently meant "the liberal group"] have shut the door on all contradictions of the opinions taken by themselves.*[48]

Arriving in France himself, Himes perceived Wright as under "extraordinary pressure" not to write about Negroes in America.[49] Wright's agent, Reynolds, expressed relief in 1954 that Wright was not inclined to comment on the American scene from Paris, since "the nuance of change would be rather hard to get living in Paris." Wright should concentrate instead on international affairs.[50]

After Wright turned in the manuscript for *Black Power*, a book he wrote on a trip to the Gold Coast (later Ghana), his agent recommended cutting any lines that "took a crack at America." The editors would not consider asking Wright to trim statements on problems Negroes faced, his agent assured him (oddly, since writing about Negroes' problems amounted to criticism of America). Harper & Brothers was "a liberal publishing house," and would publish the book the way Wright wanted it.[51] But at the request of the company's chairman of the board, Frank MacGregor, Wright added a refutation of communism to the book's introduction.[52] These precautions were not enough. *Black Power* came out in 1954, the year of the *Brown* decision, and sank like a stone. Critics noted that though Wright had given up communism, he still thought like a communist.[53]

In fact, as Wright himself said in *Black Power*, he had not abandoned either Marxist analysis of history or the hope of a socialist future.[54] His break with the Communist Party, as Sidney Hook once noted, had been more personal than political.[55] Writing about international affairs, as his agent encouraged him to do, took Wright directly onto the playing field of the Cold War. As the Soviet Union and the United States jostled for power in the disintegrating European empire, his chief subjects in the 1950s—Africa and Asia—were contested territory.

Perhaps American officials thought it was time to remind Wright, by now very much the rogue elephant, where the power lay. The State Department made a practice of using its passport power to restrict the travel of those it considered troublemakers, like Paul Robeson. According to Wright biographer Addison Gayle, on September 16, 1954, at the American embassy in Paris, Richard Wright was brought to heel. By Gayle's account, Wright not only answered questions put to him about his own party activities but also named names of people he had met in the course of those activities at a time when Communist Party members were being prosecuted under the Smith Act. If Gayle's interpretation and the documents on which it is based are accurate, then in exchange for having his passport renewed, Wright informed on communists he had known.[56]

This has been a difficult allegation for some Wright supporters to accept, but a State Department document dated a full year earlier lends credibility to the story and offers further evidence of Wright's cooperation with the U.S. State Department. During his 1953 visit to the Gold Coast, according to a memorandum from the American Consulate General in Accra, Wright "voluntarily" supplied a detailed report on what he had learned about "left-wing politics" there.[57] In what American consul William E. Cole called a "Memorandum of August 29, 1953, Prepared by Richard Wright," Wright describes "the only self-avowed member of the Communist Party" he had met in Accra, Bankole Renner, who had broken with Kwame Nkrumah's Convention People's Party. Wright had attended a meeting of a group Renner had organized, and came away "convinced . . . that their approach was that of Marxist revolutionaries."

As for Kwame Nkrumah, the man who was leading the Gold Coast to independence, Wright said that Nkrumah's "ideal is Lenin, the Russian revolutionary leader, and at the head of his bed in his sleeping room is a large portrait of Lenin." Using Marxist tactics, Wright said, Nkrumah had formed a Secret Circle, the real power behind the CPP. Wright then named the members of that Secret Circle. "I do not believe that the CPP has any direct relation or affiliation with any local or foreign Communist group" (Wright said), "but the leading members of the Party openly admit that they have conscientiously modeled their organization upon the Russian Communist Party. In short, it is a Communist minded political party, borrowing Marxist concepts and applying them with a great deal of flexibility to local African social and economic conditions." Further, Wright entertained the possibility that Bankole Renner's communist group might "successfully infiltrate the CPP. Should an occasion arise in which the CPP were in dire difficulties, with a dissatisfied rank and file following, the undercover agents of Bankole Renner might well have an opportunity to capture the CPP."

Wright's statement—three and a half typed, single-spaced pages—also includes information about infighting in the CPP. And Wright passes on the further information, derived from a man who had left the CPP, that George Padmore, who lived in London and was enormously important to freedom movements in Africa, "has access to all confidential or secret documents of the CPP." Wright even details the secret route through which Nkrumah was receiving Padmore's letters at this point, after some of Padmore's correspondence had been published in Ghana with unpleasant political repercussions. Wright closes by identifying "a West Indian businessman living in London" as the apparent "business contact between the Secret Circle and foreign business firms."

Except for a peculiar identification of Padmore as African (he was from Trinidad)—an error perhaps made by the typist who retyped Wright's memorandum on government forms—it is difficult to question the authenticity of this document, transmitted September 15, 1953, with an introduction by consul Cole, who also provided what may have been Wright's motivation for sharing the information he had collected: "Wright's intention was to write a book describing the political advances in the Gold Coast and especially the CPP, which he intended to portray in a favorable light. However, Wright found that he was not cordially received by the CPP. On the contrary he feels that he was ignored by them and that his reasonable requests for information were evaded." Perhaps, Cole suggested, the CPP feared that, because of Wright's own communist past, "he would be an alert and critical observer of CPP activities."

This cover memorandum does *not* suggest that Wright was a familiar informant (in fact, the consul provided, by way of introduction, some of the facts of Wright's life—facts of which, he said, the State Department was "no doubt aware"). There is no hint that this report was anything other than a voluntary, one-time sharing of information. Yet Wright's willingness to supply this information, betraying not only Kwame Nkrumah but also George Padmore, without whose support Wright would likely not have made this visit, suggests where Wright's loyalties lay.

The year after the session at the Paris embassy, Wright traveled to the Bandung conference in Jakarta, Indonesia, where nonaligned nations declared independence from Western dominance. Wright went to the conference with the help of the anti-communist Congress for Cultural Freedom, which paid his expenses.[58] Gayle concluded that, writing about the Bandung conference in *The Color Curtain*, Wright carefully trod "the middle path." "He would censure the West and praise it at the same time. He would suggest ways that the Third World might be saved from being devoured by the Communists. During the first years of his exile, he had attacked the evils of American hegemony as offered via the Marshall Plan; now this same hegemony was viewed as a possible good."[59]

However Wright may have tried to accommodate himself to these perilous times, he could not seem to do enough. He remained under suspicion from both the left and the right. Speaking to the historians at Memphis, William Faulkner had mentioned Wright in the same breath with Paul Robeson, implying both were disloyal (although, to avoid a libel charge, Wright's name was deleted from the speech before it was published).[60]

In March 1956, the *Reporter* ran an outright attack on Wright by Ben Burns, himself an ex-communist who had been expelled from the party for his work at *Ebony*, which the party regarded as a lackey for white capitalism.[61] Burns had known Wright when both worked at the *Daily Worker*. Now, in what Wright saw as a betrayal, Burns suggested that *Ebony* had refused to publish Wright's "I Choose Exile" because the publisher, John Johnson, believed it "verged on the subversive." In a memoir, Burns would attempt to cast his *Reporter* article in a kinder light, but the article itself stands as evidence. In it, Burns refers to "Wright's heavy-handed morose approach to everything racial." Out of touch with American life, unaware of how much it had improved for Negroes, Wright misrepresented his country to Europeans, Burns said. "Down deep inside of him there manifestly burns a relentless, insatiable loathing for white people and America that erupts whenever he sits down at a typewriter," Burns wrote. "And Wright's venom, retailed constantly by expatriates at sidewalk cafes, plus years of headlines about Dixie lynchings, has succeeded in poisoning European thinking about racial problems in America."[62] Whatever Burns's intent, Wright, with good reason, felt attacked.

Wright's friend Gunnar Myrdal, author of *An American Dilemma*, expressed himself "outraged" by Burns's comments. After all, the *Reporter* was "a liberal periodical read by good people. All of them might not know you. What can be done?" Wright considered suing for libel, but a lawyer advised against it.[63]

Several months later, writer Kay Boyle reported to Wright a rumor that he had turned informer for the U.S. government. She had heard it twice, from Americans returning from Paris. "They say that you are known to be working with the State Department, or the FBI, I don't know which, and that you give information about other Americans to these powers in order to keep your own passport and be able to travel."[64]

For more than a decade, Wright had been America's leading Negro writer, and one of its most political. As something like a revolutionary moment finally approached in his native land, Wright was an exile besieged.

Of the novelists abroad in the mid-1950s, only James Baldwin came to play a significant role in the American movement for racial equality, and the politics of anti-communism had something to do with that, too. Younger than Ralph Ellison and Richard Wright, Baldwin had come of age after the radical thirties. He had not even begun to write seriously until after the war, the radical years past. Blessed with splendid gifts as a writer, Baldwin was taken up in the late forties by the editors at several little New York magazines: the *New Leader*, the *Nation*, *Commentary*, *Partisan Review*.

The editors of these intellectual New York magazines liked Baldwin for his grace of mind and style. Writer Mary McCarthy, part of this literary circle, has left behind a verbal snapshot of Baldwin during these years. Not long before Baldwin moved to Paris in 1948, she lunched with him and *Partisan Review* editor William Phillips. Phillips seemed nervous, McCarthy thought, but Baldwin was so at ease, chatting along in his "soft, light, slightly breathy" voice, that McCarthy, a sociable person despite her sharp tongue, quite enjoyed herself.

"Baldwin had read *everything*. . . . He had what is called taste—quick, Olympian recognitions that were free of prejudice." He was neither the first black writer nor the first black intellectual she had known, "but he was the first *literary* intellectual."[65]

Charming, brilliant, well-read—and so young, with those large vulnerable eyes—Baldwin had another trait that made him attractive to New York editors: his apparent political innocence. He had marched in a May Day parade only once, at the age of thirteen. He did join the Young People's Socialist League in the mid-1940s and went through a short stage as a Trotskyist, an international socialist opposed to Stalin and Soviet-style communism. He was employed briefly as a messenger for *PM*, a newspaper that defied capitalist influence by not running advertisements. But by 1948, he was already referring to his "brief days as a Socialist" as past.[66] He escaped the singe of McCarthyism, he said later on, because he "was just a shade too young to have had any legally recognizable political history."[67] What history he had on the left was safely anti-Stalinist. His "life on the Left" was "of absolutely no interest," he said, and "did not last long." Still, he added "[i]t was during this period that I met the people who were to take me to Saul [Sol] Levitas, of *The New Leader*, Randall Jarrell of *The Nation*, Elliott Cohen and Robert Warshow, of *Commentary*, and Philip Rahv, of *Partisan Review*."[68]

Baldwin was writing for editors who had themselves turned away from the international revolution. Sol (Samuel M.) Levitas, Cohen, Rahv, and William Phillips were all former communists who had turned apostate. They were vigilantly anti-communist, hostile toward the Stalinist brand of socialism. Rahv, at least, remained a man of the left, and neither he nor Phillips was as fiercely anti-communist as Cohen.[69] But all had been caught up in the disavowal of communism sweeping through intellectual New York in the postwar years. So useful to the anti-communist cause were the *New Leader* and *Partisan Review* that both later received funds from the CIA.[70] For these Cold War editors, James Baldwin was, politically, nearly a blank slate, a new man who could be molded for a new age. He did not come dragging awkward political baggage, like Ellison and Wright. Yet he was a writer of obvious talent, which could be set to political use.

Baldwin wasted little time putting distance between himself and the radical thirties in two *Partisan Review* essays on Richard Wright. In the second and longer essay, "Many Thousands Gone," published in 1951, Baldwin took aim at the protest novel that came out of those years "when bread lines and soup kitchens and bloody industrial battles were bright in everyone's memory." The interests of Negroes and workers were not truly one, Baldwin said. That Marxist formula had failed. Rejecting Marxism and the prospect of class war, Baldwin planted his feet firmly on American soil: "Negroes are Americans and their destiny is the country's destiny."[71]

This assertion had a distinct political meaning in 1951. It was scarcely an idiosyncratic sentiment; many shared it, from the Swedish sociologist Gunnar Myrdal to Ralph Ellison to the leaders of the NAACP. It was a useful sentiment for Negroes who had no practical alternative to claiming American citizenship, but it was especially useful in the early fifties, when southern politicians tried to link the movement toward desegregation with international communism. In the international movements of the left, whatever their particular stripe, American Negroes stood side by side with oppressed peoples everywhere. To assert his identity with America, as Baldwin did, was to deny membership in the international socialist movement.

In the revised political world of his editors, allegiance to America took a central place. "Horrible *Commentary* dinner last night," literary critic Alfred Kazin wrote in his journal around 1951.

> *Insufferable to be in that gaseous anxiously self-congratulatory atmosphere of Jewish radicals of the thirties prosperously reappearing in the fifties as ex-radicals. Ideologues in every generation, no matter what their latest cause, they have not the slightest interest . . . in poverty, in race hatred (except when "they" turn on us), in workers found to be "unemployable" by the latest technocratic revolution. And now they have found their latest cause in another ideology they call "America." America is just as unreal to them as the Soviet Union was.*[72]

Baldwin later set himself apart from the anti-communist excesses of those years. Of the disillusion he experienced when he returned to New York in 1952, he would say, "I had come home to a city in which nearly everyone was gracelessly scurrying for shelter, in which friends were throwing their friends to the wolves, and justifying their treachery by learned discourses (and tremendous tomes) on the treachery of the Comintern." Reading justifications of the Rosenbergs' execution or praise for Whittaker Chambers, Baldwin learned "something about the irresponsibility and cowardice of the liberal community" that he would not forget.[73] Looking back from 1971, he wrote of this 1952 visit as a turning point: a chill fell over his relationship with the intellectuals who had taken him in. Now he saw in them "impotence and narcissism." They had been proud of him— proud that he could make himself good enough to be accepted by them. "[H]ow *I* might react to this 'acceptance,' or what this acceptance might cost me, were not among the questions which racked them in the midnight hour. One wondered, indeed, if anything could ever disturb their sleep."[74]

Baldwin was becoming his own man, if he had ever been anything else. While he completed a novel on growing up in Harlem, he developed his own political identity in Paris. He saw, through Parisians' treatment of Algerians, waging a bloody war for independence from France, that oppression was international. He himself was arrested for possession of a bedsheet stolen from a local hotel by a friend. Imprisoned for several miserable days, he entered the courtroom to find himself the object of laughter as the story was told.

It was "the laughter of those who consider themselves to be at a safe remove from all the wretched, for whom the pain of the living is not real," he wrote in "Equal in Paris," which *Commentary* published in March 1955. "I had heard it so often in my native land that I had resolved to find a place where I would never hear it any more. In some deep, black, stony, and liberating way, my life, in my own eyes, began during that first year in Paris, when it was borne in on me that this laughter is universal and never can be stilled."[75]

An old high school friend, Sol Stein, observed Baldwin's progress through these years with interest. A former ideological monitor at the Voice of America, Stein had become executive director of the American Committee for Cultural Freedom by the midfifties. The American Committee, part of the CIA's Cold War cultural apparatus, included, in addition to academics like Reinhold Niebuhr, an array of magazine editors—among them, Max Ascoli at the *Reporter,* Elliot Cohen and several others at *Commentary,* Sol Levitas at the *New Leader,* Richard Rovere at *The New Yorker,* and Norman Cousins at the *Saturday Review.* The lengthy membership roll practically constituted a Who's Who of the American intellectual establishment. Writer Robert Penn Warren belonged, and so did Dwight Macdonald. For members of the committee, communism was "the god that failed," although that did not necessarily mean they approved of Senator Joseph McCarthy, who was the target of criticism from within the group. Many of the members, like Reinhold Niebuhr, considered McCarthy dangerous because he discredited anti-communism.

Baldwin's friend Stein carried on his own war against communism with such vigor, however, that *New York Post* columnist Murray Kempton, himself a former communist, remarked in a letter, "Sol Stein's problem is that he reacts from a wounded memory." Alluding to communist influence on publishing and the arts in the 1950s, Kempton said of Stein, "He reserves his passions for the past. The Communist war on cultural freedom in the thirties has been greatly exaggerated in its effect if not in its intention; today, when Howard Fast is almost the last survivor of Communist culture, it barely exists at all. Stein has to carry on his war against mush-heads."[76]

Herbert Hill of the NAACP knew Stein well and would remember him as "the most obsessive anti-communist" he had ever known. From the vantage point of the 1990s, Hill had no doubt that Stein saw the political advantage of bringing his friend James Baldwin to the fore during this time in the Cold War, when segregation was the American Achilles' heel. Baldwin wrote about the racial problem without sounding like a

Marxist. He did not use race to discredit the whole American way of life. When Stein proposed to Baldwin that he collect his best essays into a book, the offer therefore carried distinct political overtones: their friendship and Stein's appreciation for Baldwin's talent would have not sufficed if he had not also found Baldwin's politics compatible with his own beliefs. Stein made a deal with Beacon Press to issue a set of trade paperbacks. Baldwin's *Notes of a Native Son* would be one of them.[77]

A small Unitarian publisher in Boston, Beacon was taking the lead on the issue of race in the midfifties, publishing *Citizen's Guide to Desegregation*, by Herbert Hill and Jack Greenberg at the NAACP, along with Kenneth B. Clark's *Prejudice and Your Child*. Beacon had only recently turned to publishing political books. The man responsible was Melvin Arnold, a former public relations executive at Standard Oil of New Jersey who, like Stein, was an ardent anti-communist. Arnold appeared to enjoy nothing better than the evening he spent with Herbert Philbrick, the undercover FBI agent who would become notorious as the author of *I Led Three Lives*. During their convivial session in May 1952, Philbrick had laid out for a shocked Arnold how the communists had infiltrated Unitarian operations. Philbrick told him that Stephen Fritchman, former editor of the Unitarians' magazine, the *Christian Register*, had actually held party meetings in his Unitarian office, a thought that chilled Arnold to the bone. Arnold would leave behind an array of notes and memoranda, preserved at Andover-Harvard Theological Library, that document his contacts with the FBI and his own efforts to turn the Unitarian publishing apparatus to the service of anti-communism.[78]

Arnold also turned Beacon Press to the service of the racial movement. According to Beacon Press editor Jeannette Hopkins, there was little enough interest in race in the publishing world of the mid-1950s.[79] No other press (except possibly Harper & Brothers) could approach Beacon's productivity on race in the fifties and early sixties. Just how the focus on race fit in with Arnold's anti-communism is not clear. What *is* clear is that James Baldwin's career was being shaped by editors active in the effort to stamp out all communist influence over American life and boost American fortunes abroad. For them, he was, at the least, a fine writer untainted by communism, a writer who could discuss race without turning it into a platform for the international communist revolution.

After Beacon's publication of *Notes of a Native Son*, Baldwin, living in Paris—where the left vigorously survived among artists and intellectuals—continued to position himself outside the ranks of radicalism. On assignment for *Encounter*, one of the magazines published by the Congress for Cultural Freedom, he covered the landmark Congrès des Ecrivains et Artistes Noirs, held in September 1956 at the Sorbonne's Amphithcatre Descartes. Sponsored by *Présence Africaine*, a magazine Richard Wright had helped to found, this conference brought together leading writers from Africa, interested white Europeans, and Negro Americans, including writers from the Caribbean. It was a kind of intellectuals' Bandung conference, an assertion of cultural self-determination.

Describing the conference for *Encounter*, Baldwin set himself apart from the group. He did not join in the laughter that greeted the reading of a message from W. E. B. Du Bois: "I am not present at your meeting," Du Bois had written, "because the U.S. government will not give me a passport." The laughter came at the U.S. government's expense, but the next line came at the expense of Americans present: "Any American Negro traveling abroad today must either not care about Negroes or say what the State Department wishes him to say," Du Bois said.

Baldwin thought the statement "extremely ill-considered." Although he did not belong to the American delegation, he could see the impact Du Bois's statement would have on those who did. Chatting with delegates in a sunny courtyard, he mused on the gulf between the American delegates and the African writers and artists, a gulf widened by Du Bois's statement. Unlike the Africans, who were struggling to throw off colonial rule, American Negroes had no motivation for overthrowing the American government. Their freedom, after all, lay in making the American government live up to its own promises. What, then, was the Americans' relationship with "the mysterious continent of Africa"? That would not be clear, Baldwin wrote in his article on the meeting, "until we had found some means of saying, to ourselves and to the world, more about the mysterious American continent than had ever been said before."[80]

Publishing the article in the *Encounter* in January 1957 was about as close as Baldwin appeared to skate to the Cold War politics of Paris, though that story has not perhaps been wholly told. One of Baldwin's closest friends, Mary S. Painter, was an economist with an interesting past. During World War II, Painter had worked for the U.S. Office of Strategic Services, forerunner to the CIA. Developing a statistical means of determining how many German submarines were afloat in the North Atlantic, she would prove (as the *New York Times* noted in her 1991 obituary) "startlingly accurate." After the war, she joined other economists moving to Europe to put the Marshall Plan for European recovery into play. Different stories have been told about how she and Baldwin met. The more believable is the version provided by his first biographer, Fern Eckman, based on an interview with Baldwin, that they met at a "brunch for Americans."[81] Her employer when they met was the U.S. mission to the North Atlantic Treaty Organization, where she studied the economies of Germany and France.[82]

Baldwin and Painter became very close, and he would dedicate *Another Country* to her. According to the biographer who probably knew Baldwin best, David Leeming, "He loved her more than he had loved or ever would love any woman."[83] A former employee of a spy agency, Painter worked in just the kind of job that undercover intelligence agents often held. It is at least possible, in this cloak-and-dagger time, that she maintained a link to her former employer in its new guise as the CIA.[84]

Despite his intriguing relationship with this woman engaged in high-level political work, Baldwin appeared to move through the political minefields of Paris with his mind mostly on other things: the novel he was working on, his love affairs, money, his identity as an American Negro and a homosexual, his guilt over leaving his family in New York. Not long before the writers' conference at the Sorbonne he had made a small attempt at suicide, overdosing on sleeping pills but, rescued by Mary Painter, changing his mind in time to vomit them up.[85]

Yet on the periphery of his vision he could see what was happening back home, and he was drawn to it. During Le Congrès, as he strolled down the Boulevard Saint-Germain with Wright and others, he saw in the kiosks along the way photographs of a young girl braving a mob in Charlotte, North Carolina. This image of "pride, tension, and anguish" moved Baldwin powerfully.

> *It made me furious, it filled me with both hatred and pity, and it made me ashamed. Some one of us should have been there with her! I dawdled in Europe for nearly yet another year, held by my private life and my attempt to finish a novel, but it was on that bright afternoon that I knew I was leaving France. I could, simply, no longer sit around in Paris discussing the Algerian and the black American problem. Everybody else was paying their dues, and it was time I went home and paid mine.*[86]

In the summer of 1957, while Congress was debating the Civil Rights Act, James Baldwin went home. At the suggestion of *Partisan Review* editor Philip Rahv, Baldwin prepared himself to make a reporting trip to the American South.

At this significant moment in Baldwin's life, Kenneth B. Clark, hearing he had returned, asked a friend to arrange a meeting between them.[87] Baldwin could scarcely have found a better guide than Kenneth Clark to orient him to what he could expect on his journey south. The two men had much in common besides their slight stature and powerful minds. Like Baldwin, Clark had grown up in Harlem. His strong-willed Jamaican mother, who had brought him to the United States from the Panama Canal Zone, was a union organizer in a garment factory and a follower of Marcus Garvey, the charismatic West Indian immigrant who advocated a return to Africa. She had shown scant patience with America's racial inequalities, and Clark took her example to heart. He was nearly kicked out of Howard University for demonstrating at the Capitol cafeteria, and probably would have been, had not one of his professors, Ralph Bunche, come to his aid. As a Ph.D. student at Columbia University, Clark worked on the ground-breaking study of race in America directed by Gunnar Myrdal. Teaching briefly at a Negro college in Virginia, Clark quit after the president told him his job was to make his Negro students contented with their lives, not to stir them up. Like Baldwin, Clark had never been a member of the Communist Party, or even tempted by communism. He went his own political way, as independent-minded as his mother. He worked for the government during the war, investigating Negro morale, but quit the job: his interracial team had encountered such practical difficulties working together in the South that he felt he could not go on.[88]

Clark's wife, Mamie Phipps Clark, had also gotten her Ph.D. from Columbia, and she had developed experiments using dolls to gauge the damage segregation had wreaked upon Negro children's self-esteem. Drawing on their own research and findings by other researchers, Clark helped the NAACP Legal Defense Fund mount the argument against school segregation in the cases that went to the Supreme Court. The social science research that Clark gathered weighed heavily enough in the Court's opinion to come under fire from lawyers, who, even if they supported the Court's judgment, would have preferred a legal argument not so dependent on social science. In his more political attack on the decision, Senator James O. Eastland of Mississippi singled out the social science research as "teachings of pro-communist agitators" (among whom he included E. Franklin Frazier). Clark spent some of his time in the years that followed defending the evidence, or trying to.[89]

When the Supreme Court asked for arguments on how the *Brown* decision ought to be implemented, Clark wrote another research summary, this one with the help of June Shagaloff, an NAACP staff member who later became Baldwin's friend. In the summary, Clark argued for strong, prompt enforcement of *Brown*. In countless forums, speeches, and letters to the editor, Clark called on America's leaders to put *Brown* into effect as quickly and unequivocally as possible. He took an active part in efforts to desegregate New York schools. He spoke to church groups, civil rights groups, academic conferences. Returning from his 1956 trip south, he spoke to white audiences about what he had found. He tried to speak frankly. He told one of his listeners that "only a straightforward, solid and honest approach to the racial problem by Northern whites and Negroes would be helpful at this time." He had not been certain that northern whites were prepared to hear the truth, but their response convinced him they were.[90] Seized by a sense of mission, Clark plunged into the work of change, fitting it into his already busy life at City College and the Northside Clinic, which he and his wife had founded for children in Harlem. He faced demands from every side, feeling himself, at times, caught up in a whirlwind.

Still, he took time out to meet James Baldwin, inviting him to visit the Clark home in Hastings-on-Hudson, a bucolic integrated community a forty-minute train ride up the Hudson River. "We both felt we had known each other for a long time," Clark would tell a Baldwin biographer, W. J. Weatherby. Clark found Baldwin intense, passionate, friendly, spellbinding to listen to. "His view of American racial injustice went beyond what I had read in his essays." During the course of several dinners, Clark and Baldwin exchanged views about developments in the civil rights movement.[91]

Over the next few years, Baldwin formed relationships with key figures in several civil rights organizations—the NAACP, the Congress of Racial Equality (CORE), and the Student Nonviolent Coordinating Committee (SNCC). In 1957, however, Clark was probably the most political man Baldwin knew in America. Clark could speak out of a deep knowledge about the movement and race relations. He had made a number of trips to the South, and his most recent, on behalf of the Unitarians, had left him with fresh impressions of how Negroes were faring. He offered Baldwin background and names of people he might want to see on his own first journey south.[92]

Even with Clark's encouragement, Baldwin was worried about going south. He had nightmares about the South. When he met his editor at Dial for the first time, Baldwin told him with foreboding that he was almost thirty-three, Jesus' age at his crucifixion.[93] His was a not uncommon fear. After the *Brown* decision, Lillian Smith had invited Pauli Murray, a Negro lawyer-poet who was writing her first book, to visit her in Georgia. Smith wanted the two of them to produce a dialogue—"Two Women, Talking." Murray replied that the very thought of going to Georgia frightened her into writing her will. "I tell you this only to let you know the deep-seated fear inside all of us, . . . the same kind of terror which I have in an electric storm and which my mind refuses to control, . . . a real panic . . . born of conditioning over many years." Murray was somewhat reassured when, studying a map, she saw how close northern Georgia was to North Carolina, her native state.[94]

Baldwin had no such reassuring experience of the South to turn to. In fact, he had never been south of Washington, D.C. He began his journey there, with a visit to Sterling Brown, a poet and literary critic who taught at Howard University and brought the terrors of southern history alive for Baldwin: the lynchings—the bodies suspended from trees. When Baldwin set off for Charlotte, North Carolina, Brown thought it best he arrive there before nightfall.[95]

After only two days in Charlotte, Baldwin wrote to Bill Cole, a publicist at Alfred A. Knopf, that he might not have made the trip if he had known before he came what he would "now feel in the solar plexus." He had interviewed half a dozen people, among them one of the students integrating the high school, and found himself struggling to grasp the truth of these young people's situation. He was not, after all, fifteen, nor was he the only Negro in a school of white students. But studying the boy he interviewed, watching his eyes, paying attention to what the boy was leaving out as he talked, he asked himself: if this boy could be "so clear-headed and self-contained," then could not Baldwin himself, isolated in a different way, rise to the occasion?

Baldwin was typing his letter in the office of Harry Golden, editor of the *Carolina Israelite* and a staunch supporter of integration. As he typed, a Negro girl who worked in the office took off early because, she explained, there had been Klan activity some twenty miles away. She did not want to risk walking from the bus stop one block to the taxi stand after night fell. "There is no way to exaggerate the complexity and danger of this situation," Baldwin told Cole.[96]

In Atlanta, Baldwin met Martin Luther King, "holed up" in a hotel room writing a book. Despite the interruption, King welcomed Baldwin. That night, at a party, Baldwin spotted King standing near a bookcase, listening patiently to someone but obviously weary, wishing he could go home to bed.

In Montgomery, Alabama, the bus boycott had ended with a court ruling banning segregated buses. Baldwin walked the streets, comfortable for the first time on his southern trip, detecting some familiar echo of life in Harlem. Not thinking, he entered a restaurant and was rudely welcomed with "What you want, boy?" Told to go to the "colored entrance," Baldwin ordered a hamburger through a screen that hid him from the white diners, and saw in the patience of a fellow Negro a strength he knew he did not have. That Sunday, he listened to the Reverend King preach at his church, and sensed in the congregation a particular joy—"the joy achieved by people who have ceased to delude themselves about an intolerable situation, who have found their prayers for a leader miraculously answered, and who now know that they can change their situation, if they will."

Back in New York, Baldwin retreated to a friend's home and collapsed for five days, recovering, while his family and friends searched the Village bars for him. Eventually he wrote two essays out of that journey. One was a short report that appeared in *Harper's Magazine* in October 1958, "The Hard Kind of Courage." The other, "Nobody Knows My Name: A Letter from the South," appeared in the winter 1959 issue of *Partisan Review*. The tone of the two pieces was distinctly different.

The *Harper's* piece was conciliatory—not so distant, in temper and mode, from Robert Penn Warren's *Segregation*. Restrained as it was, the *Harper's* report ended on a quiet, forbidding note, as Baldwin reflected that the troubles of the North were the same as the troubles of the South, "and that, unless we were very swift and honest, what is happening in the South today will be happening in the North tomorrow."[97] Perhaps Baldwin's careful tone in this piece derived from his knowledge of what editors wanted. *Harper's* had a reputation as a liberal magazine: liberal, but not radical. It had a circulation of around a quarter million, large enough to encompass a fairly diverse audience. Its editor, John

Fischer, was a former newspaperman who had worked for the U.S. government during the war, part of the time as an intelligence officer. Right after the war, he published a Cold War book on the Soviet Union, *Why They Behave like Russians*, in which he put forth the essential Cold War argument: "We need to make it perfectly clear that we are committed to defend certain vital areas. . . ."[98] A cold warrior on foreign affairs, Fischer belonged to the National Urban League, one of the more conservative civil rights organizations. He had edited Richard Wright's *Black Power* at Harper & Brothers, but refused to publish his *Savage Holiday* and *The Color Curtain*, and Wright did not like him.[99] Baldwin had already published in *Harper's* before this piece on his journey south, and presumably understood something of the editor he wrote for.

Partisan Review, once a project of the communist John Reed Clubs, addressed a smaller, more select, avant-garde audience, and here Baldwin pulled out more stops. The conflict over desegregation was "a criminally frivolous dispute," he wrote, "absolutely unworthy of this nation; and it is being carried on, in complete bad faith, by completely uneducated people. . . . The dispute has actually nothing to do with education, as some among the eminently uneducated know. It has to do with political power and it has to do with sex." He spoke bluntly of white sexual guilt. Negroes could trace their lineage to both blacks and whites, and white men hated them for that knowledge. Rolling toward the end, Baldwin's voice took on the timbre of dark prophecy: If the rural populations and politicians of the southern states prevented urban blacks and whites from reaching a compromise, then riots would break out. And they would not be contained in the South; they would spread to every city in the nation with a sizable population of Negroes. "And this is not only because the ties between Northern and Southern Negroes are still very close. It is because the nation, the entire nation, has spent a hundred years avoiding the question of the place of the black man in it."[100]

Forthright as the statement was, it was tucked away in a little magazine. It would be several years before Baldwin's voice reached its full force, and the man who started out a political innocent became the leading intellectual spokesman for the movement for racial equality.

PART TWO

Gathering Strength

1957–1963

CHAPTER 4

"TO BE TRANSFORMED"

B y the late 1950s, the worst of McCarthyism seemed past in the North, but in the South the repression went on. Hearing reports from colleagues, C. Vann Woodward considered taking up the conditions of civil liberties in the South in an article. From Emory University in Atlanta, historian Bell Wiley had responded in April 1957, "I don't think the civil liberties blast would be premature. I have a very strong impression that restrictions on freedom of expression concerning race are increasing all the time." Although Wiley did not claim to have much evidence in hand, he offered Woodward a two-page list of instances. Jim Silver at the University of Mississippi had written that his days there were numbered. One of Silver's colleagues, sociology professor Morton King, had resigned because of threats to free speech. A historian at the University of Alabama had reported that departures had already begun there and more were sure to follow. There were other cases, not all in higher education: a public health nurse fired for eating lunch with a Negro; an editor of a newspaper losing his job for making a speech entitled "The Right of Dissent."[1]

In spring 1958 at Allen University in South Carolina, a private Negro teachers' college, the president tried to force the resignation of three faculty members, two whites and one Negro. Writing Woodward on March 4, 1958, University of South Carolina professor Gus Williamson told him that all three were "militant NAACP men," and two of the three—one Negro and one white—had drawn the interest of the House Un-American Activities Committee (HUAC). In an attempt to force them to resign, the state board of education, headed by South Carolina Governor George B. Timmerman Jr., withdrew approval of the school's training program for teachers—in effect, barring graduates from teaching in South Carolina. The American Association of University Professors (AAUP)—the nation's foremost defender of academic freedom—tried to investigate what was happening, and the governor attacked the AAUP, too. The charges against the two professors cited by HUAC, Williamson wrote, "are clearly a cover for their integrationist sentiments and activities. . . . Since many of the dominant figures in the state government equate pro-integrationist sentiment, let alone action, with subversion, they often proclaim that there is no middle ground, not in South Carolina." Were University of South Carolina faculty in for investigation too? Possibly, Williamson thought. Indeed, the university had just terminated the appointment of an assistant professor of philosophy, apparently because the man had contributed an article on segregationists to the *AAUP Bulletin.* "This was a restrained, moderate article, but it was clearly no segregationist who wrote it." With the air growing chill, "widespread departures" might be in the offing as "the younger, marketable faculty" fled the South. "Many are rather like me, already considerably perplexed as to our conscientious duty in such a society in such a crisis as this."[2]

Teaching at Johns Hopkins University in Baltimore, Woodward had heard a number of stories from friends farther south, but he himself had escaped the harshest winds, as Howard H. Quint, a Connecticut-born history professor at the University of South Carolina, pointed out to him in a letter in May 1958. Quint had asked Woodward to write a foreword for his book on race in South Carolina, *Profile in Black and White,* and Woodward had hesitated. For one thing, he thought Quint exaggerated the difference between South Carolina and "a liberal, equalitarian, democratic America outside the South."

For another, Quint had compared southern extremists to Nazis, and that made Woodward uncomfortable. Quint defended his equation with some vigor, even bitterness:

> *For the past eleven years I have been in the trenches, so to speak, and since 1954 I have been subjected to constant bombardment. . . . I suppose that under the circumstances the enemy is much more real to us than to you who is not constantly confronted with belligerent adolescents and others who believe that any questioning of the South Carolina ideal amounts to outright heresy. . . . I'll stick by my association of the South Carolina extremists with the Nazis.*

He closed with the news that he had taken a job in Boulder, Colorado (though he wound up at the University of Massachusetts at Amherst).[3]

When Quint's book appeared, an editor's note explained that he had resigned from the University of South Carolina before the book's publication "because he believed this book should be published but did not wish to cause embarrassment to the University of South Carolina." In his own preface, Quint spoke of a young scholar who had done so much work on the book that he ought to have his name on the title page but had asked "for personal reasons to remain anonymous."[4] So strong were the southern sanctions against speaking out for desegregation that even these relatively outspoken men deferred to them.

Howard University professor Rayford Logan recorded in his journal a small incident that reveals how heavily caution weighed on college campuses. During the Little Rock crisis, Logan suggested over lunch that a law professor refute a columnist who said the president lacked authority to send in the troops. Logan recorded the lawyer's response in his journal: a person who raised such an issue would be "labeled 'controversial' " and lose effectiveness.[5] Harvard sociologist David Riesman would catch a whiff of the same caution when he visited the South in the fall of 1960. The chair of the sociology department at the University of Georgia—Raymond Bowers—told him of the difficulty he had in recruiting faculty from the North, which was virtually the only possible source of social science faculty. One prospect

Bowers had tried to recruit had turned out to belong to the NAACP—
"and while Bowers felt that any amount of scholarship could be easily
handled, political activism could not."[6]

Leslie W. Dunbar, director of the Southern Regional Council from
1959 to 1965, would say of the 1950s South,

> *It is difficult to convey to persons who did not live in the South dur-*
> *ing those years a feeling of how it was. The difficulty would be*
> *greater had not all the country experienced the ravages of*
> *McCarthyism. Imagine the emotional and political atmosphere of*
> *the McCarthy days intensified many times and compressed within a*
> *single region, and the South of the late 1950's may be suggested.*[7]

In this time of political repression and fear, on white and Negro
campuses alike, Lawrence Dunbar Reddick, the professor at Alabama
State College who had called Robert Penn Warren's hand, stood up to
be counted, and would suffer the consequences.

Southern Negro colleges had their share of talented men on their
faculties (where else could Negro scholars find positions in America?),
but Lawrence Dunbar Reddick had brought to Alabama State excep-
tional credentials as a man of the world. Working as a curator of the
Schomburg collection in the 1940s, he had played a visible part in New
York political life. He taught a class at the New School for Social
Research and invited E. Franklin Frazier and W. E. B. Du Bois to pres-
ent "The World View of the Negro Question": "the struggles of liber-
ation and integration that are now being made by Negroid peoples."
Reddick met young African leaders who were studying in the United
States and advised the African Students Association of America and
Canada, which published a Pan-African magazine. He criticized the
United Nations as a cultural imperialist. Speaking at the National
Council of American-Soviet Friendship, he offered the idea that
"Asiatic and African peoples who may not possess a single factory or
have a single paved street, may be able to teach the West a great deal

about living." He shared the bill with Ralph Ellison and Frazier in a lecture series sponsored by the progressive American Labor Party.[8]

Reddick also participated in that rancorous Harlem meeting with Ellison, Richard Wright, C. L. R. James, Horace Cayton, and St. Clair Drake to discuss publishing a collection of essays on the Negro. James was a Trotskyist; Ellison and Wright were Marxists disillusioned with the Communist Party. In the early fifties, Reddick himself would be identified by an FBI informant as a "concealed member" of the Communist Party.[9] FBI informants often got things wrong; Herbert Hill, the NAACP's labor secretary and a close observer of the Harlem intellectual scene, believes that Reddick represented "the independent black radical tradition." He was, in Hill's view, a sophisticated thinker and a marvelous man.

Weary of fighting for resources for the Schomburg and an increase in his own salary, Reddick had left the Schomburg and New York to run the library at Atlanta University Center, a consortium of Negro colleges in Atlanta. From there he moved to Alabama State, a less imposing brick campus known for summer sessions that drew teachers from all over the South. Every summer, several hundred Negro teachers would come to campus to work on their master's degrees, and the school's president, H. Councill Trenholm, would bring in Negro scholars from around the country to teach them.[10]

Despite its respected summer program, like most state Negro colleges, Alabama State had to make do with limited resources. Trenholm and his faculty, staff, and students provided much of what they needed for themselves. The campus held fish fries to raise money for the swimming pool or the gym, which campus workers would then build. There never seemed to be enough chairs for the classrooms; professors would have to round up more before class could begin. Minimal as state support was, the state still had the power to close the school down. Yet when the bus boycott started in Montgomery at the end of 1955—around the time Reddick arrived—faculty participation was strong. Both Reddick and his young colleague Norman Walton, also a historian, gathered information as the boycott unfolded. They attended meetings, talked with participants, kept notes and leaflets.

While Walton wrote about the boycott for the *Negro History Bulletin*, Reddick wrote about it for *Dissent*,[11] and it was Reddick, the more seasoned historian, who suggested to Martin Luther King Jr. that King write a book on the boycott "as told to L. D. Reddick." Worried that readers would think he could not write his own book, King agreed to a somewhat different plan: he would write a story of the boycott with Reddick's help, and Reddick would write a biography of King. It was an ambitious plan, especially for a minister in the midst of building a movement and a professor teaching a heavy load. But books could carry the movement's message farther than King himself, already exhausted by his round of public appearances.[12]

Two of King's northern advisers, Bayard Rustin and Stanley Levison, went to writer-lawyer Pauli Murray for advice on getting a book contract, and she guided King to her own agent, Marie Rodell, who arranged a contract for King with Murray's publisher, Harper & Brothers, which also became Reddick's publisher.[13] During the summer of 1957, King and Reddick met for long talks about each other's books. They divided their sessions into two halves—the first devoted to King's book, the second to Reddick's. Reddick shared his research material and helped King sort out what he should say in his story of the boycott. King, in turn, answered Reddick's questions about his life.[14]

By the start of 1958, the publisher had some of King's manuscript in hand, but Rodell was concerned enough about the book's condition that she proposed he work with a professional writer. Bayard Rustin put in a call to J. Saunders Redding, author of *On Being Negro in America*, who was writing a history of Negroes in America. Redding had already made significant contributions to the racial dialogue; here was an opportunity to make a contribution of another sort. But, unwilling to put his words under another man's name, he told Rustin that he was neither "a hack or a ghost" and would have to know more about the project before he signed on. To his editor, he expressed concern that King's book would compete with his own.[15]

A couple of white writers were actually approached to work with King. In Levison's view, however, Reddick, already on board, had an advantage over any white writer: he was Negro. Levison told King that Rodell, herself white, failed to understand that "a Negro more readily feels things that a white person comprehends with greater difficulty. This is the old story that too many white liberals consider themselves free of stereotypes, rarely recognizing that the roots of prejudice are deep and are tenaciously driven into the soil of their whole life."[16] Reddick's role in producing *Stride toward Freedom* was so important that Ella Baker, who ran the Southern Christian Leadership Conference's Atlanta office, even thought he might have written it for King. That would be an exaggeration. Several people very clearly shaped what was, after all, not an expression of individual personality but a work crafted for precise effects. While King's supporters wanted to bring national visibility to the movement, the editors were interested in both readability and political nuance. They asked for human interest stories, but they also took care that the book not present King as too radical for the times.[17]

In addition to having one of the better records for publishing books by Negro authors, Harper & Brothers, publisher of the well-circulated rejection of communism, *The God That Failed*, had a Cold War tinge. The chairman of the company's editorial board, Cass Canfield, had worked in the Office of War Information and was a good friend of CIA Director Allen Dulles.[18] More directly to the point, Melvin Arnold, the editor responsible for publishing James Baldwin's *Notes of a Native Son* at Beacon Press, had resurfaced as one of King's editors at Harper & Brothers. Still the cold warrior he had been when he worked for the Unitarians, Arnold asked King to strengthen his repudiation of communism. Where King said his "response to communism was negative," Arnold wanted him to say his "response to communism was and is negative." King made the change, but balked at weakening his criticism of capitalism.[19] Thus the Cold War penetrated this first book by the leading political figure in a movement that could so logically expand a demand for "civil rights" into a demand for economic justice—a critique of capitalism. Were the editors chiefly concerned about reader perceptions and thus trying to protect King and the movement from Red-baiting? Or did they themselves fear the radical threat that underlay the movement for racial equality? It is not easy to know, but something of a pattern was operating here: the company had made a similar request to Richard Wright, asking him to add a repudiation of communism to the introduction of *Black Power*.

In his own book on King, *Crusader without Violence*, also published by Harper & Brothers, Reddick situated King delicately, portraying him as a lover of democracy, with divided feelings about Marxism. King acknowledged Marx's appeal—"his dialectic, his critique of monopoly capitalism, and his regard for social and economic justice." However, said Reddick, "although he realizes that capitalism, too, has its evils, King unequivocally rejects communism. 'I am not a materialist. I do not believe that all history is guided and shaped by economic determinism.' " King accepted neither communism's espousal of violence nor Marxism's assertion that change comes through class struggle.[20]

After both of their books were published (Reddick's to less fanfare than King's), the working alliance between Reddick and King continued when Reddick helped King write an *Ebony* report of King's trip to India in 1959. On the way, Reddick and King, accompanied by Coretta King, stopped off to visit Richard Wright in Paris. Before the visit with Wright, Reddick told his friend St. Clair Drake that "some of the boys feel that he has pulled up his roots here and therefore his novels lack the old vitality." But he told Wright himself that he was "a sort of outpost for us, very strategically located where currents of attitudes from Europe, Africa, the Middle East and at times the Far East swirled together."[21] To Reddick, as to King, the freedom movements of Asia and Africa played a powerful role in the American freedom movement. As Reddick wrote in an essay that appeared after the trip to India, the European colonies' midcentury movement toward independence "meant as much to the Negro in the 'backward' South as it did directly to the colonials in the 'backward' lands overseas." Competing with the Soviet Union for these emerging nations' loyalty, the United States could not afford segregation.[22]

The slender volume in which this essay appeared, *The Southerner as an American*, was in its way an act of courage. This was the new southern history, John Hope Franklin announced in the lead essay. No longer held captive by southern white apologists, southern history could act as a liberating force. In his own contribution to the volume, Reddick noted that intellectuals had once shored up the social myths that undergirded segregation. Now, he said, they should help transform America peaceably into an integrated society. They could do that by reminding Negroes and whites alike what they shared—a common ground as Americans.

> *To many, change is frightfully difficult. Our social and natural scientists, historians, men of letters, editors, orators—all who communicate information and ideas—could help ease this pain if they would remind our nation, our section, our people, of the values, experiences, and dreams that we share. Therein we might discover at the least a common humanity and a universal destiny.*[23]

Reddick himself had already done more than his share to address the needs of the hour. Teaching at a college with few resources other than the talent and energy of its people, he had produced several articles and a book and had helped produce another. He did not lead the Montgomery movement; nor was he responsible for its success. But recognizing the opportunity before him, he had done his part to ensure that the world understood what was happening there. When the sit-ins began in the spring of 1960, he was situated well to play a part in the difficult days that lay ahead.

To the nation's media, the sit-ins that swept the South in 1960 blew up like a summer storm out of nowhere. Organizers themselves encouraged that notion, hoping to fend off allegations that outside agitators had planned the wave of protest. In fact, for several years, young people had been meeting and talking and planning at Highlander Center, in east Tennessee, one of the few political places in the South where Negroes and whites, even in the early 1950s, could meet in easy, relaxed camaraderie. Elsewhere in the South, chapters of the

Congress of Racial Equality and the NAACP had picked away at segregation of lunch counters, movie houses, and restaurants. At Morgan State College in Baltimore, Maryland, students staged sit-ins every year, usually in the spring, from 1955 on.[24] In Nashville, a Negro student at the Vanderbilt Divinity School, James M. Lawson Jr., had begun holding workshops in nonviolence. The Nashville students were still in training when four Negro students in Greensboro, North Carolina, sat in at a dime-store lunch counter on February 1, 1960. The next day nineteen students joined the original four. Soon students in other southern cities followed suit.

When had America ever seen a political movement more dramatic than the sit-ins that swept the South that spring? From Nashville, Fisk professor Arna Bontemps wrote his old friend Langston Hughes on March 11 that a wall in the student union was "covered with telegrams the kids have received from all over, including long ones from other student bodies like Harvard, U. of Chicago, Oberlin, Rutgers, UCLA, and the rest." Reading the board, he found himself moved nearly to tears. On March 25, he wrote again: "Police cars are circling the campus at this moment and rumors are flying." He had heard that the students were planning to demonstrate again and "fill up the jails." If that was so, he expected rough times ahead. "Many of us had hoped that Nashville just might sober up and decide to set a good example. Obviously, that is not going to happen right away."[25] Indeed, Vanderbilt University, the premier white university in the South, proving itself no more enlightened than any backwater campus, expelled sit-in leader James Lawson from the divinity school.

Lawson was unintimidated. In mid-April, sit-in organizers from across the South gathered at Shaw University in Raleigh, North Carolina, and heard him call for a nonviolent movement motivated by divine love, the love that binds God to man and men to each other. "Such love goes to the extreme; it remains loving and forgiving even in the midst of hostility." They also heard him denounce the NAACP and its magazine, *The Crisis*, a voice, he said, of the black bourgeoisie. The NAACP was wrong to rely on the courts; it was time, Lawson said, to organize the people. By the time the conference was over, a new organization—the Student Nonviolent Coordinating Committee—had been formed.[26]

Faced with direct action on an unprecedented scale, white southerners took an unprecedented step. "In community after community—more than eighty by the end of 1960—lunch counters were desegregated," the Southern Regional Council's Leslie Dunbar wrote six years later. "Never before, and this is a startling fact, had the South yielded racial restrictions without federal coercion. But more than this, the students galvanized civil-rights adherents into a movement."[27] In the unlikeliest region of the country, the radical spirit, dormant for the last twenty years, again sprung to life.

For administrators at Negro colleges, the student sit-ins offered an enormous test of courage. Even in Atlanta, more liberal-minded than most southern cities, the presidents of the Negro colleges urged students to hold back. When the students at the several Negro colleges there proposed sit-ins in February, the presidents talked them into voicing their views in a newspaper advertisement; the presidents would even pay part of the cost. A Spelman College student recently returned from Paris typed out a first draft. Other students helped finish the job, and the ad ran full-page in the *Atlanta Constitution* on March 9, 1961.[28]

"We do not intend to wait placidly for those rights which are already legally and morally ours to be meted out to us one at a time," the ad declared, and enumerated the many ways that rights were denied in Atlanta. The city's mayor responded respectfully to the ad, but Georgia Governor Ernest Vandiver called it "anti-American," and "obviously not written by students." Indeed, it did not sound to him "like it was written in this country."

Howard Zinn, a white history professor at Spelman, knew well enough that it had been written in this country; it had been written on *his* typewriter. A lean man with an elfin smile, Zinn had not come south intending to enlist in the Negro cause, but he did come primed for action. He had grown up in Brooklyn during the depression, the son of East European immigrants who had worked hard and stayed poor. On some winter days, coming back from school, he would find his mother knitting by candlelight because the electric company had turned off the power. They were always moving, from tenement to tenement, as his father worked at a succession of jobs—as waiter, window cleaner, street salesman. Zinn understood firsthand the plight of the powerless.

As Hitler and Mussolini rose to power, he had seen men from his neighborhood go off to fight Franco's fascism in Spain's civil war. After high school, he worked in a shipyard and played an active role in union organizing. He participated in the Young Communist League and might have even thought of himself as a communist, he would say later, but had not joined the party.[29] The war soured him on Marxism, but he remained a socialist. Like Norman Mailer, he campaigned for Henry Wallace in 1948. He went through college on the GI Bill and, in 1956, a new Ph.D. from Columbia University in hand, took a job at Spelman.

Zinn had no sooner arrived in Atlanta with his wife and their two children than he began crossing lines. He took his students to the state legislature, and they sat in the white section. He worked with Whitney M. Young Jr., then a dean at Atlanta University (and later executive director of the National Urban League), to desegregate Atlanta's public libraries. He published an article on desegregation in *Harper's*, arguing there were things southerners cared more about than holding the racial line.[30]

The article caused a dustup in Jackson, Mississippi, where the *State Times* published an account of it in an insert meant for Negro readers. The headline proclaimed, "Southern Whites Prefer Race Mix." Apparently a delivery boy picked up the wrong stack of papers, and some wound up on white front porches. According to a report filed with the Mississippi Sovereignty Commission, an agency established to try to control the racial story, the news item on Zinn's article had been written by the Negro journalist who put the insert together, and the editor knew nothing about it. The editor subsequently talked to the man and instructed him in the future to clear everything on segregation with him before publication.[31] Thus

Mississippi tried to keep a lid on what its Negro readers heard about desegregation, and Howard Zinn made his debut in the Sovereignty Commission files.

Already involved in the desegregation movement, Zinn was quick to support the Atlanta students when they followed up their newspaper ad with sit-ins at downtown cafeterias. He lent them his car to ride downtown in and, as they had asked him to, alerted the newspapers just minutes before the sit-ins were to begin. Seventy-seven students were arrested; fourteen Spelman students were among them. One was Marian Wright (later Marian Wright Edelman), a student of Zinn's. Her picture appeared in newspapers across the country, reading C. S. Lewis's *The Screwtape Letters* as she sat behind bars. In an article for the *Nation*, Zinn delighted in a dormitory notice that brought together the decorous past and the radical present: "Young Ladies Who Can Picket, Please Sign Below."[32] With the *Nation* article, Zinn, a white vaguely Jewish professor from Brooklyn, stepped into the supportive role he was to play in the movement as one of its more persistent spokesmen in the northern press.

The students had another, more prominent ally in Atlanta, the president of Martin Luther King Jr.'s alma mater, Morehouse— Benjamin Mays. As a private school, Morehouse was not so vulnerable as some colleges to southern politicians, and, besides, Mays was a man of independent mind. He had shared the stage with Faulkner at Memphis and supported Martin Luther King in difficult hours.[33] Now, as younger people defied the system, he stood at their side. "The demonstrations will continue, and the goals the students seek will be achieved. Their cause is just," he said in an essay entitled "A Plea for Straight Talk between the Races," published by the *Atlantic Monthly* at the end of 1960. Did the racial conflict that had followed the *Brown* decision betoken a breakdown in communication? Not at all, Mays said. "The plain truth is that, up to a few years ago, Negroes and white people in the South never had honest communication."[34]

On his visit to Atlanta in the fall after the sit-ins, sociologist David Riesman saw for himself the unease with which even that city was confronting honest speech. At lunch with a group of white newspapermen, Riesman found many of them impressed by the students' courage but worried, at the same time, that "intransigents on the Negro side" (as Riesman himself described them in his private account of his visit) might jeopardize the liberal mayor's control of the situation.[35]

In Montgomery, Alabama, the official response to the 1960 sit-ins was more unabashedly brutal than in Atlanta, and one of the victims was to be Lawrence Reddick. The Montgomery sit-ins began toward the end of February when twenty-nine students sat in at a courthouse snack bar. As soon as they asked for service, the shop shut down and the sheriff arrived "brandishing a club," the United Press International reported. "Pistol-carrying deputies patrolled halls outside the basement shop and state highway patrolmen took pictures of the Negroes, who stood quietly against the wall." Alabama Governor John Patterson said they would be investigated and expelled.[36]

President Trenholm urged the board of education to put them on probation instead. The board wound up expelling only nine. This was merely the beginning. A thousand students risked expulsion by demonstrating at the capitol on March 1. A week later, as demonstrators set off from campus, police stopped the demonstration with thirty-five arrests. Reddick was there to see police lined "shoulder to shoulder . . . with their pistols, clubs, cans of tear gas, etc. And behind them for a half block were state and county law enforcement agents with several types of guns and about thirty squad cars, motorcycles, a patrol wagon and a fire truck." Writing about the episode for *Dissent*, Reddick saw here illustrated "the essentials of the current racial war in Alabama": book-carrying Negro students versus armed white policemen.[37]

Reddick thought of himself as the movement's official historian and made a practice of attending the students' mass meetings. The meetings did not begin until seven, but people started gathering at four to be sure of a seat, so Reddick would leave his late-afternoon class in Norman Walton's charge and go off to the meeting. Walton himself was sympathetic to the student movement but had four children to put through school and so tried not to involve himself publicly.

He did his part by sitting in Reddick's empty classroom for the class hour (the students had all gone to the meeting, but a state spy might come around to make sure classes were being held). Walton did not mind helping Reddick out—he liked Reddick, an older man who had taken him under his wing. Reddick was something of a fitness buff, and he would come to swim at the pool where Walton coached the swim team. Reddick was clean-cut—he always wore a tie to class and a little smile. Walton never heard him laugh, but he wore that little smile, which Walton imagined smoothed the way for him when he mixed with whites at historians' conferences.

For this dignified man, an undignified fate lay ahead. In its meeting on March 25, 1960, the state board of education ordered the college to put on probation those students who had been arrested until (according to the minutes) "such time as they might be willing to conduct themselves in such a manner worthy of readmittance to the College." The board also ordered President Trenholm to dismiss "any and all members of the faculty of the Alabama State College who are not loyal to the College in all matters of discipline and of rules and regulations pertaining to the proper functioning of the College at all times."[38] State police had been studying photographs of protests to identify faculty members involved. By the time the board met on June 14, suspicion had fallen most heavily on Lawrence Reddick.[39]

Reddick understood that the walls were closing in on him. On April 12, he wrote a letter to Trenholm asking for "something better than an annual job contract." He asked, too, for assurance that he could "continue to discharge a few of the ordinary rights and duties of citizenship." If he was arrested for hosting a racially mixed group visiting Montgomery, he warned Trenholm, he "would have no choice but to fight [his] way out of it on the basis of principle rather than expedience." Trenholm could not give Reddick the assurance he wanted. In fact, in a long talk near the end of the quarter, Trenholm tried to talk him into resigning right away "for the sake of the college." Reddick resigned the following day, but made his resignation effective August 31, after the summer term.[40]

That was not good enough for Governor Patterson, who reported the results of an investigation of Reddick to the board on June 14. Investigators from the Department of Public Safety had encountered resistance on the part of Trenholm when they asked for Reddick's personnel file. Understanding that his own job and perhaps the well-being of the college was at stake, Trenholm had finally released it. Material in that file, along with assorted debris the investigators had come up with, went into a written report. The governor handed a copy to each member of the board. The board discussed the report and approved the governor's motion that Trenholm be ordered to fire Reddick "by sundown today."[41] One conscientious member voted nay, explaining, according to the minutes, "that he did not believe that any teacher or public official should be fired without a hearing and an opportunity to defend his record."

The report on which the firing was based has vanished from state government files. According to the minutes of the meeting, the report was to be placed in the State Department of Education along with the minutes, but a search for it in the spring of 1999 failed to locate it. The state archives had copies of the minutes but no report accompanied them. At the State Department of Education, a staff member produced the original ledger containing the minutes for this span of years—laying the large, impressive volume out on a table like a ledger from a Dickens novel. But the report, dust-covered by time, did not slip from the pages. It had vanished. At the Department of Public Safety, a staff member who inquired at a higher level was told that those old intelligence reports had all been destroyed.

So the report that cost Lawrence Reddick his job is apparently gone, but press accounts survive. The *Montgomery Advertiser* gave the story a four-column headline in the lead position on the front page: "Negro Teacher Linked to Reds, Ordered Fired." The *Advertiser* quoted Patterson's comment that Reddick's association with communist organizations suggested that "Communists are involved" in the pro-integration movement. Toward the end of the story, the *Advertiser* strung out the miscellaneous items the state investigators had come up with to make the case against Reddick.

The file on Reddick included a photostatic copy of a newspaper article with a picture showing Reddick with Andrei Vyshinsky, the then Russian delegate to the United Nations, at a "Get Together With Russia Rally" at Madison Square Garden.

The file quoted records of the Fulton County Bureau of Criminal Investigation in Atlanta, showing that Reddick was a speaker at a 1948 meeting of writers, a group later described by the Daily Worker as being made up of "Marxists and other anti-Fascist writers."

Reddick was identified further by a letter from the New York City Police Department as a lecturer at a Communist-sponsored school.[42]

There was no mention of Reddick's association with King or of his book on King or, for that matter, of his involvement with the sit-ins, the most immediate reason for the attack on him. There was no mention of anything in his past that would suggest he was a scholar—his degrees from Fisk and the University of Chicago, his positions of responsibility at the Schomburg and Atlanta University. All had vanished. He had been reduced to a link between Montgomery and Moscow.

The national press, relying on wire service reports, did no better. "Alabama Dismisses a Negro Educator," the *New York Times* proclaimed in a brief story deep in the paper. Identifying Reddick only as head of the Alabama State College history department, the story by the Associated Press reported that Reddick had been dismissed "at the insistence of Gov. John Patterson. The Governor charged that Dr. Reddick was a Communist sympathizer." According to another news account, the state's report also quoted the *New York Telegram* "as saying that Reddick was a Communist and adding that Reddick had been fired from a position with the New York Public Library because of Communist activities," an allegation that was simply untrue.[43]

It was a telling, ugly moment. "It is hard for me to understand how a man with a record like this could get a job at Alabama State College," a state press release quoted the governor as saying. Blaming communists for the student protests, Patterson called on the board of education to "clean up" the college. In a televised appearance, he made President Trenholm promise to maintain "a close watch" over the students.

Meanwhile, the Reverend Ralph D. Abernathy, a leader of Montgomery's Negro movement for integration, launched a counter-attack. If the governor meant to drive off Alabama State College's best teachers, he said, then Negro students would have to attend other institutions of higher learning in the state—white institutions. Reddick himself responded with a statement, saying, "Gov. Patterson knows that I have never been a Communist. He knows, too, that I am not an agitator, but from time to time do make serious studies of current and historical questions."[44]

Some twenty faculty members active in the movement, facing nearly certain dismissal, turned in their resignations. The board of education placed President Trenholm on what turned out to be permanent leave. The subsequent fall, students were admitted only after they signed an "oath of honor" promising to behave like ladies and gentlemen.[45] The American Association of University Professors censured the college for denying Reddick due process; the censure would not be lifted for twenty years.[46] The American Civil Liberties Union protested Reddick's firing, and so did the Southern Christian Leadership Conference, the NAACP, the University of Chicago's Department of History, and the Interdenominational Ministerial Alliance.[47] A federal court of appeals ordered the expelled students reinstated on the ground that their expulsion had violated their constitutional right to due process.[48]

The following spring, the New York City Teachers Union gave Reddick its Silver Jubilee Award "for his inspiring 'crusade without violence' for civil rights, intellectual freedom and human dignity." The *New York Times*, reporting the ceremony at significantly greater length than it had reported Reddick's firing, sharpened the story's political edge by including a comment by Carey McWilliams, editor of the *Nation*. McWilliams "warned against the 'new McCarthyism' sweeping the nation and said it was a well organized movement 'tied with the military.' He said many reserve officers of the armed forces had been addressing church and civic groups and that aircraft companies had been distributing propaganda films intended to start new 'witch hunts.' "[49]

Lawrence Reddick got a job teaching at Coppin State Teachers College in Baltimore; he continued to think of himself as the movement's historian, and he continued to offer advice to King. "Don't let them pin you down on the 'communist' issue," he warned King in 1963, with the wisdom born of experience.[50]

The sit-ins had exposed the shifting sands on which Negro colleges of the South were built. Dependent on the largesse of whites, southern Negro campuses may have looked like independent worlds, but they were not. The student assault on white supremacy shook them to their foundations. On a trip south in the late spring of 1960, James Baldwin thought he heard "the death rattle of the Negro school system."[51]

On the surface, Florida A&M in Tallahassee looked prosperous enough as Baldwin approached the hilltop campus in a taxi. So many buildings had been lately constructed in a last-ditch effort at proving that Florida's Negro schools were equal to white schools that the campus looked nearly new. In truth, Baldwin concluded after a short stay, Florida A&M was "just as poor a center of learning as almost any other university in this country." How, Baldwin wondered, could anyone be truly educated "in a country so distrustful of the independent mind"? A Negro administrator's job, so far as the state of Florida was concerned, was to keep students in line. Unable to do that, college presidents became dispensable. "It is easy to judge those Negroes who, in order to keep their jobs, are willing to do everything in their power to subvert the student movement," Baldwin wrote in his article on the visit. But consider their position and the North's responsibility for it: if Negro teachers and administrators lost their jobs in the South (as the music professor who showed him around did after Baldwin's departure), where would they go? The North would not have them.

Unsupported by campus authorities, Florida A&M students had

turned to local ministers heading the Tallahassee Inter-Civic Council. The council had proved its mettle during a bus boycott, started a few months after Montgomery's. "Every time I drove my car into the garage," one minister told Baldwin, "I expected a bullet to come whizzing by my head." Some did whiz into his living room and into the grocery store owned by another minister in the council. There had been retaliations, too, for the sit-ins, that minister told Baldwin, although he asked that Baldwin not describe them in the article he wrote for *Mademoiselle*.

Baldwin hardly needed reminding that he had walked onto a battlefield. Sitting in his hotel room at night, he was preternaturally aware of his high visibility as he typed his notes in a lighted room, the only room lighted at that hour. Beyond his room at the end of the hotel was a road lined with trees, and he thought often about what those trees hid. He talked late one night at his hotel with two young men who just happened to be there, studying together. One of them, made curious by the sound of Baldwin's typewriter, had knocked on his door, and Baldwin carried his bottle of bourbon down to their room to talk. The student who had knocked on his door sympathized with the sit-in movement, but he feared betraying his family's hopes by getting expelled. Although he had not taken part yet, his inaction bothered him. He gave Baldwin names of students more active than he, and the next day Baldwin talked with them.

The students' first sit-ins in February had failed to accomplish their goal, desegregation of dime-store lunch counters. Staging another sit-in in March, a thousand students had confronted a white mob armed with knives and baseball bats. The police, using tear gas, drove the mob off and arrested the students—twenty-nine Negroes, six whites. At the time of Baldwin's visit, the students were gathering for a new attempt. Although most participants in the sit-ins across the South were Negro, in some places white students from nearby campuses did join in, and that was the case in Tallahassee. There, as elsewhere, the taboo against racial mixing made simply organizing the sit-ins a challenge. Neither the white students from Florida State nor the Negro students from A&M could meet together on one another's campuses, so they convened instead at a church to plan an integrated prayer meeting at the state capitol. Baldwin sat in on the meeting.

They decided not to tell the police in advance. ("If you tell the police, it's just as good as telling the White Citizens' Council," one student said.) Word got out anyway. Concerned about violence, the students did not go on with their plans. Still, Baldwin was impressed by their quiet commitment. "They are not the first Negroes to face mobs," he wrote in his article for the white college-girl readers of *Mademoiselle.* "They are merely the first Negroes to frighten the mob more than the mob frightens them." That October, Baldwin, a rising voice for the movement, carried the message of revolt to college students on the West Coast. At a writers' symposium sponsored by *Esquire,* he told an audience gathered at San Francisco State College, "Now, this country is going to be transformed. It will not be transformed by an act of God, but by all of us, by you and me."[52]

CHAPTER 5

"ON THE
STAGE OF
THE WORLD"

I n the wake of the most dramatic political movement the United
States had ever seen, a group of Negro writers—among them
the future eminent historian Harold Cruse—were drawn to a
revolutionary struggle even farther south. Why, when they might
have traveled to Montgomery or Atlanta, did they visit Cuba
instead? Their journey was emblematic: the American civil rights
movement was unfolding against a backdrop of worldwide freedom
movements. Fidel Castro's overthrow of Cuban dictator Fulgencio
Batista was only the latest in a series of dramatic uprisings. From the
Mau-Mau rebellion in Kenya to the revolts against the French in
Algeria and Vietnam, to the quieter push for independence in the
Gold Coast and other black African countries, captive people around
the world were struggling to free themselves. In speeches and ser-
mons, Martin Luther King Jr. would recite like a litany the numbers,
in the millions, of Asians, Africans, and Latin Americans seeking
freedom. He situated the movement of which he was part in what had
become for him the mainstream of world history: the movement for
freedom.

King spoke out of a Negro intellectual community that identified
the world movement with its own. From Richard Wright in Paris to
Ralph Bunche at the United Nations, Negro intellectuals participated

actively in the international scene. Both E. Franklin Frazier and John Hope Franklin did work for the UN; teaching at Howard, Rayford Logan spoke at international forums in Washington, D.C. Moving in the international arena brought Negro scholars respect that white America had too often denied them—a place in the broader world. The freedom movements abroad gave them a fulcrum for greater power at home. Talking with Africans at the UN (which he covered for the *Pittsburgh Courier*), Horace Cayton realized, "We were no longer invisible men, because even if Americans ignored us we would not be overlooked by the Africans, the Chinese, the Indians, and many other peoples from far-off lands."[1]

As the United States struggled with the Soviet Union for the hearts and minds of the world's non-Western peoples, Negro intellectuals could see the role their own oppression played in that struggle. Bad treatment at home would translate into a bad image for the United States abroad. But beyond that equation, some Negro intellectuals saw in these freedom movements potential models for their own. Frantz Fanon's influential book *The Wretched of the Earth* was still several years away from publication in English, but it was hard to miss the worldwide revolt of the oppressed, from India to South Africa to Cuba, the closest of all—right on the United States' doorstep. Cuba had a significant Negro population, and Castro was making a special effort to erase racial distinctions in his new society. He was also making an effort to appeal to American Negroes as potential tourists and supporters, at a time when his relations with the U.S. government had not yet settled into the steady hostility that would characterize them over the long term. Thus it was that this little band of Negro writers from the United States visited Cuba in the summer of 1960 at the invitation of the Cuban government.

The trip was arranged by a Negro writer named Richard (Thomas) Gibson. Born in Los Angeles, educated in the United States, Rome, and Paris, Gibson had worked at Agence France-Presse but by this time was a newswriter at CBS in New York. In New York, he became prime organizer of the Fair Play for Cuba Committee. Organizing the Cuban trip, he had invited James Baldwin, who knew him slightly and signed the *New York Times* ad that launched the committee. Baldwin declined,[2] but several others were happy to go. The writers who went lacked Baldwin's visibility, but they had all begun to make their mark in New York: Harold Cruse, who would one day write a polemical history of these times, *The Crisis of the Negro Intellectual*; John Henrik Clarke, a journalist and historian of Africa; LeRoi Jones, an avant-garde poet who later changed his name to Amiri Baraka; and Julian Mayfield, an actor as well as a novelist. Mayfield was probably the best known—he had already published two novels, played a leading role in *Lost in the Stars* (a musical version of *Cry, the Beloved Country*), and produced plays for the Harlem Theater.

They formed an eclectic assortment, not wholly compatible or even respectful of one another. They approached Cuba from a range of political positions. Clarke considered himself a socialist in the traditional African mold, believing land ought to be communally owned and the community responsible for everyone who belonged to it. Mayfield and Cruse had both belonged to the Communist Party, although both had abandoned it. Mayfield retained a sympathy with socialism.[3] Of them all, LeRoi Jones was the least political.

The visit was nearly bound to have an effect on them. At a time when southern Negroes were raising a militant but nonviolent challenge to the U.S. status quo, Castro had produced an armed revolution. Here, off the United States' southern coast, stood an example of what a determined band of men with weapons could do: overthrow an old oppressive regime and, with determination and will, begin the work of transformation. Not identifying himself as a communist, Castro had nevertheless placed economic justice and racial equality high on his list of goals. Journalist Bob Taber, an organizer for the Fair Play for Cuba Committee, wrote to John Henrik Clarke before the group's visit, "If the government is sensitive about the racial situation in this country and fears that it is damaging in an external political way, all the better: then perhaps the powers that be in Washington will become a little more vigorous on the question of federal legislation in civil rights—if only to placate American Negroes and keep them from succumbing to foreign 'subversion.' "[4]

While none of the writers on the Cuban visit succumbed to "subversion," the journey did affect them. For LeRoi Jones, the trip to Cuba was transforming. Living in Greenwich Village and married to a white woman, Jones had been hanging out in Beat circles and publishing a literary magazine. By his own account, he had not been much interested in the civil rights movement. "We did not feel part of that movement," he would say of his New York circle at that time. "Most of us were isolated now from the mainstream of the black community and we did not reflect, in an undistorted way, that consciousness. Our consciousness, in the main, was that of young black intellectuals 'integrated' to within a hair's breadth of our lives." When a Cuban poet on this trip asked Jones whether Langston Hughes had become more conservative, Jones was so politically out of touch that he had no idea (he confessed later) "that Langston had testified, under duress, before HUAC, denouncing some of his own earlier work, to keep great patriots like the filthy cracker bastard James Eastland off his ass."[5]

Traveling with the others by train across the Cuban countryside, Jones talked at length with a woman who called him a "cowardly bourgeois individualist" when he told her he wasn't interested in politics. The journey itself seemed wearisome—hours first on a train loaded with other writers, then on a truck up a mountain in the Sierra Maestra, then more hours celebrating the anniversary of the July 26 movement that launched the revolution, all the time with nothing to drink, since no one had bothered to tell the Americans to bring their own water. The American group was introduced to the crowd waiting for Castro's speech as "intellectual North American visitors." Jones had a small exchange with Castro, who identified himself as a "radical humanist," not a communist. That evening Jones and three or four thousand people wandered around on the mountaintop in search of somewhere to sleep. The piece that he wrote about the trip for the *Evergreen Review*, a literary magazine, was scarcely celebratory, but it was clear that the revolution had touched him. He saw the Beat revolt as by comparison a paltry thing: "The rebels among us have become merely people like myself who grow beards and will not participate in politics."[6]

Harold Cruse, pro-Castro but leery of communists and contemptuous of Jones, recognized the appeal of the revolution to Jones and other young writers, who had not passed through the disillusion Cruse's own generation had experienced with communism. The worldwide revolutionary wave (he would write in *The Crisis of the Negro Intellectual*) "had lifted us out of the anonymity of lonely struggle in the United States to the glorified rank of visiting dignitaries." Furthermore, the Cuban example raised an issue that would become more pressing as time went on: "the relevance of force and violence to successful revolutions."[7]

For Julian Mayfield, who had lived in Puerto Rico, his wife's native land, the political meaning of Cuba had a less apocalyptic tinge: the United States *could* follow Cuba's example without staging a violent revolution—if only it would. Writing for *Freedomways*, a new magazine started by Shirley Graham Du Bois, Mayfield saw in Cuba evidence that "necessary social change need not wait on the patient education and persuasion of the bigot and the reactionary. Who can doubt that if a government as powerful and as rich as the United States were to throw its full legal and moral weight behind measures to eliminate racial discrimination it would achieve remarkable results overnight?" By the time Mayfield's *Freedomways* article appeared in the summer of 1961, the United States had sponsored the unsuccessful Bay of Pigs invasion of Cuba. An ad in the *New York Post* and the Baltimore *Afro-American*, signed by several Negro intellectuals, protested the invasion. Commenting on the ad, Mayfield said,

> *The declaration did not achieve the impact of a similar declaration by French intellectuals on Algeria, primarily because it was almost wholly ignored by our domestic communications media. Nevertheless, it was a significant straw in the winds of change sweeping the earth, a warning that some Americans of African descent are prepared to*

lock arms with combatants against racism everywhere, even those who do not enjoy the approval of our State Department.

When Castro came to New York in the fall after the writers' Cuban journey, he was welcomed by cheering crowds. His revolution, Mayfield concluded, had challenged American race relations "profoundly."[8]

Cuba had more than one meaning for American Negroes, but for some, at least, it offered a violent revolutionary alternative to the nonviolent movement led by Martin Luther King. One man on the Cuban trip with the writers would become identified with that alternative: Robert F. Williams, an NAACP official from Monroe, North Carolina, and future author of the book *Negroes with Guns.* In long nighttime conversations on the Cuban trip, Williams told the New York writers how members of his chapter had tried to desegregate a swimming pool and, their path blocked, had sued. When the Klan began driving caravans of cars through the Negro community, the community took a stand, firing back. The Klan caravans stopped, but the harassment did not, and a series of local court decisions convinced Williams that Negroes would not get justice in court. On the steps of the courthouse, Williams made this statement: "Since the federal government will not bring a halt to lynching in the South, and since the so-called courts lynch our people legally, if it's necessary to stop lynching with lynching, then we must be willing to resort to that method. We must meet violence with violence." The next day, Roy Wilkins, head of the NAACP, called Williams to ask if he had said what he had been reported as saying. Williams said he had said it and would say it again. He did just that within a matter of hours. The following day, Wilkins suspended him from his NAACP position for six months. In the annual convention in July the NAACP confirmed Wilkins's action.[9]

Williams's story made a dramatic impression on LeRoi Jones. Returning home, he joined On Guard, a group of intellectuals formed to support Williams's efforts. Williams had become a focal point for activists who doubted the wisdom of nonviolence as a road to equality. Long before the winds of Black Power swept the scene, therefore, northern nationalists envisioned a Negro community united in self-defense, violent if need be, against the white majority. To Harold Cruse, the intellectuals and nationalists who adopted Williams as their hero were misguided; they failed to see how conditions in New York City differed from conditions in Monroe, North Carolina.[10]

But the other writers on the Cuban trip were taken by Williams's story. The following winter, Julian Mayfield and John Henrik Clarke actually drove down to Monroe, and in April 1961 *Commentary* carried Mayfield's account of what was happening there. Mayfield used his moment in *Commentary* to attack both the NAACP and the nonviolent movement. As the southern oligarchy refused to yield to the students, he predicted, the students would become impatient with passive resistance. The working class would join them, and the Negro leadership would find itself in crisis, "for its purely legalistic (or passive resistance) approach will clearly not be able to control the dynamics of the Negro struggle. Then to the fore may come Robert Williams, and other young men and women like him, who have concluded that the only way to win a revolution is to be a revolutionary."[11]

The NAACP's Wilkins snapped back at Mayfield in a letter published in the July *Commentary*. Communists had been saying such things since 1930, Wilkins wrote, "predicting and working for the American Negro rank and file, the overthrow of the old leadership, and elevation of derring-do." And wasn't it interesting, he pointed out, that Mayfield met Williams in Cuba. He suggested that Mayfield and other self-appointed "gin-and-tonic rug-sitting thinkers" do some reading on the struggle they were so quick to comment on. Mayfield, in response, reprimanded Wilkins for Red-baiting. He suggested Wilkins read Franklin Frazier's *Black Bourgeoisie* to "understand the nature of his difficulties."[12]

The first notice *Commentary* had taken of the sit-in movement, Mayfield's article scarcely offered support for it. It had, besides, an Old

Left tinge that was uncharacteristic of *Commentary*. Recalling the article, Norman Podhoretz, who by the time of its publication had become editor of the magazine, said he published it because he thought that Mayfield had put his finger on a sea change in the Negro community. (IIc had also asked James Baldwin to write about the Black Muslims.) Talk of the "Negro revolution" was replacing talk of the "civil rights movement."[13]

Whatever Podhoretz's editorial motivations, Mayfield believed that his *Commentary* article encouraged young veterans of the sit-ins to go to Monroe for what would turn out to be the climactic struggle. Mayfield went, too, and found the situation intense. "It was like being in the midst of a war or a Wild West show, there was shooting and killing and all kinds of things every night."[14] Yet the national press paid little attention to what was happening. At the *New York Post*, Ted Poston, a leading Negro journalist, did put white editor James Wechsler on the phone with Mayfield, and Wechsler expressed interest in seeing reports on Monroe. When Mayfield turned in his articles, however, Wechsler turned them down. In a letter at the time, Mayfield said that Wechsler told him running the articles "would imply that the newspaper approved of Williams' approach, when in fact it favors Martin Luther King and Passive Resistance. The editor also implied that he disapproved of Williams' pro-Castro activities."[15] Wechsler's response is not that surprising. A member of the Young Communist League in the 1930s, Wechsler had become vigorously anticommunist. Although he disapproved of Senator Joseph McCarthy's tactics, he had cooperated with his committee, providing it with names of communists he had known.[16] He was not about to showcase a movement linked to Cuba.

The Monroe movement spiraled upward to a climax. While policemen looked on, whites attacked the picket line that students had set up around the courthouse. James Forman, later a leader of the Student Nonviolent Coordinating Committee, had his head bashed in by a white man with a shotgun. Julian Mayfield's car was stoned. Twenty demonstrators were arrested. When they got out of jail, Robert Williams was gone. He had been accused of kidnapping a white couple he had tried to rescue when they drove down his street and ran into an angry crowd. Fleeing from investigators, Williams and his wife went into exile in Cuba.[17] Mayfield, understanding that the FBI was looking for him to ask him about Williams, also left the country. He and his wife settled in Ghana—drawn, he would say, by Ghanaian President Kwame Nkrumah's image as a "militant, radical socialist."[18]

Ghana, like Cuba, was attracting American Negroes discouraged by the slowness of racial change in the United States. Negro intellectuals had long been drawn to Africa, understanding its importance to their own sense of themselves and their place in the world. Now, as one new African nation after another took its place at the United Nations, Africa, like Cuba, offered to American Negroes a new source of status and hope. Speaking to British undergraduates at Cambridge University in 1965, James Baldwin would recall, "Africa was suddenly on the stage of the world, and Africans had to be dealt with in a way they had never been dealt with before. This gave the American Negro for the first time a sense of himself beyond a savage or a clown."[19]

Ghana, featured in Richard Wright's *Black Power*, proved especially attractive. Led by Kwame Nkrumah, a socialist possessed by a vision of Pan-Africanism, Ghana became in 1957 the first black African country to achieve independence. Martin Luther King Jr. and Lawrence Reddick traveled there for the independence celebrations, and Ghana quickly became a magnet for Negro Americans who wanted to help create a new nation. By 1960, when the wave of sit-ins swept the South, a colony of Negro expatriates had already gathered in Accra. The American community would grow over the next couple of years to include (in addition to Julian Mayfield) Maya Angelou, W. E. B. Du Bois (who, defiantly, took out membership in the Communist Party before he left the United States), and his wife, writer-editor Shirley Graham. At a time when the United States appeared to be making a crucial turn, this particular set of writers—politically minded all—had taken themselves off to distant shores, fleeing a political climate so hostile to their points of view that they could hardly hope to make themselves heard.

Beyond the hazards of the hour, a deeper ambivalence toward the United States impelled them to settle in Africa. As Du Bois was fond of saying, what was the point of fighting for service on a train if you didn't want to go where the train was headed?[20] If white Americans were reluctant to see Negroes as Americans, then some Negro intellectuals, at least, were reluctant to *be* Americans. To the Negro intellectuals who moved to Africa, the new African nations appealed not only because they had achieved independence from Western imperial powers but also because they represented an alternative to living in white-dominated America. That was the hope that took lawyer-writer Pauli Murray to Ghana in early 1960, just as the sit-in movement began sweeping the South.

Not part of the radical political community around W. E. B. and Shirley Graham Du Bois, Murray had always played by conventional American rules. A native of North Carolina, she had attended Hunter College in New York City. Challenging the color bar, she applied to graduate school at the University of North Carolina. Denied admission, she had gone to law school at Howard; while there, she had participated in sit-ins protesting segregation in the nation's capital. In the early fifties, Murray applied to work on a federally funded project codifying the laws of Liberia—and, to her own surprise, found herself under suspicion of disloyalty. The Cornell administrator who had to approve her hiring was, in her words, "an extremely cautious man, whose main concern seemed to be the issue of loyalty." Her references, including former first lady Eleanor Roosevelt and NAACP Defense Fund lawyer Thurgood Marshall, were not conservative enough for him.[21]

Angered by the aspersions he cast on her loyalty, Murray began work on a history of her family, a mix of African, European, and Native American peoples that exemplified the cultural diversity she thought set America apart. She wrote *Proud Shoes*, a finely wrought family memoir, to counter the widespread notion that "anyone who championed a liberal cause" was inspired by communism. Like many Negroes involved politically in American life, Murray retained an unyielding commitment to American democracy. "Not Communism," she wrote, "but the ideals and influences within my own family had made me a life-long fighter against all forms of inequality and injustice."[22] She went to Africa partly with the hope of spreading American democratic ideals. She wanted to guide young lawyers in the principles of American law, which to her embodied America's great offering to the world: the belief that an *idea* can unite a diverse people. Murray was a patriot. A good Democrat who had worked in Adlai Stevenson's 1952 campaign, she saw Africa as pivotal in the Cold War. If Africa went totalitarian, she feared, then the United States would be "isolated in the western hemisphere."[23]

But for all her admiration of American ideals, Murray went to Ghana, fundamentally, because she wanted to get away from the United States. She was weary of living perpetually aware of her race. The spring before she left, she was shaken by a murder in Poplarville, Mississippi.[24] A mob had taken a twenty-three-year-old rape suspect named Mack Charles Parker out of jail and shot him. His body was pulled nine days later from the Pearl River in Louisiana. The death made a stark impression on Murray.

Seeking refuge in Ghana, she thought she might stay for several years, perhaps longer. In a journal she kept, she expressed the despair she and others had begun to feel over racial life in America: "And there is beginning to creep over some of the veteran fighters for civil rights in the United States a weariness with the struggle, a feeling of despair, a flicker of hope that perhaps in the emergent Africa there might be place for one to live without consciousness of his color."[25]

From afar, Africa had offered the opportunity of a new, freer life. Once in Accra, Murray was repelled by the reality of life in this steamy, coastal town. Cut off from friends and family, jarred by hardships and inconveniences, she felt very alone. She tried to sound cheerful in long letters home, but in her journal she confessed her depression as she struggled to adjust to life nearly alone in a place she did not really like. "What I must remember, of course, is that freedom (or the lack of it) in Ghana isn't my fight. My 'fight' is across the ocean in the U.S.A.," she told herself.[26] She wrote letters to the editor about relations between the United States and Africa, and sent them off to the *New York Times* and the *Washington Post.* An editor at the *Post* asked her to recast a letter as an article, but by the time she heard from him, she decided the timing was wrong for what she had to say.[27]

Throughout her stay, Murray corresponded with Harold R. Isaacs, a white researcher from the Massachusetts Institute of Technology who was working on what would turn out to be an important study of American Negroes' relationship to Africa.[28] Isaacs was a former journalist whose political life had made a distinct political turn. After several years in China, he had written an early history of the Chinese revolution of 1925–27 and called it *The Tragedy of the Chinese Revolution.* The tragedy, as he saw it, consisted in the influence Russia had exercised over the Chinese revolution. Leon Trotsky— Stalin's most effective communist critic—had provided a preface to Isaacs' book, published in England in 1938. In his first sentence, Trotsky introduced Isaacs as a Marxist. In 1951, when a new edition came out from Stanford University Press, Isaacs dropped Trotsky's preface and specifically disavowed "the Bolshevism of which Trotsky became the most authentic spokesman." At this point a democratic socialist, Isaacs rewrote his concluding chapters to reflect his new political understanding.[29] His newest project, a kind of sequel to a book he had written on American perceptions of China and India, *Scratches on Our Minds,* fell easily within the bounds of political liberalism.

In the course of research for his new African project, Isaacs interviewed a long list of leading Negro intellectuals and political figures. He was a skillful and empathetic interviewer—"a person who could draw things out of you," John Hope Franklin would say.[30] Yet Isaacs did not always get along with everyone he interviewed. Writing up his notes on playwright Lorraine Hansberry (fresh from the triumph of *A Raisin in the Sun* and a former member of the circle around Paul

Robeson and Du Bois), he dismissed her as "a muddlehead." After he interviewed Du Bois himself, even in his published account Isaacs could barely contain his contempt for Du Bois's weakness for communism. For all Du Bois's dignity and accomplishments, he had, in Isaacs' eyes, fallen dupe to the Soviet line.[31]

Pauli Murray's political bent was more compatible with Isaacs', and the two became friends. When Isaacs and his wife visited Ghana, they stayed with Murray, and she described to him the ambiguous position American Negroes found themselves in there, neither wholly welcomed nor at ease. As former colonies became nations and the great powers jostled for influence over them, Negroes like Murray were caught uncomfortably in the middle, trying to play a role in building these new nations but under suspicion of acting on their government's behalf to further American influence.

After Isaacs went home, Murray sent him a draft of an article she was working on: "What Is Africa to Me?—A Question of Identity." He was, she told him, "the Godfather" of the piece; it contained some of his ideas, his very expressions. "I just can't see how it will be turned down by an editor," she said. She kept him posted on her progress as she went along. She tried to turn the piece into articles for *Harper's*, the *Atlantic*, or perhaps the *Reporter*. *Harper's* did like the piece, but already had too much material on race and Africa lined up to run over the next twelve months. Someone suggested the *Saturday Evening Post* as a possibility.[32]

Letters between Murray and Isaacs flew back and forth across the ocean—letters of friends who felt themselves on the same wavelength. When Isaacs heard that Richard Wright had died at the age of fifty-two, he "felt a real pang," he told Murray in a letter November 30. "Wright has made his scratch on time and needs no one's regrets. But he was an honest searcher, and I think he would have come to face his unresolved dilemmas, and that this would have brought him home."[33] Three months later, Isaacs warned her of news he'd heard that James Baldwin had been commissioned to travel to Africa and write a book.

He will do pieces for the Atlantic *and a book—a Negro writer goes "home" to Africa and tells what he sees, feels, experiences. It will be important writing and good writing, no mistake about it; Baldwin is good.*

Hence I write to say, Pauli: get on to it.

The air is full of the new unsettling African winds blowing through the American Negro atmosphere, and it is high time someone got down on paper some solid things about the facts of Negro life in Africa.[34]

In February 1961, an event occurred that threw dramatic light on the issue of Negroes' relation to Africa. In the Congo, an equatorial African country newly released from colonial rule, Belgian rulers had barely prepared the way for an independent functioning state. While the United States, the Soviet Union, and Belgium angled for control over strategic minerals in the new nation, Congolese factions jostled for power. When the mineral-rich Katanga province declared independence from the central government and the Belgians supported the breakaway government, the Congo plummeted into political chaos. One of the key players, Prime Minister Patrice Lumumba, was assassinated, and the United States would eventually be implicated in his death.[35]

It was impossible in New York to know the American role—impossible to know for sure just whom to blame for Lumumba's death. But Maya Angelou, an actress-singer and developing writer who had worked for the Southern Christian Leadership Conference's New York office, would recall "the emptiness of the moment. Patrice Lumumba, Kwame Nkrumah and Sékou Touré were the Holy African Triumvirate which radical black Americans held dear, and we needed our leaders desperately." Angelou and some friends had recently formed a women's group to raise funds for the southern American movement, and their group gathered to plan a demonstration at the United Nations on February 15, when U.S. Ambassador Adlai Stevenson was to address the General Assembly on the topic of Lumumba's death. Other protesters gathered outside the UN, including LeRoi Jones and fellow members of On Guard, the organization formed to defend Robert Williams.[36]

What ensued, the *New York Times* would report, was "the most violent demonstration inside United Nations headquarters in the world organization's history." The *Times* reported allegations that the protests were communist inspired, and UN official Ralph Bunche apologized for the behavior of his fellow Americans.[37] The episode would become a pivotal event in American racial politics. Here the struggle for freedom in the colonies and the struggle for racial equality within the United States came together. "The demonstrators in the United Nations gallery interpreted the murder of Lumumba as the international lynching of a black man on the altar of colonialism and white supremacy," John Henrik Clarke would write in *Freedomways*. "The plight of the Africans still fighting to throw off the yoke of colonialism and the plight of the Afro-Americans, still waiting for a rich, strong and boastful nation to redeem the promise of freedom and citizenship became one and the same."[38]

A month after the demonstrations, James Baldwin—who was publishing a breathtaking run of articles in leading magazines—took them up in the *New York Times Magazine*. He had meant to be there himself that day, he wrote. If he had been there, he, too, "in the eyes of most Americans, would have been merely a pawn in the hands of the Communists. The climate and the events of the last decade, and the steady pressure of the 'cold' war, have given Americans yet another means of avoiding self-examination, and so it has been decided that the riots were 'Communist' inspired." An astonishing idea, he thought: that Negroes needed to be stirred up by a foreign power to be discontented with their lot. "When the South has trouble with its Negroes . . . it blames 'outside' agitators and 'Northern interference.' When the nation has trouble with the Northern Negro, it blames the Kremlin."[39] Lorraine Hansberry, a good friend of Baldwin's, added her own thoughts in a letter that led the *Times*'s "Letters" column on March 26. Though she was politically and religiously "non-affiliate" (she was careful to say), she would have marched readily with any Negro "who had the passion and understanding to be there." She apologized to the Congolese for the behavior of Ralph Bunche.[40]

In a 1963 *Freedomways* essay on Baldwin, Julian Mayfield would use Baldwin's and Hansberry's remarks on the UN demonstrations to illustrate the movement of "a few intellectuals" into the political arena. Intellectuals had moved into political life, he said, because Negro leaders were lagging behind the Negro community they claimed to lead. Leaders like the NAACP's Roy Wilkins were out of touch with the growing militance, Mayfield said, sounding a theme increasingly heard in both the white and the Negro press. "For a generation, neither elder spokesmen like Mr. Wilkins nor his organization had taken a public stand on any *international* issue, especially one that might conflict with the policies of the United States government. Now, here were young Negroes demonstrating in the United Nations building, of all places, because a black man had been murdered in an African country thousands of miles away."[41]

Baldwin himself reiterated the failures of established Negro leaders in a *Harper's* essay that appeared in the same month as his *New York Times Magazine* article. In "The Dangerous Road before Martin Luther King," Baldwin spoke of the danger King posed to Negro leaders, who were "trapped in such a stunning silence . . . that to say what they really feel would be to deny the entire public purpose of their lives." Aiming always toward integration, Negro leaders had had to disguise their goal in order to wring concessions from whites. In return, they led whites to believe they would keep other Negroes in line. Thus their loyalties were divided. They were caught "in a no-man's land between black humiliation and white power." In these new days, a gulf had opened between established Negro leaders and the young. Martin Luther King found himself caught between young activists and old-line Negro politicians like Adam Clayton Powell.[42]

King wrote to thank Baldwin for the *Harper's* article and for his collected essays, *Nobody Knows My Name.* "Your honesty and courage in telling the truth to white Americans, even if it hurts, is most impressive."[43] Baldwin, who had met King twice (on trips south in

1957 and 1960), replied with his own thanks for King's letter, which came to him as a supportive light in the dark of what he felt as his own isolation. Then he filled King in on his plans for the trip to Africa that Harold Isaacs had told Murray about, and mentioned an essay he was writing. It had started out as a reflection on the Nation of Islam but evolved into an exploration of Christianity's place "in the lives of black men,"[44] he said, indicating, with that choice of words, his broader subject: not American Negroes only, but "black men" everywhere.

Prompted by the demonstrations at the United Nations, Harold Isaacs produced an article out of his own research in Africa, and *The New Yorker*, the nation's preeminent magazine for literary reportage, accepted it. In making his chief point—that Negroes had not found "home" in Africa—Isaacs portrayed Africans as condescending and even hostile toward Negroes. He spoke of the "mutual prejudice between Africans and American Negroes."[45] Isaacs predicted to Pauli Murray that the article would anger some readers, both African and Negro. "At any rate, I expect to have a need for your strong prose on this same subject—nobody's writing much hard sense on this matter these days, or talking it either. Even Baldwin has lapsed into a kind of angry-young-man pose that does his intelligence small credit."[46]

Murray replied, "I don't know whether to congratulate you for doing an excellent job or to chide you for stealing most of my thunder." But she quickly recovered her composure:

> *I think the things you said had to be said and that they come with better grace from your pen than mine at this stage. If I have anything further to say, you have broken the ground. I have only one minor criticism. To have made the picture complete, you should have stressed the point of view you know I hold, and that is Africans and Africa has given to some of us a perspective on the United States, and that in that respect is a positive gain. You left the picture almost hopeless.[47]*

Murray's close friend Caroline F. Ware, a professor at Howard University, was not so forgiving. She accused Isaacs bluntly of plagiarism. Ware had read Murray's article and recognized it, she wrote to him, in Isaacs' *New Yorker* piece. She expressed the hope that he had shared the payment with Murray. Isaacs replied frostily (and accurately) that he and Murray had talked at length on this subject and that she had called him the "godfather" of her own piece. He had used only one story involving her and had urged her to include more of herself in her article. "Pauli and I esteem and value each other. You really ought to look before you leap to make statements which are a gratuitous insult to us both."[48]

Although Murray had acknowledged how much of her thought she owed to Isaacs, he had indeed scooped her. In what may have been an attempt to compensate, a few weeks after his article came out in *The New Yorker*, Isaacs suggested to an editor at E. P. Dutton that Murray could "write one hell of a book" on Africa.[49] Nothing came of the idea, and Murray's essay would remain unpublished until, years later, she included an excerpt from it in her memoir, *Song in a Weary Throat*. Only there was she able to give her own ambivalent response to the question "What Is Africa to Me?" Listening as a chief described the way his own forebears had caught and sold slaves, she had found herself at a loss for words. "I was too numbed to tell this chief that I am only two generations removed from slavery, that my own grandmother was born a slave, and that I had seen its scars on her personality." Africans shared with the white slavers the responsibility for slavery. Who knew which Africans were her ancestors, and which her betrayers? Her experiences in her ancestral home left her "deeply shaken."[50]

Isaacs had accurately predicted the reception of his *New Yorker* article on American Negroes in Africa: it was prickly. When he talked with Kenneth B. Clark during a second round of interviews for *The New World of Negro Americans*, Clark told him that many of his friends thought the *New Yorker* piece was "treacherous" and "divisive." Three years after the article's publication, Negro sociologist St. Clair Drake discussed it at some length in a speech to the American Society of

African Culture, an organization formed in the late 1950s.[51] AMSAC, one of the more important bridge builders between American Negroes and Africans, included among its members some of the best-known Negro academics and writers. Isaacs himself had spoken at its second annual conference in 1959, sharing observations based on his research.[52] AMSAC was an important and pertinent forum for Drake's provocative remarks, which he based on his own direct experience of Africa. Drake had spent two years teaching in Ghana and had traveled elsewhere in Africa on half a dozen other occasions, and he believed Isaacs oversimplified the situation. "So perceptive an observer and so diligent an interviewer as Harold Isaacs should not have missed the point in so many places and misunderstood the nuances in so many places." Probably Isaacs had not stayed in Africa long enough. Yes, some Africans rejected some Negroes, depending on who the Africans were and who the Negroes were. Politics played a role: most Ghanaians leaned toward non-communist socialism and rejected Negroes who were "propagandizing for capitalism."

Drake respected Isaacs as a "serious-minded ex-journalist now attached to an international relations research program at a large and influential academic research institution." Drake regarded him as "a man whose devotion to the cause of social justice and civil rights is beyond dispute." He therefore tried to separate Isaacs' article from a similar piece by Russell Warren Howe in the *Reporter*, published a few weeks after Isaacs'. Harder-edged than Isaacs' report, Howe's emphasized African hostility toward American Negroes. In light of that hostility, Howe questioned current efforts by the State Department and other organizations to send Negroes to Africa.[53]

Howe was the reporter who had put Faulkner's inflammatory remarks into print, and it was in this speech to AMSAC that Drake went to some lengths to discredit Howe's accuracy. Drake described a phone call he had received a week or so after the UN protests over Lumumba's death:

> It was from an editor of The Reporter, *who asked, since I was just back from Africa, if I would do an article for the magazine. He*

claimed that there is great concern in many quarters over the way in which American Negroes are tending to identify with Africans and that an article of some sort should show the American Negroes once and for all that these Africans don't care anything at all about them and that there is really no kind of tie between them. I asked him who had told him to come to me and he mentioned a couple of American Negro leaders who had said that things are getting out of hand, that some American Negro ought to write an article to get this thing straightened out and that the American Negro's identification is with America and not with Africa.

Drake had turned down the invitation—he was too busy, he said. Reading Isaacs' and Howe's articles, Drake wondered if they, too, had been approached, especially when he saw Isaacs' comments on the demonstrations at the UN. He found the close timing of the two articles suspicious in light of the phone call he had received. "I do not think it was accidental. . . . If the American journalist-scholar and the English journalist had not written them, I have no doubt at all that someone else would have written them."

Drake raised here the specter of a stage-managed public discourse, of editors and writers acting out of something more than their own political intuitions in the service of hidden political interests. In the Cold War context, too close an alliance between American Negroes and Africans could prove troublesome for national policy. Indeed, scholars have suggested that Negro organizations deliberately withdrew from international affairs in the postwar years as part of a strategy that exchanged silence on foreign policy for domestic progress.[54] If political influence was being exercised, where was it coming from? What, exactly, were the "many quarters" the editor had in mind? Was the *Reporter* responding to prompts by the Negro leaders he referred to? Or was Drake implying something more subterranean? This was a time when journalists were hiring on as CIA informants, and CIA funds subsidized *Encounter* magazine and other cultural institutions. AMSAC itself, the group before which Drake raised the issue of unsavory influence, received funds secretly from the CIA, which routed them through a foundation.[55] The CIA also helped fund the Center for International Studies, sponsor of Harold Isaacs' research, although not, apparently, Isaacs' own projects.[56] This was a time in which federal agencies with the job of managing America's place in the world used whatever cultural resources they could to shape the way Americans saw the world and the way the world saw Americans.

Drake was unwilling to entertain suspicions of Isaacs, but he appeared more ready to imagine underhanded editorial motivations. His suspicions were entirely reasonable. Although William Shawn at *The New Yorker* was not much of a cold warrior,[57] the executive editor of the *Reporter*—Philip C. Horton—had served in the wartime Office for Strategic Services and after the war became the CIA's Paris station chief.[58] He knew enough about the world scene not to need prompting to see the political implications of an alliance between Africans and American Negroes. At the same time, if the CIA or any other agency involved in national policy wanted to influence public commentary, Horton, holding a top post at the nation's leading liberal magazine, had moved into a good position to do the job.

Horton's correspondence with Russell Warren Howe did imply unusual urgency behind the effort to get a piece on Negro Americans' relations with Africa into the *Reporter*. Horton asked Howe if he could produce an article "as quickly as possible" to document "the disillusion and setbacks experienced by many American Negroes working or traveling in Africa in their contacts with the elite of the new African states." The editors regarded

> *such an article as a kind of corrective to the quite vocal sectors of American opinion, both white and black, which tend to romanticize and idealize African nationalism and to support quite uncritically whatever it produces. . . . Some of the more thoughtful and balanced American Negroes who have spent time in Africa are quite aware of the fraudulence and dangers of this viewpoint, but are understandably reluctant to go into print about it.*[59]

Whatever the editors' motivations for wanting a piece debunking American Negroes' identification with African nationalism, when the article came in, they measured the results by Isaacs' *New Yorker* piece and found Howe's wanting. Magazine editors often say unkind things about writers behind their backs (and sometimes to their faces), but under Max Ascoli the *Reporter*'s treatment of writers could be particularly harsh. Theodore White, who worked for Ascoli for a while in the midfifties, would recall that "if he did not like a writer's work, he might scream with rage and throw the pages of copy into the air like a child kicking leaves into the wind."[60] Catching his boss's contemptuous tone, Horton wrote in a memo to Ascoli, "Howe has done a slap-dash job on this and the result is such a mish-mash that I don't see how we can use it. . . . It isn't by any means an equivalent of the Isaacs, but it deals with the same general area." When the *Reporter* used Howe's piece after all, the editors cut it so much that Howe—bearing the brunt of the controversy that followed—was still miffed two years later. "What finally appeared," he said, "was a selection of quotes from my story which gave only one side of the question, left an unbalanced and biased impression on most readers and raised a furor, for which of course I took the blame."[61]

The Cold War had become a steady but complex drumbeat behind the movement for racial equality. Writing in the *Reporter*, Yale law dean Eugene Rostow, brother of President John F. Kennedy's foreign policy adviser Walt Rostow, attributed the current push for equality to "the political liberation of the colored men of Africa and of Asia," although Rostow himself rejected the Cold War as an argument for change. Changes must come, he said, "not because political forces in the North demand them, nor yet to please public opinion in Africa and Asia and score a point in the Cold War. We are struggling to accomplish these social changes because we know they are right."[62] Yale chaplain William Sloan Coffin Jr. similarly linked moral argument to foreign policy when, in *Life* magazine, he explained why he joined the Freedom Riders challenging segregated bus terminals in the spring of

1961. "Discrimination has always been immoral and now, as it undermines U.S. foreign policy, it is a matter of national concern."[63]

The Cold War had all along provided an argument for desegregation; the Supreme Court justices had considered it as they deliberated on the *Brown* decision. It went on being evoked with relentless regularity. For the new president, however, the American racial crisis did not loom nearly so large as Cold War problems on the international scene: a nuclear-armed Soviet Union—and Cuba, a nation friendly to the Soviet Union, on his southern flank. Other points of conflict peppered the globe: the Congo, Laos, Berlin. In light of East-West conflicts that could lead to atomic war, the racial movement at home was for the president an annoying distraction. He handed the racial crisis over to his brother Attorney General Robert Kennedy, who actually asked the Freedom Riders to hold off until the president's scheduled meeting with the Soviet premier. The crises at home and abroad made this a very tense time for the new president. As relations with the Soviet Union worsened, white mobs in Alabama set upon Freedom Riders—and even, in Montgomery, upon the aide Attorney General Kennedy had sent along to monitor them.

Sociologist David Riesman confided to C. Vann Woodward, "When I read about such events they fill me with horror and fear— more so, I think, than reading about equally or even more horrible events in other countries." It seemed to Riesman that a "reactionary wave" was sweeping the country.[64] Another of Woodward's friends agreed that something frightening was going on. At the end of 1961, University of Florida professor William G. Carleton visited the Woodwards in Baltimore, spending an evening chatting before a fire while sleetish snow fell outside. They discussed Woodward's fears that he might not be able to write his new book on Reconstruction. They talked, too, of the Woodwards' plans to leave the South for the North. With the encouragement of his old friend Robert Penn Warren, Woodward had accepted an appointment at Yale. Woodward was not sure he had made the right decision, and Carleton shared his doubts. All the same, Carleton wrote him after the visit, "[Y]our going to Yale is a dramatic way of proving to the world that you are what in fact you are—a national historian and not merely a regional one."

Carleton then returned to a subject much on his mind: the expanding right wing. He had spent an afternoon on a trip to Washington in the congressional library looking at newspapers from all over the country, and found them as "monolithic" as southern papers. So rapidly was the country swinging rightward that when he looked at a foundation report on the country's move to the right, he found it superficial and "already out of date." Now he was more depressed than ever, convinced of three things:

(1) that the thing that is coming is frightful in itself; (2) that it is based on a purely mythological conception of world trends, and therefore is unnecessary; and (3) that the thing could be arrested by political insight and courage on the part of Kennedy and other national leaders, but there is little evidence that they are going to handle it correctly or early enough. . . . We are approaching a terrible crisis in this country.

Carleton did not take hope from Harvard historian Arthur Schlesinger Jr.'s presence in the Kennedy circle. Schlesinger and the other "brisk young thinkers" Kennedy had surrounded himself with had been too ready to accept Reinhold Niebuhr's Augustinian belief in the triumph of human depravity and original sin and his rejection of the Enlightenment's faith in reason. Carleton himself preferred historian Arnold Toynbee to Niebuhr: "Toynbee has the outlook of a civilized man—skepticism tinged with hope, a feeling that history has provided us with some alternatives and that man is not without some ability to affect the result, to take some favorable potentialities inherent in the situation and make them actualities." This was not the stance Carlton saw operating in the Kennedy administration. Instead, the campaign and everything that had happened since—Cuba, Berlin, mobilization, bomb shelters—"has frightened the wits out of the people and moved them to the right."[65]

U.S. relations with the Soviet Union had worsened by the time

Woodward went south at the start of 1962 on an extended research trip. While a high wall divided East Berlin from West Berlin, Woodward found a new McCarthyism brewing in the South. Writing to John Hope Franklin from New Orleans, he spoke of "the curtailment of civil rights," including the civil rights of whites in just about every sector of southern life. "Much of the oppressive legislation and extra-legal coercion is directed at keeping whites in line with the system of segregation and oppression." David Riesman had suggested to Woodward that he keep notes on the "reactionary wave" sweeping southern universities, and Woodward did.[66] He had been tracking the topic for several years, yet he was shocked by what he heard.

Woodward wrote up what he found as an article, which he sent first to the *New York Times Magazine*. An editor there, Harvey Shapiro—a former editor at *Commentary*—had asked Woodward to do something for the *Times* the preceding summer. Now Woodward had something he was ready to do. He had held "scores of interviews in Tennessee, Alabama, Mississippi, Louisiana and Texas," he wrote, in order to discover "the impact of integration, racial tension and the Birch [John Birch Society] reaction on standards of academic freedom." He had surveyed Negro colleges as carefully as white and integrated colleges.

"I think I have an interesting story to tell," he said.

> It is altogether discouraging and is in many respects rather shocking. The pressures on faculty, students and administration have been severe. Some colleges have been subjected to outrageous interference by police and plain-clothesmen. Some have been shut down and the students required to reregister after screening. Professors have had their desks rifled and students have been expelled, imprisoned, and a few beaten. There are several instances of interference with student publications and with the freedom of teaching.

Shapiro responded quickly: yes, he would like to have the article. Could Woodward produce it in two weeks? Yet in the end, the *Times*'s lawyers recommended holding off publication until settlement of a libel suit involving its civil rights coverage in Alabama.[67] The article came out in *Harper's* instead. In a straightforward reportorial style, Woodward described the "wave of reaction" that had "clashed with the great movement for Negro rights." He chronicled events at white and Negro colleges, describing in particular detail Alabama Governor John Patterson's humiliation of President H. Councill Trenholm and Lawrence Reddick.[68]

The article's publication coincided with the crisis at the University of Mississippi over James Meredith's admission in the fall of 1962. In light of what happened there, Faulkner's old friend Jim Silver—eyewitness to mob violence and occupation by federal troops—thought Woodward's article "a little on the *moderate* side," although, softening the blow, he added that it was "the more effective because of that."[69]

Hard on the heels of the crisis in Mississippi came the Cuban missile crisis. The discovery of a Soviet missile base under construction in Cuba brought the United States and the Soviet Union to the brink of war. James Baldwin, visiting Brandeis University, told literary critic Edmund Wilson that if the United States were to invade Cuba, Negroes would be on Castro's side.[70] As U.S. ships steamed toward Cuba to blockade the island, Lorraine Hansberry, at a rally, said the president ought instead to send forces south to "finish the Reconstruction."[71]

The international scene had created a larger political context for the American movement for racial equality. How could the United States claim moral superiority over the Soviet Union when American Negroes had as little freedom as Hungarians under Soviet rule? How could peoples of color throughout the world look with favor on a country that treated its own citizens of color so badly? Making his plans for his Africa trip, Baldwin told Martin Luther King he hoped in the essay he was writing to analyze "the moral bankruptcy which so menaces the West, and to speculate on the role of black people in the present, and in the evolving world."[72]

The "moral bankruptcy" of the West was a common idea among intellectuals on both sides of the Atlantic. To Baldwin's friend Kenneth B. Clark, intellectuals themselves were partly to blame for the hollow heart of Western culture. Accepting the NAACP's Spingarn Medal in 1961, Clark called white intellectuals to account for their passivity in this hour of crisis, and he did not mean only the racial crisis. "Some have been silenced and intimidated. . . . Some have become captives of one set of ideologies or another, changing the color of their thought to fit the changing postures of their ideological gods. And some have just given up in despair." In light of the sorry state of white intellectuals, Clark proposed a special leadership role for Negro intellectuals like Baldwin and Ellison. Excluded from the prevailing culture, they were, he believed, less trapped by it.[73]

But American Negro intellectuals, like white intellectuals, had fallen into despair over the prospects of life in the United States, if not in the Western world. The gloom that Pauli Murray had expressed about the progress of race relations was deepening. When Harold Isaacs returned for a second interview with Baldwin in the summer of 1961, Baldwin had told him, "I expect nothing of this country." When Isaacs went back to historian John Hope Franklin, Franklin spoke with distress of his own difficulty in finding a place to live in Brooklyn and described Negroes' situation in America as "awful." "Some Negroes *feel so completely alienated* that they need something out of the country to hold on to. . . . A lot of people who were previously passive are now acutely distressed and troubled over their place in the American society."

Recording his impressions in his notes, Isaacs concluded,

John Hope Franklin obviously feels heavily embattled. He does not feel support in this situation for his kind of basic attitude, which is one of total acceptance of the bona fides and the promise of the American reality as expressed in his own ability to make his success. He feels full of confusion and unhappiness over all of this and clearly does not get much reinforcement from any quarter. He is the best we've got, and he feels very alone, or at least outside the reach of the winds he sees blowing all about him.[74]

Kenneth B. Clark, another of those Isaacs returned to for a second interview, had his own reasons for bitterness. Conducting a study of youth in Harlem, Clark had discovered "a Harlem of despair" rather than the Harlem of his youth.[75] So low had Clark's hopes sunk that he told Isaacs he was thinking of emigrating to Jamaica. Here was a man deeply involved in American political life, active in the effort to desegregate New York schools, serving on committees and boards, speaking to a wide range of audiences, appearing on television—and he, like those who had abandoned America for Ghana, was thinking of leaving. Isaacs, worried, closed his notes with the comment "It is the despair of the Kenneth Clarks that is by far the most serious aspect of the present situation. Their power to resist the onset of extremism is being eroded."[76]

In the Cold War, the United States flaunted its democratic ideals as a badge of virtue. Negroes understood how far the nation fell short of what it claimed to be—how, in its oppressive ways, it resembled countries in the Soviet bloc. The point was not obvious to everyone, as Hoyt W. Fuller, editor of the *Negro Digest*, discovered one night in Chicago that fall. Fuller had gone to witness Norman Mailer and *National Review* editor William F. Buckley lock wits in a public debate on the growing right wing. After the debate, Fuller had started off for a party when a young white man stopped him.[77]

"Well, if I had been colored I would have been embarrassed by what Norman Mailer said tonight," the man said.

Angered, Fuller said only, "Well, you aren't colored, so you have nothing to be embarrassed about." Then he moved on.

"Well, I have the right to think what I want!" the man called after him. "You can't stop me from thinking!"

Shaken, Fuller retreated to a coffee shop and reflected on what Mailer had said, in passing, about race. Mailer had proclaimed that even conservative Republican Barry Goldwater, if he were president, would have had to send in the troops, as President Eisenhower had, to enforce integration—if he wanted "to keep the Russians out of the Congo."[78]

A woman sitting behind Fuller had turned to her companion and whispered loudly, "What has the race question to do with anything?"

In her view, Fuller assumed, as in that of the young man who had stopped him,

> *the Cold War and the question of East-West morality can be debated forever without any need to deal with the problem of racism in America. . . . In the view of these people, there is no conceivable analogy between Russian oppression of Hungarians and white oppression of Negroes. It is possible for them to immortalize the young East German who was killed trying to scale The Wall to freedom while ignoring as irrelevant the young Negro girls who were shot down in Ruleville, Mississippi because they wanted for Negroes the freedom to vote.*

To triumph in the Cold War, Fuller knew, the United States would need support from other nations. To get that support, it would have to convince those nations that U.S. "freedom" was better than Soviet "freedom." The United States was a long way from making that case, Fuller thought. "[T]here is profound distrust of this country because of the racial situation here." Too many people outside the United States understood that "white supremacy lies at the core of the American dilemma, and they are not white."

That was what race had to do with the Cold War. But Fuller understood why neither the woman sitting behind him nor the young man on the street wanted to acknowledge the connection. "[R]acial hostility . . . naps like a nervous beast inside most American breasts," he wrote in an essay he published in the *Chicago Jewish Forum*. If whites did not dare let it surface, neither did Negroes, "for to do so is to force open a Pandora's box of resentment and frustration and to leave them naked and stranded on an island of very little hope."

As if to illustrate his thoughts, no sooner had he left the coffee shop than another scene—"incredible and hyperbolic"—tumbled down upon him. A middle-aged white woman forced him off the curb and turned on him.

"Nigger!" she said. "The place is crawling with niggers."

Fuller never got to the party. Most of the guests at the party he was bound for were whites. He had always been comfortable with them before, but he reflected now that perhaps he had "been approaching them, so to speak, from the wrong angle of feeling." Instead of going on to the party, he retreated to a bar, where he drank alone in the dark.

CHAPTER 6

"AND THEN CAME BALDWIN"

The Cuban missile crisis had barely ended when James Baldwin's "Letter from a Region in My Mind" appeared in the November 17 *New Yorker*. James Farmer, the national director of the Congress of Racial Equality, picked up the magazine, intending to read it over the weekend. "I made the mistake of reading the first few paragraphs," he wrote Baldwin, "and found myself asking the switchboard operator to hold calls while I finished it. It is a very great piece. . . ."[1]

To Lorraine Hansberry, it was "one of the extraordinary documents of our time; perhaps any time." Sending along a copy to Henry David, president of the New School for Social Research, she said, "When I read it it seemed to me to articulate the inarticulable; as if Billy Budd had finally found the words to match his passion." Norman Podhoretz ranked it "among the classics of our language."[2]

New Yorker writer Lillian Ross remembers the day Baldwin handed in the essay he called "Down at the Cross" to the magazine's editor, William Shawn. Shawn immediately saw in it what the others saw: a document of nothing less than historic importance. Shawn could not stop talking about the piece, Ross remembers, "the historical importance of it, not only as a piece of writing, but as a 'revolutionary' document." The decision to publish it had been entirely Shawn's. Some at

The New Yorker opposed publication of "serious" journalism, and Shawn "didn't want to have any other opinions or to be drawn into any arguments about publishing it. . . . He responded wholeheartedly to Baldwin and to the piece immediately. He edited the piece himself and worked with Baldwin on a one-to-one basis." He also gave the essay its *New Yorker* title, "Letter from a Region in My Mind."[3]

After the essay appeared—it occupied nearly all the space in the issue—letters poured in to *The New Yorker*, mostly from readers who liked the piece. To those who didn't, the magazine had a terse reply: "If you are unable to understand and appreciate James Baldwin's 'Letter From a Region in My Mind,' we're afraid we can't help you." Occasionally a disgruntled reader suggested an enemy power was at work here, but more often the response was favorable. By April 1963 (when the essay won the prestigious George Polk Memorial Award), readers were being told that demand for reprints of the article had exhausted the supply.[4]

According to the Minneapolis Sunday *Tribune*, "Baldwin's *New Yorker* article came as a shock to many white people, particularly to liberals and other 'men of good will' who never had suspected the depths of Negro hatred and contempt."[5] Nat Hentoff, a white New York journalist who knew the jazz world, fielded questions from surprised whites. "Is this really true?" an editor asked him. A labor union official told Hentoff he had not realized Negroes felt this way about whites. "Anger, yes. I know the anger. But so much contempt. . . ."[6]

Baldwin had broken through the wall of restraint that had kept Negroes from speaking their minds to whites for so long. The context of the essay would be blurred in later years, and not all readers then would understand its audacity, or the apocalyptic context in which it appeared, directly in the wake of the University of Mississippi and Cuban missile crises. Even if hysteria had not already been in the air, "Letter from a Region in My Mind" would have made an impact. In November 1962, very few black writers were publishing in white magazines. Those who did, wrote with measured care. "And then" (in the words of Julian Mayfield) "came Baldwin."[7]

"The brutality with which Negroes are treated in this country simply cannot be overstated," Baldwin wrote, "however unwilling white men may be to hear it. . . . [A] Negro just cannot *believe* that white people are treating him as they do; he does not know what he has done to merit it. And when he realizes that the treatment accorded him has nothing to do with anything he has done, that the attempt of white people to destroy him—for that is what it is—is utterly gratuitous, it is not hard for him to think of white people as devils."[8]

If it had not been for the Cold War and the African liberation movements, Baldwin said, the Supreme Court would not have gone as far as it did in *Brown v. Board of Education*. But even *Brown* did not go far enough. Baldwin saw "no possibility of a real change in the Negro's situation without the most radical and far-reaching changes in the American political and social structure. And it is clear that white Americans are not simply unwilling to effect these changes; they are, in the main, so slothful have they become, unable even to envision them." White good will—"sloppy and fatuous"—would not bring change; change would come because Negroes, powerless to take control, were not powerless to undermine it. "The Negroes of this country may never be able to rise to power, but they are very well placed indeed to precipitate chaos and ring down the curtain on the American dream."

With that doomsday prediction he issued a final warning: if white Americans could not regard Negroes as men like themselves, they would forever abandon the attempt to be free. The answer to the American dilemma—James Baldwin's answer (and he knew he was asking "the impossible")—lay in a change of consciousness. A term at the nexus of Marxist and Freudian thought, "consciousness" substituted for Christian grace an acceptably modern idiom. Everything depended on the "relatively conscious whites and the relatively conscious blacks" who, together, could create "the consciousness of the others." Now at the end, despite the secularity of his language, Baldwin spoke as a preacher, stretching out his rhetorical arms to the congregation. The organ sounding, he offered an invitation to repent, to change, to kneel at the foot of the cross, to be cleansed, and to take up the burden of salvation: "If we do not now dare everything, the fulfillment of that prophecy, re-created from the Bible in song by a slave, is upon us: *God gave Noah the rainbow sign, No more water, the fire next time!"*

However bitter Baldwin had seemed in the past, his *New Yorker* essay signaled a deeper alienation from his native land, and a deeper radicalism than any he had expressed. In 1956, at the black writers' conference in Paris, he had resisted identification with Africans, and in essay after essay he had meditated on his identity as an American. In the *New Yorker* essay, he repositioned himself outside the United States—outside, even, the entire Western world. He had not transformed himself into a nationalist: he did not imagine Negroes were Africans—"the American Negro is a unique creation." But he had detached himself from the American identification with Western civilization. At a time when the Soviet Union was so often portrayed as the great threat to Western civilization and, thus, the world, Baldwin portrayed Western civilization itself as the threat—Western, *Christian* civilization, which, through the atomic bomb, had brought the world to the brink of extinction: "We have taken this journey and arrived at this place in God's name."

The essay flowed directly out of the political currents that swirled around Baldwin in the early 1960s: the demonstrations at the United Nations, the talk of Cuba, the heady faith that Western culture need not dominate the world, the rhetoric of Malcolm X and the Black Muslims. Baldwin had signed the Fair Play for Cuba ad and appeared on a platform with a South African freedom fighter.[9] He had talked deep into the night with Maya Angelou, John Killens, Julian Mayfield, and novelist Paule Marshall in Marshall's apartment.[10] Baldwin's own New York apartment, a kind of way station of New York intellectual life, was filled with cigarette smoke and arguments. Sometimes Baldwin and Lorraine Hansberry talked until morning came, arguing over history.[11]

In Paris, he had watched Algeria's struggle for independence from France; he had spent time in Turkey. He had taken his trip to Africa, on assignment from *The New Yorker*, although he had not written the

African report *The New Yorker* expected; he had turned in this piece instead—a piece arguing frankly for a *radical* transformation of American society—indeed, of Western culture. What had started out as a critical look at the Nation of Islam (the article that *Commentary's* Norman Podhoretz had suggested) had become a critical examination of Western civilization and the religion that undergirded it— Christianity. "If the concept of God has any validity or any use, it can only be to make us larger, freer, and more loving. If God cannot do this, then it is time we got rid of Him."

Baldwin did not have any compensating faith in Islam. He could not imagine a separate black American nation, such as the Nation of Islam envisioned. In a *Mademoiselle* interview a few months later, he spoke of the Nation of Islam as "irresponsible . . . as all racists are irresponsible." The Nation fed on Negro despair.[12] But in *The New Yorker*, he made clear his belief that Christianity served white supremacy as its handmaiden. Baldwin had cast a critical eye on Christianity in *Go Tell It on the Mountain*, but never had he so set himself against the culture it had helped to produce, Western civilization.

Within months, as if belatedly understanding the import of his own words, James Baldwin would back away from the position he had staked out in *The New Yorker*. He would return to his earlier stance, telling interviewers that he was a "committed Westerner."[13] Negroes who identified with African freedom struggles were romantic, he would say; he identified with the southern students instead. But the position he took in *The New Yorker* put its stamp on him, not only because of what he said but also because of the fierceness with which he said it.

If Baldwin burned hotter than most, he was not the only pugnacious writer around. This was a contentious time. Norman Mailer did not just argue with opponents; he got into fistfights with them. He once reprimanded Baldwin for "being incapable of saying 'Fuck you' to the reader."[14] Writing for *Esquire* about Mailer's own sparring at parties, Baldwin wrote as if he, Baldwin, were a mild-mannered bystander when in fact he was already becoming notorious for berating liberals in social situations. That spring, he had let fly at liberal lawyer Joseph Rauh in a gathering at Arthur Schlesinger's home after a White House dinner for Nobel laureates.[15] Television, a medium that took kindly to Baldwin, probably loosened his tongue, as did the example of Malcolm X, with whom he had appeared on television. "He loved debate and spirited dialogue," his sister, Gloria E. K. Smart, has recalled.[16]

The times were right for him. Combat was in the air, and it broke over his head after Dial Press published his *New Yorker* essay in *The Fire Next Time*, along with a shorter essay that had appeared in the *Progressive* magazine.[17] In a long, scornful review for the *San Francisco Examiner*, white poet Kenneth Rexroth called Baldwin "the most effective and widely read spokesman for the American Negro," then launched into a recitation of his faults. Baldwin's novels were "contrived, shallow . . . and sensational," and written for white, not Negro, readers. *The Fire Next Time*, as its title revealed, was "designed to make white liberals feel terribly guilty and to scare white reactionaries into running and barking fits." Baldwin had characterized the Negro's history in America as "centuries of blood, fire, rope and prostitution of his womenfolk." Baldwin had identified Christianity "with imperialism and slavery." Baldwin had portrayed "the Negro as boogie man." Baldwin had portrayed the "Negro problem" as apocalyptic. The Black Muslims, in Baldwin's view, "were honing up for the Night of the Long Knives." To Rexroth, Baldwin's picture was overblown. To Rexroth, the race problem amounted simply to "annoyance and frustration" for middle-class Negro families. Even for the poor of Harlem, he thought, "there is no fire, rope and rape"—only poverty. The race problem would not be solved until "white and black in America have broken through into simple ordinary life." After five columns of scorn, Rexroth turned at the end to say, sardonically, "Still, I'm all for James Baldwin, just as I'm for Malcolm X and Elijah Muhammad."[18]

Someone sent a copy of Rexroth's review to Hoyt Fuller at the *Negro Digest*. Fuller admired Baldwin's work and kept a growing file of reviews and articles about him. Angered by Rexroth's attack on Baldwin, Fuller wrote a response that began in the bleakest terms:

> *It may very well be that the racial puzzle in the United States is unsolvable. If it is, then ultimately one of two alternatives seems like-*

ly. Either Negroes will have to be forcibly re-enslaved or extermi-
nated; or they will have to be totally segregated, confined to a select-
ed area of this country (as the Black Muslims advocate) or deported
to some other country.

Fuller raised the possibility that American culture was irre-
deemably racist. White Americans preferred not to think so. They
preferred to think it was only a matter of time before the race problem
would be solved. They felt guilty about their racism, knowing how it
violated the great American principles "of freedom and equality and
justice." No writer had done more of late to stir up that guilt than
James Baldwin, but now, Fuller said, a reaction to Baldwin and his
message was setting in. "The signs and sounds of reaction began with
Baldwin's third novel, *Another Country*, published in 1962, and they
have grown in volume with *The Fire Next Time*, his most recent book.
Look now, his denigrators are saying, we have had enough of this: we
have conceded our guilt; we have made our gesture; now leave us in
peace."

Dismantling Rexroth's argument point by point, Fuller arrived at
the Black Muslims, who seemed to Rexroth "the only significant rip-
ple of discontent in the Negro community." Rexroth obviously did not
know the new generation. Nor did he know the Negro problem. "If the
'Negro problem in America' is not sensational, then nothing is. In
every area where Negroes and whites live in any considerable numbers in adjacent communities in this country, the threat of racial violence is ever present." Nor did Rexroth know the history of the Negro
problem—nearly four centuries of dehumanization had left wounds
"deep and hideous." Nor did Rexroth take account of the forces rising
in the world beyond. Fuller ended with the affirmation that the
"Negro problem" *was* solvable, if white Americans wanted to solve it.[19]

Fuller sent the essay to *Contact*, a magazine in Sausalito, apparently without result. Some weeks later he sent it to *Dissent*. Editor
Irving Howe accepted the article, commenting, "The points you make
seem to me essentially correct, and I'm glad to see Rexroth slapped
down a little in his pretentiousness." Howe was planning a section on

race for the summer issue. He intended to include a piece he himself had written about Baldwin and Richard Wright, but he would add Fuller's essay to the mix. Howe did want to cut a page and a half or so out of the essay to fit it in. He wanted to take out some statements about "Rexroth's *intent*" that would only provoke denials by Rexroth. And he wanted Fuller to add a sentence or two signaling the broader significance of Rexroth's review, which Howe felt "indicates a kind of withdrawal of sympathy and understanding on the part of white liberals, which helps explain the desperation, militancy and anger of many Negroes, including Baldwin and not at all merely the Muslims."[20]

Then Howe had second thoughts. Ten days later, he returned the piece to Fuller, asking him to have another go at it—"a reworking structurally." Howe worried that Fuller was following Rexroth's review too closely. He suggested Fuller reframe his thoughts as an essay on "white Liberals and Negro discontent." "You would be talking about the reasons for the curious withdrawal (which I've also observed & consider ominous) among white liberals once Baldwin refuses to let up, once he keeps hammering away." Howe was *not* asking Fuller to soften the piece, he said. Rather, he wanted it to be less of "a polemic against a review few people will have seen in any case."[21]

Fuller's defense of Baldwin never appeared in *Dissent*. Howe's infamous critique of Baldwin, "Black Boys and Native Sons," did. In *The Fire Next Time*, Howe wrote that Baldwin had reached "heights of passionate exhortation unmatched in modern writing." Baldwin had joined Richard Wright in protest, and in doing so had learned "that to assert his humanity he must release his rage. But if rage makes for power it does not always encourage clarity, and the truth is that Baldwin's most recent essays are shot through with intellectual confusion."[22]

Although Howe had the most to say about Baldwin and Wright, he made the mistake of taking a few whacks at Ralph Ellison, who called Herbert Hill and asked, with some indignation, *"Who the hell is Irving Howe?"* Hill knew the left wing of literary New York well, and he filled Ellison in on Howe's background. Howe had been a member of the Schachtman group of the Socialist Workers Party, and Ellison was interested in that. Hill and Ellison talked for hours, late into the night. Ellison thought he had better cool off before he replied to Howe, but reply he did.[23] At the request of an editor at the *New Leader*, Ellison penned a polemic as passionate as any Baldwin had ever produced. Ellison warmed to his attack as he went along, his more urbane abstractions giving way to direct hits. Wright "had his memories and I have mine, just as I suppose Irving Howe has his—or has Marx spoken the final word for him?"[24]

Howe responded in the *New Leader*, and Ellison responded to his response, spreading out his part of the exchange across thirty-six pages in his 1964 collection *Shadow and Act*. Ellison implied that Howe (rumored to have anglicized his family name) was "passing" for white, and Ellison chastised him for it: Jews ought not to identify themselves with the white "power structure." He made fun of Howe for cobbling together "verbatim" sections of writing he had already published to make up this "paste-and-scissors job." As a writer, Ellison said he feared the state of Mississippi less than he feared Irving Howe's ideas. "Dear Irving," he said at one point, speaking as if they were old friends when in fact they were not. Indeed, anyone whose only knowledge of Howe came from Ellison's essay would think him a perfect fool.

Howe had implied that Negro life was unremittingly impoverished and desperate, drearily the same from one Negro to the next. Ellison denied that and denied, too, that as a writer he could not claim all literature as his heritage—Ernest Hemingway no less than Richard Wright. Against Howe's narrow vision of what a Negro writer ought to do, Ellison posed his own: to transform his unique experience and give readers "a broader sense of life and possibility." That was Ellison's contribution to the freedom movement, he said, and it was what Negroes wanted him to do.

In a swipe at Baldwin, Ellison told Howe that "Negroes want no more fairly articulate would-be Negro leaders cluttering up the airways. . . . Their demands, like that of many whites, are that I publish more novels . . . . [T]hey recognize what you have not allowed yourself to see; namely, that my reply to your essay is in itself a small though necessary action in the Negro struggle for freedom."

The Fire Next Time had set off fireworks all around. A dozen years later, one reviewer, F. W. Dupee, explained that the book came at a time when "most of us were alarmed by the Muslims." Dupee's review led the first issue of a new publication, the *New York Review of Books*. There, Dupee, a Marxist Columbia University professor who had been a founding editor of *Partisan Review*, expressed the fear that *The Fire Next Time* would stir up white bigots and "confuse" Negroes.[25] Once the Negro darling of the New York intellectuals who edited the *Partisan Review*, Baldwin had become the literary equivalent to Malcolm X.

Baldwin riled even Robert Coles, a psychiatrist ordinarily generous to a fault. After his awakening to the racial problem that day at the beach near Biloxi, Coles had devoted his life to interviewing children attending newly desegregated southern schools. He had also begun to work with the young activists of the Student Nonviolent Coordinating Committee. Starting out as a janitor in SNCC's Atlanta office (the duties he was assigned when he asked if he could do interviews), Coles had become a kind of resident counselor. He spent hours listening to these young people and to the school children he would eventually call "Children of Crisis" in his book of that name. Throughout this process, he tried studiously to avoid imposing judgment, and he talked with children on both sides of the racial divide. He tried to understand these young people's lives, the ways they thought. He tried not to impose his own psychiatric or political views. Characteristically, confronted with "Letter from a Region in My Mind," Coles deliberated whether or not he ought to write down "in some clarification for myself, just what Mr. Baldwin said, and meant to say." The review that resulted was decidedly uncharacteristic of Robert Coles.

What set Coles off, apparently, was Baldwin's remark "The Negro boys and girls who are facing mobs today come out of a long line of improbable aristocrats, the *only* genuine aristocrats this country has produced." For one thing, Coles responded, white children, too, had walked through mobs to attend integrated schools. For another, just how aristocratic were Negroes? He told the story of a Negro boy who had started going to a white school and, seeing a razor drawn at a Negro high school football game, said to his mother, "They're animals, they're animals, and you know it when you go to a white school and see how civilized people behave."

That was to be Coles's method throughout the review: out of his deep well of research, in the interest of granting Negroes "the truth of their lives," he called up one Negro after another to discredit Baldwin. Coles threw in his own description of "large numbers of Negroes in the South" rendered by their oppression "dispirited, worn people, and, from a doctor's viewpoint, very often sick; sick with vitamin deficiencies and their sequelae; sick with a high incidence of venereal disease, hypertension, alcoholism, paranoid schizophrenia . . . diseases of the poor, the ignorant, of the wayward and backward." He pinned their failure to register as voters on the fear-induced weakening of body and spirit rather than on the white authorities who refused to *let* them register. Hope could reverse the fear, but "hope comes rarely to these grim settlements of shanties with littered yards along frowzy, unpaved streets, the inhabitants barely literate, really illiterate, with ragged, unsightly, outlandish clothes and ill made, tasteless furniture." They hardly appeared aristocratic to Coles, who saw their lives instead as "an endless matter of merely automatic or sometimes wanton twitches and exertions."[26]

Here was an unexpected echo of that insulting lead piece for the *Antioch Review* ten years earlier—the one Lillian Smith protested; or of an astonishing 1962 piece by *Harper's* editor John Fischer, who suggested—to a storm of response from readers—that Negroes needed a first-class citizens council to help them learn how to behave.[27] Here, spilled out on the pages of *Partisan Review*, the magazine where Baldwin's own words once appeared, was evidence of the contempt that even a dedicated liberal like Coles could tap, if he needed to. Such contempt had been a surprise coming from Fischer. How much more shocking was it to hear these words from Coles, a man who was by this time virtually a resident psychiatrist for SNCC? It was a measure of how Baldwin's words could stick in the craw.

If some whites were feeling edgy about Baldwin, so were some Negroes. In the spring 1963 issue of *Freedomways*, Julian Mayfield— still living in Ghana yet in touch by mail with the American scene— analyzed the mixed feelings Baldwin stirred up among Negroes. Detractors' reasoning went like this:

> *"There must be something wrong with Baldwin because his books are on the best-seller list and his articles appear in prestige mass-circulation magazines. Worst yet, he's always on television giving his opinion about this or that; and although I usually say 'hear, hear' to his ideas, tell me—since when did Mr. Charlie White Man Boss become so interested in the opinion of any black man but an Uncle Tom?"* On the left, militant intellectuals—Negroes inclined to nationalism and socialism—pointed out Baldwin's ignorance of political science, history, and economics. *"Were it not for this ignorance* They, *those who control American communications media, would never have permitted him to become so prominent."*

Mayfield could grant "some merit" to the argument from the left, "but it is not so much a criticism of Baldwin as of the society in which he functions." For one thing, he said, Baldwin's knowledge of political science, history, and economics was deeper than these detractors imagined. For another, Baldwin was a "creative writer," whose job was "to synthesize and illuminate in human terms," not to work within the definitions of these disciplines.

Nor could Mayfield (perhaps an innocent on this point) imagine a "board of censors" raising and lowering the bar to let some and not others into the nation's media. Rather, the real censor was the economic system. "The people who run this country, and who also run a large part of the rest of the world, do not belong to a single club. They don't have to. They only have to have enough common sense and common self-interest not to allow socialists and spokesmen for genuine revolution to use their media." They had the good sense to know that they needed to improve the lot of Negro Americans in order to reap the economic riches of Africa. Racial tolerance at home was a price they were willing to pay for economic control abroad. They would let radicals speak if letting radicals speak served their purpose. "The only thing a genuine capitalist fears, hates, and will not tolerate, is a genuine socialist revolutionary." Baldwin was not that. He was a radical, but not a socialist radical. "I believe the power elite could survive a dozen Baldwins broadcasting day after day, month after month, as long as he does not spell out socialist alternatives."

To Mayfield, Baldwin was doing as well as a man could when he was poised between "white publishers and his militant fellow-Afro-Americans who will damn him loudly if anything he writes seems to lend support to white stereotypes of Negroes." What set Baldwin apart from other "militant black intellectuals" was this: he was still trying to talk with whites. "Baldwin, almost alone, still talks to the whites, in love and compassion, offering them a way out, if only they will listen."[28]

In his critique of Baldwin's *New Yorker* essay, Robert Coles had found one positive thing to say about it: its publication "indicates that we are moving into that important time when the Negro and white people of this country are not simply politically or economically more nearly equal or 'free,' but socially, personally, humanly face to face." One of the whites with whom Baldwin talked face to face was Norman Podhoretz. During what Podhoretz called "an angry conversation" about Baldwin's giving his *Commentary* piece on the Nation of Islam to *The New Yorker*, Podhoretz described his experiences as a boy. Baldwin encouraged him to write his own essay about race.[29]

Podhoretz had grown up in a tough Brooklyn neighborhood, where he was often bullied by Negro boys. One hit him on the head with a baseball bat, an experience that did not incline him toward the stereotype that Jews were rich and Negroes persecuted. Acknowledging his own dislike for Negroes, Podhoretz imagined that other white liberals shared some of his feelings. "And it is because I am convinced that we white Americans are—for whatever reason, it no longer matters—so twisted and sick in our feelings about Negroes that I despair of the present push toward integration," he wrote in "My Negro Problem— and Ours," his response to *The Fire Next Time*. Thus Negroes and whites were locked in mutual hatred, since, he said, "We have it on the authority of James Baldwin that all Negroes hate whites."

When would the racial madness end? In a comment that must have made *Commentary*'s Jewish readers uncomfortable, Podhoretz framed his answer in terms of the Jewish experience.

> *Did the Jews have to survive so that six million innocent people should one day be burned in the ovens of Auschwitz? It is a terrible question and no one, not God himself, could ever answer it to my satisfaction. And when I think about the Negroes in America and about the image of integration as a state in which the Negroes would take their rightful place as another of the protected minorities in a pluralistic society, I wonder whether they really believe in their hearts that such a state can actually be attained, and if so why they should wish to survive as a distinct group.*

Unlike the Jews, who had "a memory of past glory and a dream of imminent redemption" to set them apart, Negroes had only the stigma of their color and their past. The best hope for them, he imagined, was to escape their color through "miscegenation," or "the wholesale merger of the two races."[30]

Before the essay appeared, Podhoretz sent a copy to Kenneth B. Clark (who had known *Commentary* editor Elliot Cohen and had even once contributed to the magazine). In his cover letter Podhoretz anticipated "angry protest from various organizations in the field of intergroup relations." If Clark agreed with the central argument, would he supply a comment that could be published? "If, in addition, you believe that the kind of candor I've striven for here is helpful rather than damaging to the fight against bigotry, I'd of course be pleased if you would say something about that, too."[31]

Clark did what Podhoretz asked, starting off with praise for the article as "important, at times profound, and above all, honest." Clark did not agree that either miscegenation or intermarriage was the answer. Miscegenation had not solved the racial problem so far, and intermarriage would be evidence that the problem had already been solved. Clark led the letters column for April, followed by David Riesman, Elizabeth Hardwick, Hilton Kramer, and other noteworthies, all praising Podhoretz for his candor and courage (although not agreeing with him down the line) and all, presumably, invited, like Clark, to respond. Two of Podhoretz's fellow magazine editors rallied around. *Harper's* editor John Fischer did not think blacks and whites hated each other as much as Podhoretz claimed, but he thought it "a healthy thing to have such questions raised." Gilbert A. Harrison, editor of the *New Republic*, wanted to give Podhoretz a Pulitzer Prize for his "landmark" piece. It is easy to spot the letters that were not solicited. "The solution is so easy I wonder how no one else ever thought of it. If we had no Negroes or Jews we would have no minority problems," wrote one reader. Wrote another, "His vision of the future is of erasing the stigma on the white man's past by erasing the Negro."[32]

Baldwin himself approved of Podhoretz's candor. He told *Mademoiselle* (which published one of the bolder, wide-ranging interviews with Baldwin at this time) that Podhoretz had done just what he, Baldwin, wanted white liberals to do: "to tell the truth, what he really feels about Negroes." Long critical of white liberals, Baldwin explained to *Mademoiselle* why he was voicing that criticism more openly.

He had realized something, he said, after an exchange with radio talk-show host Barry Gray. Baldwin had gone on Gray's show to criticize the Anti-Defamation League's award to President Kennedy for what he had done for civil rights (which in Baldwin's opinion was not nearly enough). Baldwin had also wanted to protest the government's prosecution of Negro journalist William Worthy Jr., for travel to Cuba (Worthy would win his legal challenge of the State Department's ban on travel in communist countries).[33] Angered by Baldwin's on-air comments, Gray had replied that Baldwin ought to be criticizing Mississippi Governor Ross Barnett instead of his friends.

Thinking over the exchange with Gray, Baldwin came to feel that what motivated many people who claimed to take Negroes' side was "a will to power that has nothing whatever to do with the principles they think they are upholding. . . . Their status in their own eyes is much more important than any real change. If there were no Negro problem, I don't know what in the world they would do." As for liberal columnists—"the professional bleeding hearts"—they were chiefly trying to reassure the public. "If reality broke into one of those columns, God knows what would happen! And when it threatens to, they get up on their hind legs and say, 'Don't attack your friends!' "[34]

Although Baldwin led the attack on white liberals, his feelings were widespread among the Negro intelligentsia, as *Dissent* reported in its summer 1963 issue. "The honeymoon between white liberals and Negroes is over," Charles B. Turner Jr. wrote (probably exaggerating the degree of trust that had ever prevailed). Discovering they could not have integration without "cost or inconvenience to themselves," liberals had beat a retreat.[35]

From a quiet corner of Kentucky, a white Trappist monk named Thomas Merton, poet and author of *The Seven Storey Mountain*, said much the same thing in a series of magazine pieces he would describe as "Letters to Liberals." Merton had read Baldwin's "Letter from a Region in My Mind" and, despite its attack on Christianity, admired it so much that he wrote Baldwin a long letter about it.[36] In essays published toward the end of 1963 in the Catholic magazine *Ramparts* and other small magazines, Merton put Baldwin's message in his own Christian terms. America had arrived at a "moment of unparalleled seriousness," he wrote. America's liberals had been put to the test. Negroes had challenged an unjust social system; they had mounted, in effect, a "revolution." To respond to their challenge would require large changes. Privileged white Americans would have to give up something. Quite apparently, Merton saw, they did not intend to do that. Through "a well-meaning liberal policy of compromises and concessions," they were trying, instead, "to placate the Negro and to calm . . . conservative whites." They had failed the challenge of this "providential 'hour.' "[37]

As the centennial of the Emancipation Proclamation approached, the U.S. Commission on Civil Rights had asked John Hope Franklin to write the story of civil rights over the last century. When Franklin had done the job, he was told he had not sufficiently emphasized the racial progress thus far. To the commission director's request that he contribute to the revision of his manuscript that the commission itself was undertaking, Franklin replied, "I am not at all certain, after reading your letter, that my efforts will satisfy you or the Commission. In time I shall send them along for whatever they are worth; but I am afraid that I cannot 'tidy up' the history that Americans themselves have made."[38]

That history lurched onward. In early 1963, the year both *The Fire Next Time* and the commission's report emerged, three SNCC workers were driving from Greenwood to Greenville, Mississippi, when they were fired upon from a '62 Buick that pulled alongside them. The SNCC driver, Jimmy Travis, was shot in the shoulder and the head. (He survived, barely.) A week later, more shots came crashing into another SNCC car in Greenwood, this time without injuries. A few weeks after that, fire swept through SNCC's Greenwood office. Next, shots slammed into the home of a couple of teenagers who had been helping with voter registration. The following day, during a march from a church to the courthouse, the city police jailed eight SNCC staff members. In April, a white postman from Baltimore, William Moore, set off for Mississippi carrying signs that protested segregation. He was murdered on a road in Alabama. SNCC continued his Freedom Walk, but as soon as the walkers crossed the Alabama line, state troopers arrested them.[39]

James Baldwin had caught glimpses of southern terror early in the year when, in Mississippi, he accompanied the NAACP's Medgar Evers on an investigation of a killing. Whenever Evers and Baldwin stopped to talk with people who might have information, Evers parked his car so that no one on the road could see the license plate. When they went inside, the lights were turned off as they talked. Was this, Baldwin wondered, what Jews must have felt in Hitler's Germany?[40]

Here was scarcely the hopeful picture the U.S. Commission on Civil Rights had wanted Franklin to paint. Much of the brutality in the South took place in small towns and along back roads, out of sight of the national media. But in the spring of 1963, with *The Fire Next Time* fresh on at least some Americans' minds, television was about to bring southern brutality in Birmingham, Alabama, into millions of American homes.

CHAPTER 7

"THIS "TERRIFYING CRISIS"

At the Gaston Motel, the center of operations for the Birmingham campaign in the spring of 1963, worried leaders crowded into the living room of Martin Luther King's suite to decide the next step. It was a small room, smoky from cigarettes, and too warm. They were frustrated, unsure what to do next. Birmingham minister Fred Shuttlesworth, impatient, asked, "Where is the Justice Department? Where is Bobby Kennedy when we need him?" Demonstrations had already sent several hundred marchers to jail when a state injunction was served banning further marches. Should King leave Birmingham to raise bail for those in jail before others, defying the injunction, went in? King listened to the arguments quietly, then stood and went back to his bedroom, followed shortly by the man often by his side, the Reverend Ralph Abernathy.[1]

Without King to hear them, the arguments died out. The room had fallen nearly quiet when King and Abernathy reappeared. King had changed out of his dark suit. He wore his denim jacket and jeans: his work clothes. He had made the decision to go to jail, defying the injunction. On Good Friday, 1963, King led a march down the usual route toward Kelly Ingram Park, a small rectangle only a block long, studded with century-old oak trees. As the marchers approached the park, the police moved in with their dogs and nightsticks to arrest them.

From solitary confinement, King wrote the document that became the movement's most famous statement: "Letter from Birmingham City Jail." Responding to white Alabama clergymen's criticism that the campaign was "untimely" because it denied the new city administration time to act, King argued that the administration was not likely to act unless it felt pressure to act. "[P]rivileged groups seldom give up their privileges voluntarily."[2]

For this writing, King did not have around him a phalanx of helpers; this was a solitary effort, by a man alone, in jail, filling the edges of newspapers or the blank sides of legal documents. Reading the letter as it emerged piece by piece, King's young assistant Andrew Young, himself a minister, saw that here King was "articulating the religious basis for the nonviolent movement in Christian theology."[3] Like martyrs before him, King called Christians to repentance:

> *I have traveled the length and breadth of Alabama, Mississippi and all the other southern states. On sweltering summer days and crisp autumn mornings I have looked at her beautiful churches with their lofty spires pointing heavenward. I have beheld the impressive outlay of her massive religious education buildings. Over and over again I have found myself asking: "What kind of people worship here? Who is their God?"*

At the *Atlantic Monthly*, editor Edward Weeks, receiving King's "Letter," found it so powerful that he read passages aloud at an editorial meeting. He asked King if he could make some cuts so it could be squeezed into the August issue.[4] Other magazines published it, too. "Letter from Birmingham City Jail" traveled far and wide, throughout the world, intensifying media interest in the Birmingham crisis. When Birmingham Police Chief Bull Durham unleashed his dogs and fire hoses on teenage marchers on May 3, television cameras captured the images: dogs attacking young Negro marchers, water blasting them off their feet. In homes across the nation, families sitting down to dinner saw a scene that might have been beamed from apartheid South Africa: the power of police unleashed against a peaceful protest.[5]

In an interview with the Associated Press, Ralph Bunche at the United Nations spoke of the harm the scenes from Birmingham had done to the country's standing in the world. "There is a real social revolution in progress, involving the unshakable determination of the Negro to escape from second-class status."[6] Bunche's comments were surprisingly strong. As a high official of the UN, Bunche had not played the public role in the movement that he might otherwise have. Although he once listed fifteen southern speeches he had given between 1956 and 1963 as evidence he had not dropped out altogether, by and large he had kept a low profile. His comments on Birmingham, "perhaps the fullest expression of Bunche's views on the civil rights movement," according to one biographer, were all the more significant—evidence that Birmingham marked a turning point.[7]

Militancy had escalated on both sides: Negroes were showing a new, stronger determination, and white law enforcement was responding with naked force. Here was the violence that liberals had long foreseen if Negroes pushed too hard for their rights. In a poem published in the *Liberator*, "Northern Liberal: 1963," Langston Hughes took a caustic view of northern liberals who would now say,

> *"Dogs have vindicated me—*
> *I knew that it would come."*[8]

But neither Hughes nor Bunche appeared on the cover of *Time* magazine the week Birmingham became its lead story. As television news showed the attack dogs and demonstrators downed by the force of water, eager journalists circled James Baldwin, luminous from the controversy swirling around *The Fire Next Time*. To put a face on Birmingham, the country's leading newsmagazine, *Time*, featured Baldwin on the cover. He was not "a Negro leader," *Time* said, but "nevertheless, in the U.S. today there is not another writer—white or black—who expresses with such poignancy and abrasiveness the dark realities of the racial ferment in North and South." Noting his "effeminate" manner, *Time* presented him as a spokesman for "Negro rage." A week later, *Life* magazine ran a feature spread on a speaking tour

Baldwin had made on CORE's behalf earlier in the year. In its title, *Life* proclaimed (picking up Baldwin's own words), "At a Crucial Time a Negro Talks Tough: 'There's a bill due that has to be paid.' "[9] Transformed into an icon of black anger, Baldwin was about to become an even more central figure on the political scene.

During the Birmingham crisis, Baldwin had sent Attorney General Robert Kennedy a cable blaming the violence on the FBI, J. Edgar Hoover, Mississippi Senator James O. Eastland, and President Kennedy himself for not using "the great prestige of his office as the moral forum which it can be."[10] Now, as the attorney general was embarking on a series of private meetings in preparation for a new civil rights bill,[11] he invited Baldwin to meet with him. Over breakfast in Kennedy's Virginia home, Baldwin "laid it on the line," he told Kenneth B. Clark in a telephone call after the meeting. Clark was working late at his office that night when Baldwin called to invite him to the second meeting with the attorney general, this one at Kennedy's Manhattan apartment.[12] Driving back to the Justice Department from Hickory Hill, Kennedy had asked Baldwin if he could gather some people to suggest what the government should do in the cities.[13] Immersed though he was in the problems of Harlem, Clark was not sure what he had to contribute. What did Baldwin want him to say?

"Just come and talk, because my feeling is that the guy really doesn't understand the seriousness of the problem."

For Baldwin and Clark, as for others frustrated by the Kennedys' failure to take hold of the racial issue, the midnight hour had arrived. Negroes' exasperation with white America had risen to a pitch that the Kennedys did not appear to comprehend. It was past time for the nation's highest leader to act with force and conviction.

To build the strongest delegation he could to make this case, Baldwin had invited Martin Luther King to join the group, but King had other obligations. King designated Kenneth Clark as his spokesman. Since the two men had met on a train seven years earlier, Clark had helped King in whatever ways he could—meeting him at the airport when he flew to New York, even raising money to help the Kings pay for babysitting. Now King talked by phone with Clark about what Clark might tell the attorney general. The Kennedys should come out clearly for Negro rights to back up leaders like himself, "rather than permitting the more disruptive forces to develop," as Clark put it later. For a start, President Kennedy should stop appointing segregationist judges.

"Be sure and point this out," King told Clark. "This is detrimental and it should be changed. You don't play politics with a problem as important as this. You tell him that this would be what I would say."

Just a few weeks earlier, writing in the *Nation*, King had called Kennedy to account for his timid approach to civil rights. Following a path of political expediency, Kennedy had accepted "tokenism." He had settled for symbolic rather than significant change. "Token gains may well halt our progress, rather than further it," King had written. "The time has come when the government must commit its immense resources squarely on the side of the quest for freedom." So great were the violations of federal law in the South that "only enforcement machinery of vast proportions will be equal to the task."[14]

The Baldwin meeting with Robert Kennedy would go down in movement history as a peculiar affair. Arthur Schlesinger Jr. would help set that stamp on it in his history of the Kennedy years, *A Thousand Days*, where he quoted Robert Kennedy's comment about those who came: "They don't know anything. They don't know what the laws are—they don't know what the facts are—they don't know what we've been doing or what we're trying to do."[15] Baldwin himself would say, when he was interviewed about the meeting by Jean Stein, that the people he brought with him were "fairly rowdy, independent, tough-minded men and women." They were not the kind of people Kennedy had in mind—people who would provide specific policy proposals or, as Baldwin put it, tell "what's wrong in the twelfth ward."[16]

But they *were* political people, and at least two of them knew very well what the Kennedys had been doing in Birmingham. Singer Harry Belafonte and lawyer Clarence Jones both knew that the Kennedys had secretly raised funds to help pay bail for demonstrators jailed in Birmingham. Both Jones and Belafonte belonged to King's

New York "kitchen cabinet" and had a hand in delivering the money to Birmingham.[17] Jones had handled Baldwin's legal affairs but was also close to King, and surely knew a great deal more of what the Kennedys had done—and not done—in Birmingham and elsewhere.

Others in the group brought different kinds of knowledge. Ed Barry, director of the Chicago Urban League, was a reasonable choice, considering the potential for violence in the cities, as was Jerome Smith, a young CORE worker and veteran of the Freedom Rides. Smith had been assaulted in McComb, Mississippi, for trying to desegregate the bus station there; he bore marks of the beating to the meeting. Lorraine Hansberry came, as did actress Lena Horne, who had had a brush with blacklisting during the McCarthy years. These celebrities, political in their way, were important links between the movement and mainstream white society, including white money.

It is true, of course, that they were not likely to provide policy proposals. Others present seemed even more peripheral to the purpose of this meeting: actor Rip Torn, a friend of Baldwin's and a white Texan; and Baldwin's brother David, who often accompanied him. Clark and Baldwin were scheduled to tape a television interview after the meeting, and the producer for the program came along, too. They all added to the impression that this was, as Baldwin's friend June Shagaloff would call it, "a motley crew."[18]

Diverse as they were, they *could* give Kennedy the message Baldwin wanted to get across: not the policy suggestions Kennedy expected, but rather a sense of crisis. *"This guy doesn't understand the seriousness of the problem"*—that was what Baldwin had told Clark earlier. And that was the message this group was prepared to convey.

They arrived at Robert Kennedy's apartment on Central Park South around two in the afternoon of May 24, 1963. Almost immediately, Kennedy began what became his refrain: that the Kennedys "had done more for Negroes than any other Administration, and *implying* that we should be grateful," Clark would recall in a 1970 interview with Jean Stein.

Jerome Smith, beaten for trying to assert his rights, said he was not grateful. How could the Kennedys ask him to go to Cuba, to fight for "freedom" when the government could not protect his rights in his own nation? Robert Kennedy flushed, then counterattacked. Lorraine Hansberry had met Smith the year before, and now, her emotions stirred, she came to his defense. She said to Kennedy, "Look, if *you* can't understand what this young man is saying then we are without any hope at all because you and your brother are representatives of the best that a white America has to offer; and if *you* are insensitive to this, then there's no alternative except . . . chaos."

Under the force of the attack, Kennedy withdrew into himself. "It became really one of the most violent, emotional, verbal assaults and attacks that I had ever witnessed before or since," Clark would tell Stein. "Bobby became more and more silent and tense, and he sat immobile in a way in the chair. He no longer continued to defend himself about it. He just sat there, and you could see the tension and the pressure building in him." Harry Belafonte had socialized with the Kennedys, and he tried to intervene, but the others brushed him aside.

"The rest of us came right back to the issue," Clark would say. "And it went on for hours! . . . It was about three hours of this kind of searing, emotional interaction and confrontation. And the point that we were trying to put over was: 'Look. The Kennedys have a tremendous amount of credit with the American people. This credit must be used by them. You and your brother must use this credit to lead the American people into an awareness and understanding of the nature of this problem, and what has to be done.' " They wanted President Kennedy to do more than make a statement. They wanted him to go south and lead a child into a school. And Robert Kennedy said that would be "phony."

"And this was the abrasive clash here," Clark would say: "our insisting that the crisis demanded extraordinary acts; and Bobby retreating and saying no, and occasionally coming back and implying that we were ungrateful; that we were insatiable, et cetera." When Kennedy brought up what the administration had done for the movement, his visitors brought up the FBI, which they felt had done so little.

Clark did not see Bobby Kennedy as a racist. He saw him as

Baldwin and Hansberry saw him, as "the best that White America had to offer." Yet even *this* man, representing the best of white America, lacked the empathy needed to act. Clark commented later, "There was no sensitivity on the part of Bobby on the basic problems and issues here." At one point Kennedy pointed out that his brother, the grand-son of an immigrant, was now president of the United States. In fifty years, he said, a Negro could be president. Baldwin's terse reply: "You know, my family has been here for generations."

To Clark, it had been "an extraordinary meeting . . . all the more extraordinary because it was the most intense combination of uncen-sored feelings and thought. It was not just an explosion of feelings."

By the time the meeting was over, Clark and Baldwin were already late for their television taping, but Baldwin wasn't sure he had the stamina for it. In the taxi he kept saying, "Kenneth, all I need is a drink. Can't we stop at the nearest bar? I must decompress." They were so stirred up by the encounter with Kennedy that, in the taped interview, they hardly knew what they said.[19]

Later, Baldwin and Clark kept going over the meeting, replaying it between themselves in fury and despair. June Shagaloff, their dinner companion that night, could not tell which was the stronger. Many years later, she told the story as she had heard it, preserving what was possibly the most bitter and charged moment, when "Jerome leaned forward and said to Mr. Kennedy,

> *"Let me tell you what happened to me. Let me tell you about voter registration in Mississippi." Jerome was so eloquent and elegant, although they knew exactly what had happened to him, at his telling of it they were all very moved, deeply moved. When Jerome finished, Bobby Kennedy leaned forward, eyeball to eyeball with this young black man, and said to Jerome, "We've all had hard times." And the meeting erupted. Harry Belafonte tried to keep it going, but they left in anger and despair.*

When, later on in the 1960s, Shagaloff read that Bobby Kennedy had found in himself greater empathy for the movement and Negroes, she could never believe it. She always thought that "a man who could respond that way to Jerome Smith wasn't capable of change."

In an unrelated interview before the meeting, Baldwin had mentioned his upcoming "secret" meeting with Robert Kennedy to a *New York Times* reporter. The next day, the *Times* gave the meeting front-page coverage. A bold double-deck headline proclaimed, "Robert Kennedy Consults Negroes Here about North / James Baldwin, Lorraine Hansberry and Lena Horne Are among Those Who Warn Him of 'Explosive Situation.' "The following day, the *Times* carried the story again on the front page, under a smaller headline: "Robert Kennedy Fails to Sway Negroes at Secret Talks Here." Now, unnamed sources called the meeting a "flop." Baldwin disputed that. The meeting had been, he hoped, "significant" and "beneficial."[20]

The meeting resurfaced for an astonishing third day in a row on the front page of the *Times* in a story about another meeting held by Kennedy: "A source close to Kennedy conceded today that his meeting in New York Friday with Negro intellectuals had been unfortunate." Another *Times* story the same day reported a warning by the chairman of New York City's Commission on Human Rights—"Negro Violence in North Feared"—and again referred to "the views of a group of prominent Negroes who met informally with Attorney General Robert F. Kennedy in New York on Friday."[21]

Three days later, in what by now had become a barrage of publicity, Baldwin and Clark appeared yet again in the *Times*. This time they showed up in a review of Clark's interview with Baldwin, broadcast before its intended show date because of the extraordinary interest the session with Kennedy had aroused. *Times* television critic Jack Gould called the half hour "a television experience that seared the conscience of the white set owner. . . . The writer, coming to the studio almost directly from his celebrated confrontation with Attorney General Robert F. Kennedy, looked directly at the camera and said he was not a 'nigger' but a human being."[22]

A few days after that, the *Times* ran a front-page report of an interview with Baldwin. There was no news peg this time, no event that made his remarks relevant. What Baldwin said, this time, made news by itself not only because of what he said (he predicted more racial violence in both the North and the South) but because *he* had said it.[23]

On June 7, the meeting with Kennedy, fast turning into a legend, surfaced yet again in the *Times* when James Reston, the Scottish-born dean of Washington journalists, wrote a column about it. Basing his account on only superficial familiarity with what had transpired, Reston revealed, through his own attitude, the liberal establishment's failure to understand the impatience and despair that Baldwin and his companions felt. Two events had convinced the Justice Department that it faced opposition from both "militant white segregationists" and "militant Negro integrationists," Reston said. One event was the Birmingham crisis. "The second," Reston wrote, "was a meeting held in New York recently between Attorney General Robert Kennedy and a group of Negro leaders." With dry disdain, he referred to "a savage comment by one of the Negroes against 'the Kennedys' " and said that "the Negro leaders in the New York meeting gave the Attorney General and Burke Marshall, one of his aides, a hard time." Reston's reference to the group led by Baldwin as "Negro leaders" was peculiar enough; even more oddly, throughout Reston's lengthy column, he omitted the names of those he so designated.[24]

Years later, June Shagaloff, herself white, said that white journalists considered Baldwin a Negro leader simply because they did not distinguish one Negro from another. In their ignorance of the movement, they bestowed leadership status on whoever was speaking out. Shagaloff made a special point of denying that Baldwin was a "civil rights leader." He was not a leader; nor did he think of himself as such, she said.

Neither did leaders of civil rights organizations. According to an FBI report, in the summer of 1963 King told someone (the name was blacked out) that he was not eager to appear on television with Baldwin, because Baldwin "was uninformed regarding his movement." The press might consider Baldwin a spokesman, King was reported as saying, but King himself did not think of him as a civil rights leader.[25] FBI reports were notoriously inaccurate, and this one indeed could be. Nevertheless, other civil rights leaders expressed unease with the spokesman's role the press had cast Baldwin in. The National Urban League's Whitney Young dismissed both Hansberry and Baldwin in a talk with Robert Penn Warren, who in 1964 did a round of taped interviews for a new book, *Who Speaks for the Negro?* "While Lorraine Hansberry is a gifted playwright and while Baldwin is a gifted writer, these are not people who either by their experiences or by their training or by their whole emotional orientation, are by any means leaders of the Negro Revolution," Young told Warren. Baldwin's chief appeal, Young added, was to white masochists.[26]

The NAACP's Roy Wilkins did not like Baldwin, either, according to Shagaloff, who as NAACP education director worked closely with Wilkins. "He didn't like Jimmy, because Jimmy was gay, among other things, and he didn't like the kind of statements that Jimmy made. Mr. Wilkins was very pragmatic, and Jimmy was very mystical and ethereal in his political comments." Neither Baldwin or any other intellectual participated in planning or policy meetings, to her recollection. If their names even arose, they were treated dismissively. If one were to judge Baldwin's role in the movement from the meager references to him in the memoirs by movement leaders, Baldwin was at most a peripheral figure—a striking contrast to his star role in the media at the time.

In its initial story of the Baldwin group's meeting with Kennedy, the *Times* had erroneously included Shagaloff in its list of those present. (Baldwin had invited her, but she had had another commitment.) When she arrived at the NAACP's offices on Monday morning, Wilkins told her she was fired. It wasn't simply because he thought she had shown up at a high-level meeting without the organization's authorization. Wilkins's motivation was more directly political, Shagaloff believed. "Mr. Wilkins had a political relationship with Johnson, and with Kennedy, and here was a representative of his office, at a very nontraditional meeting with a Kennedy, with James Baldwin, whom he didn't like." She had to convince Wilkins that she had *not* gone to the meeting; only then did he hire her back.

What *The Fire Next Time* began, the meeting with Kennedy completed: James Baldwin had become a front-line player on the political scene. In an unlikely transformation, this small, anguished gay man had become an Old Testament prophet, standing outside the walls of white America and calling her to repentance.[27] In late June the Associated Press, the wire service that supplied more news to the nation's media than any other, sent out a story that began, "Suddenly, men like 38-year-old novelist James Baldwin have become the crest of an historic wave. Some feel that it was he and other Negro intellectuals who indirectly convinced President Kennedy that Negroes would no longer buy gradualism and would fight in the streets to get their rights." *The Fire Next Time* had "vaulted him from a fairly limited circle of intellectuals to international prominence." Baldwin demurred at the spokesman's role the AP writer assigned him. "I am not a spokesman for anyone," he said. "What must be understood is that the movement for justice and action is on. It's a wind and nobody can stop it."[28]

The wind had caught him up. In London, on the eve of British publication of *The Fire Next Time*, the *Sunday Times* filled a page with an extract arranged around a large photo of Baldwin. The caption: "JAMES BALDWIN, seen in a Harlem slum, has emerged recently as a leader of his people. A month or so ago, at the request of Robert Kennedy, he arranged a New York meeting between the U.S. Attorney General and a group of prominent Negroes. The depth of feeling shown surprised Attorney General Kennedy. Now the Negroes are appealing for justice and threatening violence—'the fire next time'— if it is not given to them."[29]

In a later age when novelists and most other intellectuals have largely retreated from political life, the extraordinary attention paid to James Baldwin in 1963 has become almost incomprehensible. He had built his career as a writer in tandem with the rising civil rights movement. Now, as what King called the midnight hour approached,

Baldwin had the ear of the media. He held no position in any civil rights organization; he did not join in sit-ins, did not ride a bus in the Freedom Rides, did not take the risk of marchers facing armed southern sheriffs; he was not even in the country for much of the time. Yet he had become—by virtue of his frankness, eloquence, and reputation—a spokesman for the movement. He was speaking out publicly on events as they happened: releasing statements, appearing at press conferences, making speeches, giving interviews, going on television. He spoke for political organizations when they asked him to help raise funds or spirits; but he spoke on his own, too. Unfettered by strategic political considerations, he spoke as he pleased, frankly, honestly, directly from the heart of his own convictions. He was, in the terms of the trade, a great interview: he took journalists' questions and ran with them. He enjoyed the give-and-take of talk; he enjoyed having people around. He did not seem to mind his celebrity, although he would talk about how paradoxical it really was. By trying to break through stereotypes in his own personal life, he told an interviewer later that year, he had found himself "in the center of the civil rights hurricane."[30]

Baldwin and his friends had thought their meeting with Robert Kennedy had made no impact. Kennedy had not understood them, and his brother the president would not go beyond "the trite and usual words."[31] Then, less than a week later, Vice President Lyndon B. Johnson, speaking on Memorial Day at Gettysburg, seemed to do just what they had asked. "One hundred years ago the slave was freed," Johnson said. "One hundred years later the Negro remains in bondage to the color of his skin. The Negro today asks, 'Justice.' We do not answer him—we do not answer those who lie beneath this soil—when we reply to the Negro by asking 'Patience.' "[32]

On June 3, discussing strategy for getting a civil rights bill through Congress, Johnson further told Theodore Sorenson, speechwriter for the president, that the president had to go south and "without cussing at anybody or fussing at anybody . . . be the leader of the nation and make a moral commitment" to the Negroes. In the taped telephone conversation with Sorenson, Johnson went on to mention Baldwin specifically, saying, "You see, this fellow Baldwin, he says, 'I don't want to marry your daughter, I want to get you off my back,' and that's what these Negroes want. They want that moral commitment." And coming back to Baldwin again: "So the only big problem is saying to the Baldwins and to the Kings and to the rest of them, 'We give you a moral commitment.' "[33]

A crisis at the University of Alabama gave the president the opportunity to make the speech Johnson suggested. In a showdown contrived with President Kennedy to save Governor George Wallace's segregationist face, the governor had blocked the entry of two Negro students, then given way. In a televised address on June 11, 1963, the president told the nation, "We face . . . a moral crisis as a country and as a people."[34] Historian Mark Stern, examining Kennedy's record on civil rights, would say this speech had a tone "unlike any other made by John Kennedy. He appeared to have made an absolute commitment to the issue in starkly moral terms."[35]

Others besides Baldwin had pressed Kennedy to take a moral stand. Yet that messy, rude, impolitic session with Robert Kennedy may have made a difference. In an essay several years earlier, C. Vann Woodward, writing about intellectuals' role in the populist movement, had said, "One must expect and even hope that there will be future upheavals to shock the seats of power and privilege and furnish the periodic therapy that seems necessary to the health of our democracy. But one cannot expect them to be more decorous or seemly or rational than their predecessors."[36] The meeting with Robert Kennedy had not been "decorous or seemly or rational," but it had helped do what needed to be done. Baldwin and his companions had spoken truth to power, and power appears to have listened.

The night of Kennedy's speech, Medgar Evers, who had driven Baldwin over Mississippi back roads just a few months earlier, was shot to death in his own driveway. Baldwin heard the news in Puerto Rico, where he was working on *Blues for Mister Charlie*. "It was a wonderful, bright, sunny day, the top to the car was down, we were laughing and talking, and the radio was playing. Then the music stopped. . . ."[37]

The death of Medgar Evers, a man who had worked so hard and so well for freedom in Mississippi, set off waves of sorrow across the country. In Jackson, the state capital, Eudora Welty, a white Mississippian whose short stories had brought her national renown, was so moved that she sat down and wrote out a story from start to finish, imagining herself into the mind of the murderer. *New Yorker* fiction editor William Maxwell reworked the June 26 issue to make room for "Where Is the Voice Coming From?," which begins at that crossroads of television and life where Americans had begun to live: "I says to my wife, 'You can reach and turn it off. You don't have to set and look at a black nigger face no longer than you want to, or listen to what you don't want to hear. It's still a free country.' "[38]

Pauli Murray, home from Ghana and a graduate fellow at Yale Law School, expressed the anguish that so many felt when she spoke on June 14 to Radcliffe's Alumnae College. She took stock of all that had happened in the preceding week—demonstrations around the country, Governor Wallace's stand at the University of Alabama, Kennedy's televised address, and now this sorrowful event, the death of Medgar Evers. She told those assembled, "Clearly, this is our most serious domestic crisis since the Civil War."[39]

In Puerto Rico later that month, James Baldwin and an old high school friend Richard Avedon (by this time a celebrated photographer), mapped out a book they planned to produce together. Avedon would provide the photographs, Baldwin would provide the text, and the theme would be (as Avedon told a journalist) the "despair, dishonesty, the alienation of all things that keep people from knowing each other." Several months later, toward the end of summer, Baldwin, back in Paris by this time, had still produced no copy for the book. After dinner with Baldwin and Mamie and Kenneth Clark one evening, Avedon took Baldwin to the home of a friend and put him in a guest room with a typewriter and paper. Forty-eight hours later Baldwin reappeared, worn down by his effort, with the first five pages of what became "Nothing Personal."[40]

That essay, completed over the next few tumultuous months, rolled out a critique that took in not only America's racial sins but much more besides: the nation's great crime, Baldwin said, was "placing things above people." He poured out the despair he felt about a country that paid psychiatrists to adjust human beings to the terrible reality in which they lived. "One day, perhaps, unimaginable generations hence, we will evolve into the knowledge that human beings are more important than real estate and will permit this knowledge to become the ruling principle of our lives. For I do not for an instant doubt, and I will go to my grave believing, that we can build Jerusalem, if we will."[41]

In this essay, Baldwin spoke as he could not possibly speak on a political platform. He was, as his friend June Shagaloff said, a "mystic." The power of his thought, inextricable from his powerful sentences, had no chance at all of coming through the news reports of his interviews and speeches—the tight, pusillanimous grid of American journalese. "We live by lies," he would say in the finished essay. Journalism, with its narrow ways, told its own lies. Only in Baldwin's own writing could he hope to get through the lies to some deeper, more honest reality.

And yet Baldwin continued to speak publicly, to play the political man in Paris, organizing support there for the March on Washington that climaxed a summer of protests. He did not plan to be present for the march, but he spoke out in its favor at the American Church in Paris. And on August 21 he led several hundred writers, artists, actors, and musicians to the American embassy. They carried with them a statement signed by three hundred, expressing support for the forthcoming March on Washington. Novelist James Jones was in the group, along with pianist Hazel Scott and actor Anthony Quinn. A secretary at the embassy, hoping to meet Baldwin when he arrived—maybe even shake his hand—found a lobby so packed she could not even get close to him.[42]

A couple of days later, a *New York Post* columnist quoted Baldwin as saying he was going to have to "disappear" if he was to fulfill his "real responsibility" to the people he represented, and that was "to be a writer." The words were no sooner out of his mouth than the *New York Times Magazine* featured him as one of "five Negro leaders" addressing the question "What the Marchers Really Want." The others were Kenneth B. Clark, the Reverend Martin Luther King, Roy Wilkins, and James Farmer.[43] On August 26, just before the march, Baldwin flew back to the United States.

Future commentators would make much of the fact that Baldwin was not asked to speak on that climactic day, televised to the nation. Although King himself had urged the "participation" of celebrities in the march,[44] the actual speakers were religious leaders and political people, representing political organizations, their presentations so carefully orchestrated that SNCC's John Lewis was coerced into modifying his own strong words. During the speeches, June Shagaloff sat with Baldwin and his brother David near the front of the crowd that flowed down from the Lincoln Memorial to the Washington Monument. Contrary to later reports, being on the program, she believed, never occurred to Baldwin. Whatever his private feelings about not being part of the ceremony, he was at least there, observed and photographed. When writer Kay Boyle described the scene for *Liberation*, she brought him into it, likening him to one of France's best-known political intellectuals, Albert Camus.

> It is good for a writer to be able to express himself in action. And it is good to remember that our American Revolution is not the only revolution in history that did not destroy the intellectuals who had given it a framework and a tongue. Albert Camus knew how to come out from behind the writer's closed door and act, not only act on the stage, but as a socially aware citizen. James Baldwin knows when to push the typewriter aside and march through the streets. . . .[45]

Across the ocean in Ghana, Maya Angelou, who had demonstrated at the United Nations but was now living in Accra, joined other Negro exiles who had gathered at midnight at a park across from the American embassy. They, too, were marching, in support of the march back in the States. Julian Mayfield, usually a man who arrived on time, came late, but finally he came bearing the bleak news that W. E. B. Du Bois, nearing a century old and no longer American, was dead. "Suddenly," Angelou wrote later, "someone whose voice I didn't recognize began singing, 'Oh, oh, Freedom, oh, oh, Freedom, oh, oh, Freedom over me.

> *And before I'll be a slave*
> *I'll be buried in my grave*
> *And go home to my God*
> *And be free.'"*

They marched to the embassy, remembering this man who had received his doctorate from Harvard in the last century, this man who had said, "The problem of the twentieth century will be the problem of the color line." As dawn lightened the dark, a great torrent of rain came down. At the embassy, two soldiers, one white, one black, were raising the American flag. The crowd jeered, and in the intensity of their jeers Angelou heard not only disappointment but also ambivalent hope. "Many of us had only begun to realize in Africa that the Stars and Stripes was our flag and our only flag, and that knowledge was almost too painful to bear."[46]

Two and a half weeks after the March on Washington, a bomb exploded in the stately 16th Street Baptist Church in Birmingham, just across from Kelly Ingram Park. Four young girls died in the blast. In a long statement released to the press, James Baldwin laid the blame on the Kennedy administration, which had failed to stand up to the southern political power. "This shameful day," Baldwin said, "utterly destroys any claim the Kennedy administration in general, or the Justice Department in particular, may make concerning its zeal or dedication in the field of civil rights; it is a day which imposes on anyone who still cares about this country the obligation of challenging the extreme power held by J. Edgar Hoover." Could America expect even more violent repression of the Negro movement? Baldwin raised the specter of Nazi Germany. Perhaps, he said, Birmingham would be America's Reichstag fire. "Let no one say that it can't happen here: it happened here Sunday, and has been happening for a long, long time."[47]

Appearing later at a press conference with Bayard Rustin, Baldwin picked up themes from his statement and added others. Talking to journalists at Harlem's Utopia Club House, he focused on the intensity of the hour, this "terrifying crisis." He called for a Christmas boycott of stores. He called for a nationwide campaign of civil disobedience. In the *Liberator*, a magazine with which Baldwin was associated (not to be confused with *Liberation*), Harold Cruse was advocating the start of a third political party, and Baldwin picked up that idea as well. He called for a party that had nothing to do with either the party of Jim Eastland (the Democrats) or the party of Barry Goldwater (the Republicans). "We are here to begin to achieve the American Revolution. It is time that we the people took the government and the country into our own hands."[48]

Baldwin talked with reporters from several radio stations and networks. At one point, as he stood in a backyard littered with broken bricks and decaying leaves, he told a latecomer, "If you do not let these people go, there will be blood in all American streets."[49] *Liberation*, the pacifist magazine associated with Rustin, published the text of his remarks that day, and a press release went out from the March on Washington office in New York: "Novelist James Baldwin and Bayard Rustin, two leaders of the Negro movement, stated at a press conference held in this city that the Negro's patience and his faith in American Constitutional Government have been pushed to the breaking point."[50]

Bayard Rustin, Baldwin's ally at this moment, was the nonviolent movement's best northern strategist; he had organized the March on Washington. A longtime pacifist with close ties to socialist labor leader A. Philip Randolph, Rustin was an integrationist and a man, like Baldwin, who had many white friends. Yet after appearing at the press conference with Rustin, Baldwin shared the Town Hall stage with novelist John O. Killens, a very different kind of political man.

Author of *And Then We Heard the Thunder* and *Youngblood*, Killens was characteristically so angry at white people that his friend Maya Angelou would remark in a memoir on the intensity of his rage. Describing a stay with the Killens family, she would say, "I had heard white folks ridiculed, cursed and envied, but I had never heard them dominate the entire intimate conversation of a black family."[51] However much Baldwin might berate white liberals, he had not given up on either whites or integration. When Baldwin and Killens appeared together at a Town Hall memorial service for the children who died in Birmingham, Baldwin criticized President Kennedy for his "lack of passion" and whites for their silence in the face of Negro suffering, while Killens took aim instead at the nonviolent course taken by Martin Luther King and spoke out for Negroes' right to defend themselves. "Negro Passivity Is Held Outdated," the *New York Times* proclaimed, picking up on Killens's more provocative remarks.[52] Killens and Baldwin were not close, nor did Baldwin belong with Killens politically, but Baldwin's willingness to travel from one political circle to another was not that remarkable. Maya Angelou, for instance, had managed Martin Luther King's New York office for a time, but she also had demonstrated at the United Nations and turned to Malcolm X for help when the situation got out of hand. Kenneth B. Clark raised money for King and supported him in other ways, yet he questioned King's emphasis on loving one's enemies, and he, too, liked and respected Malcolm X, who paid visits to Clark's Harlem youth project and seemed to Clark (as to Baldwin) a gentle man.

The truth was, northern Negroes' support for the southern nonviolent movement was mixed in the artistic and intellectual circles to which Baldwin belonged. Killens's skepticism about the nonviolent approach was not so rare. Northern intellectuals and artists could scarcely help supporting the nonviolent movement, since it was the most powerful racial movement in process. Yet there were those who longed for the greater militancy that Malcolm X stood for. At a time when Hannah Arendt was blaming Jewish leaders for their passivity in the face of fascism (a position she took in a controversial 1963 *New*

Yorker account of Adolf Eichmann's trial), nonviolent resistance could seem the wrong road to take.

In an essay published in the Jewish magazine *Midstream*, LeRoi Jones attacked the very goal of the nonviolent movement: "a proposed immersion into the mainstream of a bankrupt American culture." To Jones, middle-class Negroes who put their faith in assimilation were like middle-class European Jews who had imagined that assimilation (and their class) would protect them. Jones dismissed the nonviolent movement as a tool of the white and black middle class: "King's main function . . . is to be an agent of the middle-class power structure, black and white," he wrote.[53]

Baldwin was not likely to join Jones in that position. Not personally committed to nonviolence, he still saw the power of this movement, and he was not likely to undermine it. Swimming through the conflicting currents in a stormy hour, he stayed afloat by focusing his own criticism on white politicians. He attacked the southern "oligarchy" and the Kennedy administration, which deferred to it. He found common ground, with others, too, in a call for a Christmas boycott: protesting the children's deaths by refusing to shop for Christmas.

A new organization took shape to call for the boycott: the Association of Artists for Freedom, and Baldwin was part of it. Several members came from Harlem's artistic left wing, among them John Killens and actor Ossie Davis, author of the play *Purlie Victorious*, and Davis's wife, actress Ruby Dee. Dee and Davis, unintimidated by the political climate, had remained supporters of Paul Robeson; they also allied themselves with Malcolm X.[54] Davis served with Baldwin on the board of the *Liberator*, which described itself as "the voice of the Afro-American protest movement in the United States and the liberation movement of Africa." But the political range of the Association of Artists for Freedom was broad enough to include Louis Lomax, a Georgia-born journalist who had written a provocative account of the movement, *The Negro Revolt*, and Clarence Jones, the attorney Baldwin shared with King. The organization's first move was a call for the shopping boycott to protest the deaths in Birmingham. The money that would be spent on Christmas shopping would go instead to organizations fighting for equality.[55]

Baldwin explained the call for a boycott when he appeared on September 22 with Reinhold Niebuhr on a New York television program, organized by the Protestant Council, to talk about the children's deaths in Birmingham. Christmas was a "commercial enterprise," Baldwin said, and America was apparently more of a commercial nation than a Christian nation. He accused the white Christian majority of "a really staggering level of irresponsibility, an immoral washing of the hands." Niebuhr agreed with him on that. The theologian's support for what he now called a "revolution" had stiffened,[56] helped along perhaps by Baldwin's *New Yorker* essay, which Niebuhr had clipped for his files. In what was by this time a familiar analogy, Niebuhr compared the behavior of "good Americans" to good Germans who had stood silent under the Nazis. But when Baldwin turned the question toward economics, suggesting that real estate interests and banks kept Negroes trapped in ghettos, Niebuhr was less willing to follow. "That gets way beyond the racial issue. These are very complex economic issues," he said.[57]

The dialogue closed with an invitation to listeners to attend a demonstration that afternoon in front of the Justice Department building at Foley Square—part of a nationwide day of mourning for the children killed in Birmingham. The *New York Times*'s front-page coverage of the event featured "denunciations of President Kennedy and calls for civil disobedience campaigns." At a time of high tension, Bayard Rustin stressed adherence to nonviolence. Baldwin, too, holding that line, called for "a mass campaign of civil disobedience."[58]

In the end, the boycott idea, failing to win the support of the major civil rights organizations, came to nothing. In *Liberation*, which had published Baldwin's call for it, a white instructor of history at Stanford University, Theodore Roszak, expressed concern about the smallness of the gesture.

I am disturbed by the limited grasp of this situation which even the best and noblest minds in our society seems to have. In response to the deed, James Baldwin calls for rent strikes in Harlem and proposes a Christmas-buying boycott. Again, these things may be good as far as they go. But we must go further. For what has happened in Birmingham is not a matter simply of civil rights in Alabama. It is not simply a matter of race relations throughout America.

Children around the world were being "held hostage" in the Cold War, Roszak said. How was killing four children in Birmingham for a political cause different from the American government's readiness to kill millions of children with atomic bombs? "I put the question to the Negro community and its leaders: what can it be, ultimately, but a futility to expect this society, the colored and white within it, so acquiescent in the preparation for thermonuclear war, to take moral resolve from the deaths of four children?" Baldwin's speech, Roszak concluded, was "a fine address, charged with revolutionary implications, a frontal attack on the whole order and ethos of white America. And still it left unexpressed (I ask, why?) the indissoluble ethical alliance of race relations with the cause of peace."[59]

The truth was that Baldwin was no pacifist. In his conversation with Niebuhr, Baldwin had complained that "the only time that nonviolence has been admired is when the Negroes practice it." He avoided marching in southern demonstrations because he did not imagine that if someone attacked him, he would respond nonviolently. James Baldwin was a fighter, and he had found in the heat of this hour a fight worthy of his talents. Yet, increasingly combative in the North, Baldwin turned south in the fall of 1963 to play a quieter role.

Selma, Alabama, an old town on a curve of the Alabama River, had its pretty places: the dark river itself, the Victorian homes where white people lived. The streets of the Negro part of town were unpaved, the houses often ramshackle, but the Negro community had several handsome churches, and in one of them on an early October night, comedian Dick Gregory spoke, saying things to the crowd that they were not accustomed to hearing in Selma.

Historian Howard Zinn was there, an unobtrusive presence, as a scribe. His involvement in the movement had deepened. Noting the articles he had published on desegregation, the Southern Regional Council had tapped his talents to produce two reports on the Albany movement, which dragged on inconclusively from one year to the next. He had published articles in *Harper's* and the *Nation*. Now he was writing a book on SNCC for Beacon Press (which had asked him, first, for a book on the NAACP). He had time to devote to the work since he had lost his job at Spelman (fired not so much because of his civil rights activities as because he had supported Spelman women's rebellion against campus rules so restrictive that one of his students, the future novelist Alice Walker, transferred to a northern college).

After the evening program when Dick Gregory spoke, Zinn waited with several others at the home of Amelia Boynton for James Baldwin and his brother David to arrive.[60] A gracious, determined woman, Mrs. Boynton, recently widowed, was the pillar of the Negroes' effort to register voters against the will of white Selma. Neither Mrs. Boynton and her few allies nor field-workers from SNCC had been able to break through the unyielding barrier whites had placed before voters in Selma. In a campaign of intimidation, the sheriff and his deputies arrested hundreds for unlawful assembly or parading without a permit. When arrests in the last two weeks of September mounted to more than three hundred, the U.S. Department of Justice filed a suit that would have to wend its way through recalcitrant white juries.

To shore up local courage and bring national pressure to bear, SNCC had designated October 7, 1963, a Freedom Day. As SNCC leader James Forman would explain in *The Making of Black Revolutionaries*, the goal of Freedom Day was to attract to the courthouse a large number of Negroes wanting to register to vote—far too many to register during the two days the county normally allotted for registration (which could take a full hour per person, in the case of Negro applicants). Coming down to the courthouse would take courage; anyone who did ran risks, from job loss to imprisonment, to physical harm. To boost spirits, Forman, a Chicagoan and former student of St. Clair Drake, had invited James Baldwin and Dick Gregory, a celebrity who, like Baldwin, had supported the movement at every turn.

As usual, Mrs. Boynton had opened her home to the visitors, whose choices of lodging were limited. She did not try to cook for all the visitors who stayed with her; she simply turned over her kitchen to them.[61] Forman scrambled eggs while they waited. Once he appeared, Baldwin did not say much. "You fellows talk," he said. "I'm new here. I'm trying to find out what's happening." The atmosphere was tense. Each time a car passed, everyone fell silent, expecting bullets, or a bomb.

Although this was not Baldwin's first journey south, he had not seen anything before to match the scene he witnessed the next day in front of the Dallas County Courthouse, a modern building on a side street. A long line of people wanting to register waited—young mothers with their babies, elderly women and men. Sheriff Jim Clark's deputies, wearing helmets and armed with guns and clubs, stood guard over them. Some candidates had been standing there for hours without food or water when two SNCC workers with a load of sandwiches from a shopping cart defied the deputies' efforts to keep them away and walked toward the line. State troopers moved in with electric cattle prods. They smashed a reporter's camera, pushed him against a truck, and struck him in the mouth.

A lawyer from the Justice Department took the name of the photographer who had been hit, but when Zinn asked an FBI agent why he didn't arrest the sheriff and the others for breaking federal law, the agent told him, "We don't have the right to make arrests in these circumstances."

Zinn knew that the U.S. Administrative Code authorized FBI agents to arrest people without warrants when crimes were committed before their eyes. Yet again and again, in situations like this, they refused to step in. Just a few weeks earlier, he had proposed, as an alternative, a special federal force to be stationed in the South to protect "the lives and liberties of Negroes, and of whites who break with segregation." The president had the power to create such a force, he argued in an impassioned but unpublished letter to the *New York Times*, co-signed by journalist Murray Kempton and Harvard professor Thomas Pettigrew.[62]

Now once again the federal government failed to act. Zinn and Baldwin sat glumly on the steps of the Federal Building, along with one of the Justice Department attorneys and a black attorney named John Conyers, a future congressman, who had come down from Detroit. "Those cops could have massacred all those three hundred Negroes on line, and still nothing would have been done," Conyers observed. That night, after only a handful of those who had waited in line had managed to register, Baldwin rose to speak before an audience crowded into a church. He blamed Washington, "the good white people on the hill," for creating this "monster they can't control."[63]

The experience made a powerful impression on Baldwin. Right after his return to New York, he talked with *New York Post* reporter Fern Eckman about what he had seen, and his indignation poured out with all the vigor of new, calamitous understanding. That morning, coming to the courthouse, he had been scared, but his fear had soon turned to rage. He felt himself wanting to kill these men who, like parrots, told him and the others to "move along." Here before him were Americans trying to exercise their American right to vote, and the U.S. government, which in the name of democracy supported invasions of Cuba and a despotic government in Vietnam, could not protect its own citizens. If the government could not protect Negroes, Baldwin told Eckman, then the government ought not to draft Negroes or make them pay taxes. But the simple, maddening fact was that the government *could* protect Negroes. It could send in federal troops to break up the southern police state (although he knew that could send the white South reeling into full-scale paranoia). He blamed Bobby Kennedy for the failure to act. He blamed both the Kennedys. They were afraid of the southern congressmen. The Kennedys, Baldwin said, did not "give a damn."

After that first visit to Selma, Baldwin came and went quietly, "like a shadow," J. L. Chestnut Jr. would say.[64] As Selma's lone Negro lawyer,

Chestnut tried to get people out of jail after Sheriff Jim Clark put them there. When Baldwin came to Selma, he spent most of his time in Chestnut's office, in the back of Mrs. Boynton's real estate business.

Baldwin would arrive unannounced, calling Chestnut from the Montgomery airport or simply driving up in a car with his brother David. He became for a time Selma's secret muse, a kind of "griot," sitting with David in a corner of Chestnut's office—staying there not only because he did not like to demonstrate but also because he knew that if he appeared in public, reporters would write about him instead of about the people they ought to be writing about: the people marching and standing in line. He thought, too, there was danger in building a movement around a few individuals. Chestnut believed that Baldwin "did not want his notoriety to be in competition with the struggle for *liberty*, as he put it, that was going on here."

That was why Baldwin remained in Chestnut's office, sipping his scotch and reassuring those who came and went that what they were doing was important, not just to Selma but to the nation. Baldwin had the most flexible mind, Chestnut observed, and Selma needed that. The Negro community was divided, and Baldwin helped bring them together. He understood what different people had to bring to the movement; he understood what *he* had to bring to the movement.

"He was shrewd enough and intellectual enough to know exactly where his talents and his skills would fit," Chestnut would say. "He was also one of those rare individuals who objectively looks at his own limitations and then operates accordingly. He knew he was not nonviolent, and so he didn't get in a position where he would do something that would undermine what Martin and all the rest of them were trying to do."

Many years later, as if it had been only yesterday, Chestnut talked about the impact of Baldwin's presence in Selma and the impact of Selma on Baldwin.

> Let me explain this to you. If you were black and of my generation, Harlem was almost a mythical place. People in this area looked

forward to getting out of this area and finding freedom and rest and peace and dignity in Harlem. That was where Duke Ellington and Joe Louis were—all of the black heroes—that's where Langston Hughes was. Jimmy was from Harlem. . . . In Harlem there were black policemen. That was unheard of down here. In New York at least there were superficial motions that the justice system would go through. Down here they didn't bother to do that. They were not literally lynching black folk on 125th Street in Harlem down by the Apollo, but they were literally beating black men to death in front of the local theater here in order to send a message to black men. Jimmy had not really come face to face with that sort of reality in discrimination until he came to Selma.

That's partly what kept drawing him back here, and that's why he felt he had to give whatever he could to help keep this movement alive. . . . His sense of black suffering and the apparent lack of white shame created in him a kind of intensity and dedication that in a different way equaled Martin King's. I also don't have any doubt in my mind that while Jimmy, like Martin, had no intentions of committing suicide, he was fully prepared to die in that cause if it became necessary.

In "Nothing Personal," written during the months after he first went to Selma, Baldwin spoke of awaking at 4 A.M., that "devastating hour," not knowing if he had the courage to go on but knowing he had no right to end his life, although he put it more abstractly: "one has no right, at least not for reasons of private anguish, to take one's life" because "all lives are connected to other lives and when one man goes, much more than the man goes with him."[65] Alongside his despair he placed his faith in love, the relationships human beings form with one another.

Many elements went into Baldwin's despair, not least the anguish of being black in America and homosexual in a society that regarded homosexuality as perversion. What is surprising is not that Baldwin despaired but that despite his despair he persevered in his public role. His highest hopes lay in personal relationships, yet he had been called upon by his times to live many of his days as a public, political man. Wherever he went in New York, people came up to him—in restaurants, bars, on the streets—to tell him they admired him, to ask how they could be published, to get his signature on a scrap of paper. When his mother asked why they couldn't take the train instead of a taxi, he replied, "Mama, it's easier. On the train, people come up to me for autographs or bring me their troubles. And I have enough of my own."[66]

If he usually bore the crowd pressing in on him with good grace, his could not have been an easy life. When the group that met with Robert Kennedy decided Baldwin should be the one to make public pronouncements about the meeting, his agent had protested: Baldwin was a novelist, he said—a "great novelist, and will become even greater—but not if he gets so involved in politics that he cannot survive."[67] There was truth in his warning. The work Baldwin did for the movement was hard on the man and hard on his writing.

In a 1964 piece for the *New York Herald Tribune*, LeRoi Jones, himself transformed into a celebrity by *Blues People* and his play *Dutchman*, would speak of his own fears of what celebrity could do to him and whatever he had to say. The wave was already upon him, in fact—the commercial wave that undermined serious speech with invitations to write a musical or report on the movement or teach in college or advertise soap. "I write now, full of trepidation because I know the death this society intends for me. I see Jimmy Baldwin almost unable to write about himself anymore. I've seen Du Bois, Wright, Chester Himes, driven away—Ellison silenced and fidgeting in some college. I think I almost feel the same forces massing against me, almost before I've begun."[68]

As Jones understood, Baldwin stood in jeopardy. Depending on white readers and editors, depending on a publishing world that had beaten a retreat from anything radical, Baldwin had spoken too many times without regard for fear or favor. His old sparring partner Norman Podhoretz prepared a table for him where he could eat his humble pie: a *Commentary* roundtable on "Liberalism and the Negro," held toward the end of 1963. Podhoretz would tell writer Marvin

Elkoff later that he invited Baldwin "to get him off the personal kick and make him talk about solutions and programs."[69] If that was what he had in mind, Podhoretz had the wrong man.

According to Elkoff, Baldwin himself turned to one of the other panelists before the talking began and wondered "what the hell he was supposed to say to them in there about all this sociology and economics jazz." Baldwin might well have wondered if he was being set up. The men arrayed with him on the otherwise white panel were academic heavyweights. There was Sidney Hook, who had locked horns with Hannah Arendt over Little Rock. There was Nathan Glazer, co-author with Daniel Moynihan of a new book, *Beyond the Melting Pot*. There was Swedish social scientist Gunnar Myrdal, author of *An American Dilemma*, the book that framed the racial problem as an issue of conscience. Baldwin's friend Kenneth B. Clark, who might have reasonably been asked to speak, too, watched from the audience.

All the panelists except Baldwin came armed with academic training. Baldwin was no lightweight, but he was a different sort of intellectual altogether. Moreover, unlike the others, he had involved himself in the direct-action movement. He had given speeches, raised funds, talked to the press, become a celebrity—and made unkind comments about liberals. He stood out among the rest like a lightning rod.

To launch the debate (which was to appear in *Commentary*),[70] Podhoretz brought up a subject that had stirred controversy: "preferential treatment" (or, as it came to be called, "affirmative action"), a remedy proposed by the National Urban League's Whitney Young. It was a suitable topic for a magazine meant for Jewish readers. Jews had fought long and hard to get rid of quotas for Jews in the nation's universities, which used quotas to limit the numbers of Jewish students. "Preferential treatment" was meant to increase the numbers of Negroes present in schools and jobs, but it sounded suspiciously like quotas in disguise.

The idea had critics within the movement. Lawrence Reddick counseled King against it. Negroes could demand "maximum" opportunities, but Reddick did not think "white boys who have struggled hard to prepare themselves for jobs should be asked to step back for

Negroes. We can never get away with this. It violates our principle of equality. And it is so contrary to the American spirit that our opponents would fasten upon it as our main objective and mobilize opposition against us." At issue, as Reddick understood, was support from the labor movement, already smarting from criticism by the NAACP's Herbert Hill. Reddick thought the civil rights movement had already erred by alienating the labor movement. Preferential treatment would make matters worse.[71] King and the SCLC had not yet settled where to stand on this proposal, but another who disliked it was King's New York attorney Clarence Jones, who had accompanied Baldwin to the meeting with Robert Kennedy.[72]

It is hardly surprising, then, that Baldwin did not defend preferential treatment. In fact, judging from the edited transcript of the session, only Hook gave it any support, and his was lukewarm. Myrdal argued against preferential treatment. He favored a broad program to lift the "underclass" out of poverty and affirmed that "the system works." The whole discussion would have sunk under the weight of optimism if Baldwin had not been there.

"You and I around this table and everyone in this room may agree that our institutions are really working to liberate the Negroes. But the *Negroes* don't believe it," Baldwin said. If it had not been for street action pressing against the institutions—"the people who got their heads broken and were put in chain gangs"—there would have been no change at all.

Loftily, Hook replied that it was not street action that had handed down the *Brown* decision or sent troops to protect individuals' rights.

Podhoretz, changing the subject, picked up on the theme of Glazer's new book to ask Baldwin if he could foresee Negroes taking "their place . . . as one of the competing groups in the American pluralistic pattern."

Baldwin implied that from his point of view, the American venture was scarcely worth joining.

Hook asked if Baldwin spoke for himself or all Negroes. "If I read his most recent book properly," Hook said, "he actually believes that all Negroes hate white people; . . . But that's not true of the

Negroes I know, and it can't be true for Negroes who have married whites. . . ."

Baldwin said *he* did not hate white people. "And as far as I know, Mr. Hook, I never said that all Negroes hate white people either. What I *have* said is that I cannot imagine any Negro in this country who has not for at least one of the twenty-four hours of a day hated all white people just because they were on his back."

The dialogue bumped along, a chasm widening between Baldwin and the rest. In a question period, Charles Silberman, an editor at *Fortune*, asked what Baldwin meant when he told a reporter, "There is no role for the white liberal, he is our affliction." In no time at all, Baldwin and Hook were off and at it again.

Baldwin said liberals were an affliction because they seemed to think "they must help me into the light." Hook said, on the contrary, liberals believed in letting people be different. He accused Baldwin of developing a "myth of collective guilt."

Baldwin said he wasn't trying to make people feel guilty. What he wanted was acknowledgment of the crimes whites had committed. Hook said whites who hadn't committed crimes shouldn't have to take responsibility for crimes other whites had committed.

At this point, Kenneth Clark, who had worked with Myrdal on *An American Dilemma*, spoke up from the audience. Clark agreed with Baldwin's critique of the white liberal, "a curious and insidious adversary—much more insidious than the out-and-out bigot." Universities, social work, public schools, unions—

> *We could go right down the list of areas of American life that are not controlled by out-and-out bigots, but that are controlled by individuals who define themselves as liberals, and find that the predicament of the Negro in each of these areas is incomprehensible. . . . With all due respect to my friend and former colleague and boss, Professor Myrdal, I have come to the conclusion that so far as the Negro is concerned, the ethical aspect of American liberalism or the American Creed is primarily verbal. There is a peculiar kind of ambivalence in American liberalism, a persistent verbal liberalism that is never*

capable of overcoming an equally persistent illiberalism of action. And so I am forced to agree with James Baldwin that so far as the Negro is concerned, liberalism as it is practiced—I am not talking of it as it is verbalized—is an affliction. It is an insidious type of affliction because it attempts to impose guilt upon the Negro when he has to face the hypocrisy of the liberal. The Negro doesn't have to feel guilty when he faces out-and-out bigotry. Mr. Baldwin has been put on the defensive all throughout this discussion by people who don't want to be made uncomfortable by him. Professor Hook is, in effect, saying, "Jim, don't make me uncomfortable. Don't make me face the fact that my Negro friends. . . ." I almost expected Professor Hook to say, "My Negro cook. . . ."

Afterward, an editor from Pantheon Books wrote Clark to thank him for speaking up. He and another editor who had accompanied Myrdal to the session were "both depressed by the discussion and appalled by Professor Hook's statements. Hearing you made us feel a little less ashamed about the whole business."[73]

A few months later, Marvin Elkoff mentioned the roundtable in his attack on Baldwin in *Esquire*. He described Baldwin's performance with the half-respectful disdain that marked his whole piece: "*[H]e*, James Baldwin, was damn well going to get these liberals to accept his black reality before they talked of ethics and the future of society and housing programs."[74]

Throughout Baldwin's time of political celebrity, there had been those who scorned it, and scorned him for the strength, even arrogance, of his views, the poundings he gave to whites, and perhaps, too, his scorn for white American capitalist culture. Even as he published him, *Esquire* editor Harold Hayes had kept his distance from Baldwin. Hayes was a white ex-Marine from North Carolina, conventional in many ways despite the iconoclastic flair he had brought to *Esquire*. He thought Baldwin ought to give liberals credit for keeping things from being worse than they were. Favoring irony and satire, Hayes saw "Letter from a Region in My Mind" as a polemic, and believed that William Shawn ought not to have run it. Not long after Hayes published Elkoff's piece, he spoke contemptuously of the "virulent strain in some of Baldwin's recent work, more related to the political philosophy of RAM [Revolutionary action movement] than to Martin Luther King."[75]

Always ready to take celebrities apart, *Esquire* found in Elkoff a writer who was happy to set to work on Baldwin. Considering himself a radical, Elkoff would say later that he felt no liberal guilt about blacks, and he went at Baldwin with a will, exploring his celebrity and what he saw as his exhibitionist personality. In a snide play on Baldwin's collection of essays *Nobody Knows My Name*, Elkoff's piece bore the title "Everybody Knows His Name." "How does a man of so unorthodox and disorderly a mode of life become so persuasive and pertinent a spokesman for the Negro protest movement. . . ?" Elkoff asked. His answer: the unaccustomed honesty with which Baldwin spoke to white liberals. "He is the first who has gotten beneath their skin, . . . the first to make them see what it is like to be a Negro in America." The article, one of the richer portrayals of Baldwin during this time, nevertheless hurt him; Hayes told Elkoff that Baldwin even threatened to sue. It would be several years before Baldwin published again in *Esquire*.

Yet, whatever the consequences to his own work as a writer, Baldwin felt absolutely obliged to go on doing what he was doing. If he spoke sometimes like one possessed, his voice clipping rapidly along in anger and despair, it was because he *was* possessed by his mission to describe, as honestly as he could, what was happening to the nation he went on claiming as his, even as he spent much of his life beyond its shores. Other intellectuals and artists set their creative lives aside to do the work of the movement, but none with greater effect than James Baldwin.

Many years later, *New Yorker* writer Hilton Als would refer to Baldwin as an "intellectual carpetbagger."[76] It was an unkind remark, carrying the implication that Baldwin engaged in the southern movement in order to profit from it. While the movement *did* thrust Baldwin into the limelight, expanding his celebrity, Baldwin was well on his way to respect as a writer before the movement entered its most active years. Nor, except for the added attention it brought him, did his work for the movement profit him as a writer. Baldwin was a middling journalist. *Blues for Mr. Charlie*, his main attempt to capture the movement in a major creative work, does not wholly fail as a work of art, but it does not wholly succeed either. "Going to the Meet the Man," a short story written out of his time in Selma, was a strong and bitter piece, an exploration of the sensual depths of racial sadism. Yet Baldwin's experience with the movement did not yield his best writing, which came out of himself and his personal life, not out of his reportorial encounters with the South.

The South remained for him an alien country, and he did not write about it with any special understanding. Nor did he write about the movement itself with special insight or eloquence. What he did do was articulate, in terms many white Americans could understand, the anguish and anger Negroes had hidden from whites for so long. Through his essays, interviews, and speeches, through television appearances and press conferences, through conversations in barrooms and living rooms, he stretched the limits of what could be said.

PART THREE

The Last Campaigns

1963–1965

CHAPTER 8

CALLING THE QUESTION

M ississippi had carved out for itself an ugly place in America's racial crisis. Three of its deadliest dramas had drawn national attention: the murder of Emmett Till, rioting at the University of Mississippi, and the assassination of Medgar Evers. There had been other deaths, too, and countless acts of brutality. By the reckoning of James Silver, the historian who had delivered William Faulkner to the Southern Historical Association at Memphis several years earlier, it was time for someone to call Mississippi to account. Silver volunteered for the job.

Never timid, Silver had nevertheless exercised caution in the past. He had avoided identifying himself with the little newspaper put out with P. D. East and William Faulkner. He had once talked maverick journalist I. F. Stone out of running an excerpt from a historical speech he had given, on the ground that it might get him fired.[1] Throughout the 1950s and into the early 1960s, reporting on the South for the British magazine *Economist*, Silver signed his reports only as "a Correspondent in Mississippi."

Watching James Meredith live through his ordeal at the University of Mississippi had changed Silver profoundly. Born in the North but educated in the South, Silver had seen the South he knew transformed before his very eyes, as the cruelty behind the screen emerged into public view. After gunfire and smoke filled the campus in the fall of 1962, Mississippi politicians blamed the Kennedys for what had happened there. Silver was outraged. Writing the *Time* magazine bureau chief in Atlanta to correct errors in the magazine's account, Silver said, "This whole business has been the most emotional experience of my life, and I have gone through a number of crises in my own thinking and actions." His caution did not, however, fall away all at once. When he sent an account of the crisis to the *Reporter* magazine, he asked that his name not be attached to it, and the *Reporter* used it only as background. His *Economist* article on the riot also appeared without his byline.[2]

Yet Silver had not hesitated to put himself in harm's way. He and his wife had mingled with the crowd the night Meredith arrived on campus in the hope of discouraging violence. Because he openly supported Meredith, he endured phone calls in the night and harassment by politicians. He received threats of violence, and once someone sent his young daughter a doll with a pin stuck through its heart.[3]

There were days when his commitment faltered. "Yesterday was one of my bad days," he wrote to a friend in March 1963. "My skin has been acting up, as it does after a few days of tension." He felt trapped by his circumstances. He had just gone to Clarksdale to see Aaron Henry, head of the Mississippi NAACP, and he was about to take a little group of professors down to Tougaloo College, a Negro school, in an effort to get acquainted with Negro leaders. Now he found himself committed to a steak dinner with colleagues and Meredith even though, he confided, he felt "fed up with the whole damned Negro business and certainly didn't want any more involvement." Silver had gone on to dinner, which turned out fine, despite the interruptions by phone callers who hung up as soon as the phone was answered. As they ate in the kitchen, every now and then the thought crossed Silver's mind that a brick might fly through the window.[4]

Given the awfulness of the situation, friends encouraged him to take a job elsewhere, but he was determined to stay in Mississippi. He had a plan. He had accepted the vice presidency of the Southern Historical Association because as vice president he would become president, and would deliver a presidential address in the fall of 1963. He meant to use the occasion to tell Mississippi the things he felt it needed to hear.

Long before time came for the speech, Silver began to lay plans to extend its reach beyond a few historians gathered in the North Carolina mountain town of Asheville. He stirred interest in the speech in the very way he prepared it. First he traveled the state talking with community leaders. Then he sent letters out to professors and lawyers, along with a handful of businessmen and newspaper editors. Nearly half of those he wrote were historians. The majority were native Mississippians. Others had either lived in Mississippi or were living there still. His letter asked a simple question: What made Mississippians act as they did? The answers flowed in, thirty-eight in all.[5]

Tom Clark at the University of Kentucky said he had turned the question over in his mind himself without coming up with an answer. "It seems to me there is such a deep psychological thing involved that a historian has a hard time laying his hands precisely on what makes people act like they do." From Stanford, David M. Potter offered the idea that white Mississippians belonged to a single "reference group." Unlike most Americans, who felt allegiance to several reference groups, white southerners felt allegiance to only one. Consider William Faulkner, who didn't agree with segregationists but had said that in a showdown with the federal government, he would cast his lot with his native state. "Of course, the tighter the reference group, the more repressive and extreme will be the demonstrations of conformity to it, and the more harsh will be the penalties for not conforming." It was an idea, but Potter feared that perhaps his answer offered merely a restatement of the question.[6]

George B. Tindall at the University of North Carolina proposed a potpourri of explanations: that the population was mostly rural, that the white population was relatively homogeneous, that educational standards were low. All these factors made Mississippi a place where "variety, knowledge of the outside world and different cultures and different ways of doing things, remain unknown." Besides that, the state was poor and, unlike North Carolina and Georgia, had almost no middle-class liberals. The newspapers were "impossible." The South was a patriarchy, with ties forged by family and clan, not by economic roles as in the "open modern society." But Tindall, like Clark, suggested that what was truly needed was psychological insight, which was not something he felt equipped to offer.[7]

John W. Wade, dean at Vanderbilt, raised the fact of Mississippi's "Scotch-Irish pedigree," with its "heritage of being persecuted."[8] Someone else pointed out Mississippi's lack of a metropolis to break up its provincialism. Another said that in Mississippi, Negroes represented a higher percentage of the population than in any other state; equality would therefore bring greater changes in how people lived. Although one college president disapproved of Silver's plan for his speech (he assumed, correctly, that Silver meant to indict Mississippians), most who replied took the question sympathetically. More than one expressed surprise at being asked by Jim Silver to analyze Mississippi. They shared David Potter's opinion that Silver was "the top authority on this."

Silver was investing heavily in this project, and he planned to disseminate the results as widely as possible. He and Leslie Dunbar at the Southern Regional Council had talked of issuing an expanded version of the speech as a pamphlet. A Pascagoula lawyer wanted to start raising money from foundations for "massive distribution" throughout the state. This would be "the biggest bomb-shell to hit Mississippi since the Civil War," the lawyer said.[9]

By October 1963, the month before the Asheville meeting, Silver had a ninety-five-page manuscript in hand—the draft for the pamphlet. He had sent it to C. Vann Woodward and other historians for feedback. He wanted his analysis as solid as he could make it. He had promised the speech to *Newsweek* and the *New York Times*, and the *New Republic* and *Harper's* were interested in publishing excerpts. He had also drawn the interest of Harper & Row and Harcourt, Brace & World. Should he issue the pamphlet quickly, or wait for book publication? Silver was not sure. Harcourt, Brace & World was moving more aggressively to sign the book, inviting him to stop over in New York on his way back from a lecture at Brandeis. An editor there imagined the book as both a history of Mississippi and the story of Silver's relationship with James Meredith and William Faulkner. Harcourt, Brace & World saw this as "a big book . . . but a complex one." Recognizing the book's potential, the publisher moved to protect its commercial interest. Would Silver please copyright the speech? And refrain from publishing an expanded version before the book came out?[10]

Silver was not yet convinced that he ought to give up the idea of publishing the pamphlet instead of a trade book, which would take so much longer to reach the public. On the other hand, despite the effort both Silver and Dunbar had poured into it, the pamphlet was not even ready. Silver had worked fifteen-hour days to complete the manuscript, and Dunbar had put so much of himself into the revision that Silver told him, "Sometimes I haven't been sure whether this was my paper or yours."[11] Like Martin Luther King's *Stride toward Freedom*, the book that would be called *Mississippi: The Closed Society* would be the product of a group effort, a work collaboratively crafted for political effect.

It was too late to get a pamphlet printed by the date of the speech, November 7, as they had hoped, but at least they could get it out by Christmas. That would be faster than a book could appear, especially since Harcourt, Brace & World wanted to expand the current manuscript, with Silver's personal story added in. "Now, I'm at an impasse," Silver confessed to Dunbar, "and I guess that I'm not thinking too clearly about the whole business anyway. My major concern is to set the record straight and to have some impact on Mississippi thinking. The first I have largely done and the second is damned unlikely." He was not eager to write a hundred more pages on top of the work he had already done. He had not given his classes the attention they needed, and that could give authorities an excuse for firing him. He knew what he had written was "going to be not only timely but enormously provocative," and he didn't think he should wait to publish it as a book. He put the question to Dunbar: "What is the best thing to do, for all of us, under the present complicated circumstances? I want this material, in whatever form, widely distributed in Mississippi, even if it is as a sort of last will and testament."[12]

Dunbar knew that a trade publisher could bring *Mississippi: The Closed Society* the attention that an SRC pamphlet would never draw; he weighed in on signing with a publisher for a book. Furthermore, he intervened on Silver's behalf with Harcourt, Brace & World, persuading the editor to scale down his expectations and make an offer for a smaller book.[13] Thus, before Silver ever gave his address in Asheville, the wheels were turning to deliver its message to a national audience.

As the moment approached, Karl Fleming from *Newsweek*'s Atlanta office knew what was coming and planned to be there. Bennett H. Wall, secretary treasurer of the SHA, had written half a dozen press people he knew to let them know Silver was going to "lower the boom."[14] Silver himself had sent out advance copies of the speech. Arriving in Asheville, he went over it with the *New York Times*'s Claude Sitton, pointing out the parts he thought were important. A television camera was set up in front of the podium, but Silver, afraid it would be distracting, asked that it be removed.[15]

By the time he began to speak, most in the audience had an idea of what he was going to say. They might not have known before they came, but once they arrived in Asheville, they heard what was coming soon enough. Silver himself was elated; all this attention was heady wine. As Bennett Wall saw the situation, "The man had been living on nerve for a long time."

Yet after all the fanfare, it was characteristic of Silver that he began as he did, not on a solemn note but with a protracted joke that developed the theme. "The Mississippian and the American should each stick to his own kind," he said, to gales of laughter. "If the good Lord had intended Mississippians and Americans to live and work in the same way, he would not have created a Mississippi and an America in the first place." Of course, he did not *really* feel that way, Silver said, ending the comic warm-up and getting down to the serious business of Mississippi's "closed society."

Not since W. J. Cash had conjured up "the mind of the South" had a writer attached to the region such an illuminating phrase. It was masterful politically, invoking the totalitarian world behind the Iron

Curtain. Countering the rhetoric of white resisters, who portrayed the civil rights movement as a communist plot, Silver portrayed Mississippi itself as a totalitarian society, out of George Orwell's *1984*.

"In committing itself to the defense of the bi-racial system, Mississippi has erected a totalitarian society. . . . The more embattled the closed society becomes, the more monolithic, the more corrupt, and the more willing to engage in double-think and double talk." But the Cold War spelled an end to Mississippi's resistance to the national will. A nation fighting communism had to fulfill its democratic promise. "[I]t will not much longer indulge the frustration of its will."

The speech built powerfully to the end, when Silver delivered his hardest blow, the last thing the white resistance wanted to hear: a call for federal intervention—"the massive aid of the country as a whole, backed by the power and authority of the federal government." His audience rose in standing ovation. Of the hundreds there, only two or three had walked out.[16]

The speech was not much reported in Mississippi, but Claude Sitton's account appeared on the front page of the *New York Times*: "Mississippi Professor Declares That His State Is 'Totalitarian.'" At the end, on the inside jump page, the *Times* tucked in a one-inch Associated Press story reporting Mississippi Governor Ross Barnett's response: "Old Silver's liable to say anything. I wouldn't waste words on that man. He ought to have been kicked out a long time ago."[17] The Associated Press also distributed a story on Silver's speech to newspapers and broadcast outlets across the country. Dozens of newspapers and magazines featured the speech in some way. The *St. Louis Post-Dispatch* ran a long article headlined "Most Hated Man in Mississippi." In the *Saturday Evening Post*, Ralph McGill referred to the speech as "a documented and damning indictment of thought control in that state."[18] *Newsweek*'s Karl Fleming wasn't happy with the report his own magazine ran, he told Silver. "Not enough of the goddamn speech in it," he said. "And there were one or two near-miscues. But then what the Hell can you expect from the kept press."[19]

Expressions of appreciation (along with hate mail) flooded Silver's office. Historians at City College of New York sent him a telegram. They thanked him for his "courage in speaking plainly in the present crisis." The *Journal of Southern History* was publishing a longer version of his speech, and Silver wrote to Philip F. Detweiler, its managing editor, "In Asheville, I was really apprehensive about even returning to the state; now I realize that I have a few strong allies."[20] By mid-December, Silver had received around six hundred letters, so many that he told Leslie Dunbar he planned to send out a mimeographed reply.[21]

Less than a month after the Asheville speech, the Mississippi Board of Trustees for Institutions of Higher Learning received a letter from the director of the state Sovereignty Commission. A surveillance-propaganda machine, the Sovereignty Commission tried to control what was said about Mississippi's racial situation, and Jim Silver was obviously someone who needed to be controlled. Irritated especially by an earlier speech Silver had made in Atlanta, the commission's director, Erle Johnston Jr., suggested that Silver's comments on Mississippi, delivered outside state borders, constituted such disloyalty that he ought to be fired for them. Johnston understood that firing Silver might endanger the university's accreditation. He understood, too, that Silver was working on a book and that firing him would just draw attention to it. On the other hand, he thought the accrediting agency could scarcely make a case against Mississippi for firing a man for "extreme disloyalty." Nor would dismissing him draw more attention than Silver was already drawing with his "inflammatory speeches."[22]

Thomas J. Tubb, chairman of the board and a lawyer, replied that nothing would please him better than firing Professor Silver. At the same time, he really did not want to jeopardize the university's accreditation. Nevertheless, the board appointed a subcommittee to explore grounds for ridding Mississippi of this meddlesome man. Support for Silver's dismissal was gathering. In February, a lawyer from Rosedale, Mississippi, Walter Sillers, with no apparent irony, wrote the trustees' chairman of the board to say that Silver's repeated allegations "that Mississippi was a 'closed society' " had taken Silver over the line: his university employment ought to be "promptly terminated."[23]

Toward the end of April, Silver received a letter from the trustees' secretary asking him to respond under oath to fifteen questions. Five dealt with the Asheville speech. Five referred to other speeches he had allegedly made (including one in Denver, where he had never spoken). The final five seemed to Silver "an even greater fishing expedition." They hinted at general interrogation, possibly at length, under oath. The goal, he thought, was to entrap him into saying something that the board could call perjury. Then the board could fire him for "contumacious conduct."[24]

Silver had expected retaliation for the things he said. Even before his Asheville speech, Dunbar had alerted the American Civil Liberties Union to the possibility of retaliation, and the ACLU stood by to help. After a speech at Brandeis, Silver stopped off in New York to talk with ACLU officials. Then he went to Washington to talk with the American Association of University Professors. The AAUP offered to pay for a Mississippi lawyer if Silver could find one brave enough to take the job.[25]

Silver did in fact find a Mississippi lawyer willing to take his case—Landman Teller of Vicksburg. On June 15, 1964, one week before publication of *The Closed Society*, Teller wrote Silver a letter laying out the terms under which the firm would represent him. In the hope of settling this matter quietly, the lawyer asked Silver to steer clear of controversy. Silver wrote Teller a couple of months later that he *had* turned down "a number of requests," using what was, for him, "some restraint."[26] But if the Sovereignty Commission had slowed him down, it had hardly silenced him. He gave several hundred lectures around the country in the months after the book's publication. And why not? By this time, his days in Mississippi were numbered. Although the trustees abandoned their efforts to bring him to heel once they heard from his lawyer, Silver, weary of the pressure, had left Mississippi by the following year to take a job at Notre Dame University, in Indiana.

If southern professors were less outspoken than they might have been, Silver's ordeal suggests why. Heroism was hard work. Even before Silver gave his speech, *New York Times* reporter Johnny

Popham told Bennett Wall, "He's a great guy, Bennett, and some day some historians must record his magnificent role at Oxford, indeed single him out for honoring solely in that context—Lord, when you think of the pressures and crises he has met, and the skill with which he handled the whole thing in the highest interests and devotion to the real meaning of pedagogy and just plain decent civilization."[27]

It takes nothing away from Silver's courage to point out that he drew support from the community to which he belonged: his handful of allies at the University of Mississippi, along with professors at other institutions, as well as national organizations—the AAUP, the ACLU, the American Friends Service Committee. Writing to Bertram H. Davis at the AAUP when his troubles were nearly over, Silver said that without the AAUP and other organizations that lent support, "I would have been a lost soul in Mississippi from the beginning. It is pretty damned hard to fight a whole community by yourself."[28]

Two weeks after Silver's dramatic speech in Asheville, President John F. Kennedy was assassinated in Dallas. The *New York Times* asked James Baldwin for a comment, and June Shagaloff was with him when he met two reporters, one from the *Times*, the other from a wire service, in a friend's Manhattan apartment. Baldwin went into a bedroom and typed out a statement. He handed a carbon to Shagaloff as he reemerged. A nation that had not been roused to act by bombings in Alabama and the assassination of Medgar Evers had finally been stirred, he said. "It is entirely possible that if we *had* been aroused by these events, our President would still be alive." He also gave a warning: "If we, the President's survivors, do not have the courage to continue the work to which he has set his hand, the effect of this assassination will be nothing less than a *coup d'etat* on the part of the extreme right. . . ."[29]

The president's death shook the country profoundly. What would it mean for the movement? The signs were not clear. Was Kennedy's assassination, as Baldwin feared, a sign that right-wing extremism was escalating? In the face of the right-wing threat, what could be expected from the new southern president, Texan Lyndon Baines Johnson, a man under intense political pressure? Johnson would have to submit himself to the voters within a year, and his most formidable Republican opponent was Senator Barry Goldwater, who stood on the right end of the Republican wing. Meanwhile, U.S. involvement in the Vietnam War was deepening. By the summer of 1964, Johnson would seek a resolution authorizing more aggressive action while at the same time asking Congress to approve a new civil rights act. The one move would eventually undermine the other, as the war diverted political attention from civil rights. But that outcome still lay in the future in the spring of 1964, as the Mississippi movement laid plans that would test the new president's support: the Mississippi Project—or, as it came to be called, Freedom Summer.

Within the Student Nonviolent Coordinating Committee, the most radical of the organizations involved in the Mississippi Project, there had been debate about whether the whole plan was a good idea. How would bringing hundreds of white college students to Mississippi affect the developing movement? Would local Negro leaders falter, and lose confidence and control? Yet without federal protection from the coalition of Klansmen and Mississippi law enforcement, the killings would go on.

No one who had worked for civil rights in Mississippi could fail to understand the danger the summer volunteers would face in the closed society. Most of them were white, but that would be no protection. Staying with Negro families, teaching Negro children in Freedom Schools, registering Negro voters for a "Freedom vote," they would challenge racial division by their very presence. They could expect hostility and scorn; they could expect to be arrested, to be injured, perhaps to die. Would the federal government, which had done so little to protect the movement, intervene to protect these white students from elite colleges?

Few had pressed harder for federal intervention than Howard Zinn, the history professor who, with James Baldwin, had watched federal agents standing by at Selma. Earlier, Zinn had seen the need for federal action when the SRC sent him to Albany, Georgia. There he heard chilling stories from two young SNCC workers trying to register voters in surrounding Terrell County. Someone in a truck tried to run over one of them and, failing in that, beat him up. At a voter-registration meeting in Sasser, a small community in Terrell County, the sheriff appeared with a dozen white men and began taking down names. With reporters on hand watching, the sheriff broke up the meeting. As those present left the church, a deputy sheriff told one of the Negroes, "I know you. We're going to get some of you." A few days later, two SNCC field-workers were arrested. Finally and belatedly, the Department of Justice asked a federal judge to order law enforcement officials not to intimidate Terrell County residents who wanted to vote. The judge refused.

"Two days later," Zinn would write, "a church that was used as a voter-registration center in neighboring Lee County burned to the ground. . . . Two weeks later, in another night shooting incident, the homes of four Negro families active in voter registration were riddled by bullets, while children slept inside." A shotgun blast wounded a SNCC worker. The same week, the Mount Olive Church in Sasser went up in flames.[30]

At the time, Zinn was teaching constitutional law at Spelman. Applying the material of his classroom to the situation at hand, he came to a startling conclusion. "It suddenly struck me that constitutional rights were being violated and the federal government was absent—not only absent, but complicit," he would recall. The federal government was supposed to protect Americans' civil rights, wasn't it? Zinn called the national office of the ACLU and said he wanted to talk with someone who knew constitutional law. William Kunstler, emerging on the civil rights scene as a dynamic force, came on the line and told Zinn he was right.[31]

The SRC was not immediately convinced that the theme of the report Zinn was writing on Albany ought to be the irresponsibility of the federal government, instead of the hostility between Negroes and whites. But in the end, Leslie Dunbar issued the report with a strong introduction. The November 1962 report portrayed a southern police state in action. While local law enforcement officials rode roughshod over the rights of Negroes and some whites, the federal government had failed to act. Zinn called for prosecution of local officials. He called on the government to station federal agents in Albany to protect those who were being intimidated. In fact, he called for a creation of a special unit of federal agents who would protect civil rights (a proposal that Dunbar did not support). He asked for a presidential address on desegregation. The *New York Times* picked up his criticism, including comments critical of the FBI (which attempted to discredit him by spreading the rumor that he was communist).[32]

But instead of strengthening its support for the Albany movement, the federal government actually turned on SNCC, indicting nine people working in the Albany movement on misguided charges. To the movement, the Albany indictments represented a major betrayal by the Justice Department. Zinn tried to recruit Yale and Harvard law professors to pay a call on Attorney General Robert Kennedy to protest. He found the professors he approached sympathetic but unable to make the trip. As an alternative, he suggested that SNCC "do something dramatic in Washington." Increasingly, he felt that SNCC ought to reconsider its demonstrations in the Deep South. Beatings and jailings seemed to have little redemptive effect on white segregationists. As he wrote to SNCC's Jim Forman and John Lewis on October 1, 1963, "Something very dramatic, very stark, very intense needs to be done in Washington to make clear that *here* is the root of Southern repression. Not Congress, not anyone; but the executive branch, which has the power, and which is not using it. I think people like James Baldwin and others would go along with something dramatic."[33]

But SNCC's focus at that point had been Freedom Day at Selma. There Zinn, watching with Baldwin, again saw evidence of the executive branch's failure to act. Afterwards, he published an article in the *New Republic* calling for a special federal force—a thousand agents, at least, "to stand guard throughout the Deep South in protection of the constitutional rights of the people of that region." The *New Republic* endorsed his call. True, such a force might foment more white rebellion and less willingness among local police to enforce the law, the magazine acknowledged. It could even lead to "a full-fledged national police force." Still, perhaps that would be necessary to "secure the Negro his full rights as a citizen of the United States." This was a strong statement, and the *New Republic*, long a member of the country's liberal establishment, was a strong platform from which to make it. Burke Marshall, the assistant attorney general in charge of civil rights, took the article seriously enough to write a lengthy response, which the *New Republic* published in its issue of November 16, 1963. Marshall defended the Justice Department's record in the South and labeled "a national police force" an "extreme alternative."[34]

In the spring of 1964, however, Marshall acknowledged to an audience at Columbia University that the restrained Kennedy policy had failed. The executive branch had tried to play by the traditional rules of federal-state relations, but some southern states had flatly defied federal law. In the face of outright and widespread defiance, what could the federal government do? Very little, Marshall appeared to be saying. Even if Congress were to grant the federal government greater enforcement powers, would that be a good idea? He doubted it. Aside from the enormous strain on federal resources, policing the states would give the federal government enormous power to define the nation's political life.[35]

But if the federal government did not intervene, who would protect southern Negroes and the whites working with them to secure their rights? "Right now a Negro or white civil rights worker in the Deep South risks his life every moment with no chance of protection by the Federal Government," Zinn wrote in a long letter published by the *New York Times* on February 19, 1964.[36] In the May 18 issue of the *Nation*, he offered a litany of the kind of violence he believed the federal government could bring to a halt if it tried.

In towns in Georgia, James Williams had his leg broken by police. . . ; Rev. Samuel Wells was kicked and beaten by police. . . . Mrs. Slater King, five months pregnant, was punched and kicked by a deputy sheriff, . . . and later lost her baby. In Winona, Mississippi, Mrs.

Fannie Lou Hamer and Annelle Ponder were beaten by police. Men, women and children were clubbed in Danville, Virginia, by police. In a Clarksdale, Miss. police station, a 19-year-old Negro girl was forced to pull off her clothes and was then whipped. The list is endless.

The FBI had "faithfully recorded it all," and nothing of consequence had resulted. Police brutality was not new in America, he acknowledged, but that did not make it right. Drawing a comparison so often made in these years, he said, "It is very much like the Germans and the death camps. There they are, all around us, but we honestly don't see them."

He had an idea what to do about it. The federal government needed to interpose itself between citizens and the police. Once again, Zinn proposed "a nation-wide system of federal defenders" who would have the power the FBI already had but did not use: the power to arrest violators of federal laws, including police officers who violated citizens' rights. "Either we put up with jailing and brutality for thousands of Negroes and whites who have done nothing but ask for rights asserted in our Constitution, or we put into jail—*without* brutality—enough local policemen and state officials to make clear what the federal system really is." That job was the president's.[37]

In *John F. Kennedy and the Second Reconstruction*, historian Carl M. Brauer would single out Zinn as the only critic of Kennedy's policy to specify what the federal government ought to do.[38] But Zinn's role in the movement was larger than that. When he described it himself in later writings, his description would fail to capture the full extent of his engagement. In his writing at the time, he was even more self-effacing; he barely suggested his role in the events he described (though sometimes he appeared as a witnessing "I"). He had kept himself out of his articles because, he explained later, he had been taught, as an academic, to stand back. But he was also sensitive to his role as a white man in a predominantly black movement. Whatever the reasons for his reticence, he showed no inclination toward celebrity, and none came his way. So quietly did he play his role that later historians would miss it altogether.

As a member of SNCC's advisory committee, Zinn stood near the heart of the action.[39] Even after his move to Boston, he made strategy suggestions, especially regarding publicity, the area he had taken on as his particular province. In Boston, he was in an even better position to connect SNCC to intellectual centers in the North, mustering support from academic and political communities there. As Freedom Summer approached, he conceived a plan to bring the Mississippi struggle to the capital—and show why the federal government needed to intervene.

A fellow scholar-activist at Spelman, white historian Staughton Lynd, had what he later characterized as a "comradely difference" with Zinn over so much emphasis on federal intervention.[40] Son of prominent sociologists Helen and Robert Lynd, Lynd had joined Zinn on the Spelman faculty after the sit-ins began in order to be close to the developing movement. To Lillian Smith, he was one of several outsiders who had led SNCC's "starry-eyed" young people astray with "a mixed up mess of 19th century anarchism and 1930s communism."[41] Smith's hostility was odd since Lynd and his wife, Alice, were committed Quakers. Smith, for her part, was a member of pacifist CORE's advisory board and had recommended nonviolence as a strategy long before it was adopted in a widespread way. Nor was Lynd a communist. But he *was* a radical, and his radicalism set him apart from Smith's Cold War liberalism.

Committed to radical, local transformation, Lynd questioned the wisdom of emphasizing federal intervention over "building a strong grassroots organization." He told Zinn that he might wind up owing Zinn his life for "putting forward the question of protection so early and so insistently." Yet he also said that "there is no clear sense . . . as to whether the purpose of the Summer Project is to provoke Federal intervention or to build the Mississippi movement." While asking for federal intervention was a "sound tactical demand," more fundamental changes were needed. After Freedom Summer was over, Lynd would write C. Vann Woodward, "I have long had a difference with Howard about massive Federal intervention, he feeling clear about its necessity, I (much more confusedly) feeling that what was needed was a change in the economic substratum of daily life—comparable to 40 A[cres] and a mule—which would set Negroes and whites free to find a new pattern of relationship by themselves."[42]

Zinn shared Lynd's vision of radical transformation, but he thought that demanding federal intervention could help to build the movement and safeguard people while they built the movement.[43] The two men were not really so far apart. Lynd knew as well as Zinn the need for protection—he would make out his will before he left for Mississippi that summer to direct the Freedom Schools.[44] And so, despite their comradely difference, as Freedom Summer approached, Lynd helped Zinn and SNCC's Julian Bond mount a carefully staged appeal for federal intervention in Mississippi.

Zinn's first notion had been to collect a group of "nationally known figures" to meet with President Johnson and urge him to exercise a firm hand in Mississippi.[45] Lynd floated the idea to Arthur Waskow, a research fellow at the left-leaning Institute for Policy Studies in Washington. Waskow suggested an alternative: sending the president a registered letter, without any publicity, asking for protection. That way, they could hold in reserve the threat of publicity if he didn't do anything. At the same time, they should invite all the candidates for the presidency to come to Mississippi during the summer to observe what was happening.[46]

By April, the plan had shifted. Zinn and Bond were now hard at work putting together a showcase hearing in Washington. Before a panel of leading intellectuals, Mississippians would bear witness to the violence directed at them for trying to exercise their constitutional rights. It was a good idea, Waskow thought, though he did not want them to abandon the letter to the president and the invitations to the candidates. "Keep kicking the Establishment in the shins; and if someday it falls over from the pain, fine. In the meantime it will keep hobbling along in the right direction."[47]

The letter to the president was forthcoming. Oscar Handlin signed it, and so did several of his colleagues from Harvard, along with faculty members from Boston University, Boston College, Brandeis University, Tufts University, and the University of Texas. Ready as they were to sign a letter, the professors were harder to pin down for the hearing. Near the end of April, Zinn told Julian Bond that the Harvard law professors he had hoped would testify as legal experts could not. One would be grading blue books while the other was involved in commencement and faculty meetings. Even if they had not been otherwise occupied, the professors he had asked could not give him what he wanted: an expert statement that the president had the constitutional power to intervene on behalf of the civil rights workers. Neither would commit himself on this key point without further study. Zinn badly needed a legal scholar who would be willing to make the point. He had nearly called Charles Black, a southerner and law professor at Yale; they had met in the home of Yale dean Eugene Rostow, and Zinn thought him "a very good man." Black had gone on record saying that the attorney general had more powers than he had yet used in the civil rights area. But Zinn had decided Black's invitation to the hearing ought to come officially from SNCC or the Council of Federated Organizations (COFO), the coalition organizing Freedom Summer. Better for Bond to make the call. Better, in fact, for Bond to run the operation from Atlanta, with Zinn contacting people around Boston when that was helpful. Zinn did offer suggestions for the panel. A social psychologist like Thomas Pettigrew would be good, as would Jim Silver, who could talk about Mississippi's closed society. Perhaps actor Sidney Poitier would join the jury.[48]

A lot of energy was going into this project, with little assurance of success. Another group had tried this very strategy earlier, in May 1962, with no apparent effect. The Congress of Racial Equality, which was also participating in Freedom Summer, had asked former first lady Eleanor Roosevelt to chair the Commission of Inquiry into the Administration of Justice in the Freedom Struggle. Commission members included psychologist Kenneth B. Clark and lawyer Joseph Rauh, among others. Over two days in Washington, civil rights activists described reprisals against them and the failure of the Justice Department and FBI to come to their aid. The press paid little attention, and even Eleanor Roosevelt was unable to attract congressmen to the hearings.[49]

Despite this ominous example, SNCC moved on with plans for the hearing. On May 4, Zinn wrote to Clyde Ferguson, dean of Howard's law school, to see if he would serve as interrogator. "A number of Northern liberal academicians have always claimed that strong executive action in the deep South would bring white uprisings, near-warfare, or extreme social dislocation. Tom Pettigrew has argued as I have—that firm action will, in the long run and perhaps even in the short run, diminish sharp Southern white reaction."[50] Ferguson turned down the invitation. June was a bad time for academicians, he said; he had another obligation on the day of the hearing. Thus far, with the hearing only a month away, sociologist David Riesman and historian Henry Steele Commager had both declined the invitation. C. Vann Woodward had promised to come, but in the end he canceled in order to attend another meeting.[51]

But the final lineup turned out to be strong. It included Robert Coles, who by this time was a research psychiatrist at Harvard University Health Services and already deep into his extraordinary documentation of the movement. Coles had begun to publish articles in which he tried to counter a common suspicion that young civil rights activists were little better than juvenile delinquents acting out of neurotic impulses. He had signed on to counsel volunteers at orientation and throughout the summer project. He had made a serious commitment to the movement.[52] Coles was joined on the panel by Joseph Heller, best-selling author of the novel *Catch-22*, a satiric indictment of war; anarchist Paul Goodman, author of *Growing Up Absurd*; New York journalist Murray Kempton, and several others. Harold Taylor of the Eleanor Roosevelt Foundation presided. The panel gathered at the National Theatre in Washington on June 8, 1964, just as the students began traveling south for Freedom Summer. A large audience was in attendance, and television cameras recorded the event, which took place on the set of *Camelot*, a musical about political idealism and betrayal.

The heart of the Mississippi movement was there on the National

Theatre stage that day. There were Lawrence Guyot and Fannie Lou Hamer, and there was Robert Moses, who introduced the others. Jimmy Travis was there to tell how he had been shot in the head and shoulder as he drove toward Greenville from a voter registration meeting. Greene Brewer described how he and his brother were bludgeoned by a store owner who apparently just didn't like their attitude ("When a damn nigger goes North and comes back, he gets beside himself, and he gets where he can't respect white folk," the man had said before he launched his attack). George Greene told about his beating by a police officer in Ruleville. Fannie Lou Hamer recounted her arrest on her way from a voter-registration workshop. Taken to jail, she was beaten with a blackjack by two Negro prisoners under the supervision of a state highway patrolman. Mrs. Louis Allen described the death of her husband, killed for witnessing the murder of Herbert Lee. Bessie Turner told about being beaten at city hall. Hartman Turnbow told how he was arrested on a charge of firebombing his own house. Mrs. Vera Pigee told of being arrested for boycotting stores to protest the exclusion of Negro school bands from the Christmas parade; then she was hit by a gas station attendant after she asked him for her change. When she reported that incident to the police, the chief of police arrested *her* for disturbing the peace. The stories, told in detail, built up a picture of lawlessness and corruption.

Lawyers then took the stand, stating their opinions that the federal government had the power to intervene in Mississippi. One congressman, William F. Ryan from New York, stopped in to say he was drafting a letter asking the president to send marshals to Mississippi for the summer.

Throughout the hearing, members of the panel occasionally asked questions that seemed innocently naive, as if they had no real idea what was happening in Mississippi. "Is it possible that a white man in Mississippi can commit any kind of crime against the colored person and escape without punishment?" asked Joseph Heller. To Mrs. Pigee's story of being hit by the gas station attendant, Robert Coles asked, "[D]o you think that there is something wrong with this man's mind that would cause him to suddenly leap out and strike you?"

Despite the presence of nationally known figures and leaders of the Mississippi movement, local and national media largely ignored the production. Television stations showed a few brief clips, and transcripts of the hearing were hand-delivered to the Justice Department and the gates of the White House.[53] A week later, in the House of Representatives, California congressman Phil Burton read a portion of the hearing transcript into the *Congressional Record.* The next day, June 16, several other members of Congress rose in succession to place other portions of the transcript into the record. In all, twenty pages of transcript were read into the *Congressional Record.*[54] President Johnson read the *Congressional Record* every morning. It is possible that the testimony at the hearing entered his thoughts as he was called upon to respond to the violence about to break in Mississippi. If it did, he gave no sure sign of it. Far from committing himself to intervention, as Zinn had hoped, he ignored the appeal altogether.

Zinn himself wrote a long account of the hearing, but no one published it. By the time his agent sent it to the *Reporter* in early July, three summer workers had disappeared in Mississippi. On a routing sheet, an editor commented (with a smugness characteristic of such editorial comments at the *Reporter*), "It's about a busload of Mississippi Negroes who testified in Washington on June 8 before a panel of citizens . . . about the need for federal protection etc. in Miss. But all this is all too well known now."[55]

The deaths of James E. Chaney, Andrew Goodman, and Michael Schwerner finally brought the federal government into Mississippi. FBI agents and navy men swarmed across the landscape around Philadelphia, Mississippi, searching for the bodies of the three volunteers. The FBI set up an office in Jackson. After the bodies were found, the state refused to prosecute the men implicated in the murders. The federal government then brought charges in federal court. Seven defendants were convicted, among them the deputy sheriff.[56]

In July, the Congress enacted the Civil Rights Act of 1964, guaranteeing equal access to public accommodations and jobs. Despite this seeming victory, the summer left a bitter taste, sharpened when Democrats refused to seat the Mississippi Freedom Democratic Party's delegation at the August convention. Staughton Lynd would ultimately see Freedom Summer as a tragedy in the Greek sense—"a good thing with a tragic flaw." Bringing in white northerners had proved an effective strategy; without question, the summer project had helped pass the 1964 Civil Rights Act and the Voting Rights Act that would follow in 1965. At the same time, the summer project had opened the door to greater influence by northern liberals.[57]

All along, northern liberals had worried about the movement's potential for radicalism. The Kennedys and J. Edgar Hoover had focused their own concern on alleged communists in the movement, even pressing Martin Luther King to separate himself from advisers like Stanley Levison, once associated with the Communist Party. In fact, the radicalism of the southern movement was not at all rooted in communism of the party kind. SNCC's own particular brand of radicalism was more akin to utopian socialism or anarchism, or the democratic egalitarianism of the Highlander Center. But it was still radicalism, and northern liberals worried about it.

In *The Making of Black Revolutionaries*, James Forman, SNCC's most passionate chronicler, would tell of a meeting in a congressman's office that summer, when Arthur Schlesinger Jr., out of the blue, brought up the work of the National Lawyers Guild (a group often Red-baited) in the Mississippi Project. "There are many of us who have spent years fighting the communists," Schlesinger said. "We worked hard during the thirties and forties fighting forces such as the National Lawyers Guild. We find it unpardonable that you would work with them."[58]

Robert Penn Warren, who was writing a book on the movement, heard from *New York Times* reporter David Halberstam that the National Council of Churches, a sponsor of the project orientation in Oxford, Ohio, was worried about SNCC. Halberstam had covered the sit-ins in Nashville in 1960, then made his name nationally with early skeptical reports on the war in Vietnam. Back in the United States,

Halberstam (later the author of an affectionate chronicle of the young movement activists, *The Children*)[59] told Warren that some of the students at Oxford seemed "so alienated that they might just as well, psychologically, have been Communists—because they hated their own country so much, and distrusted its every word and action." There were those in the National Council of Churches (itself the target of Red-baiting) who were concerned, he said, about what they called "the hotheads from SNICK."[60] Without question, the attacks on SNCC were escalating, both in the press and behind the scenes. Even C. Vann Woodward, civil libertarian though he was (but never fond of communists), worried. When the summer of '64 was over, he asked a surprised Staughton Lynd, "Staughton, what are we going to do about the communists in SNCC?"[61]

By summer's end, Jim Silver, Howard Zinn, Staughton Lynd, and Robert Coles—engaged intellectuals all—had left the South. That fall, Alfred A. Knopf published Zinn's *The Southern Mystique*. In it Zinn put forth a thesis that directly countered Silver's point in *The Closed Society*. Silver had described Mississippi as set apart from the national will—so set apart that the nation would have to force change on it. Zinn argued that the South was not so special, so different. Americans ought to shrug off the idea of a "Southern mystique." The South only exaggerated some of the characteristics of the nation, including racism. The South was "a distorted mirror image of the North." The southern mystique—the idea that white southerners were innately violent or xenophobic—was only an excuse for inaction. The truth was that "compromise and vacillation on the race question are intrinsic parts of our national political heritage." If national leaders failed to act now, they followed a long tradition: "The Negro has always been a hitchhiker in American history."[62]

Reviewing *The Southern Mystique* for the *New York Herald Tribune's Book Week*, Ralph Ellison remarked on Zinn's optimism about executive action.[63] Zinn was "far too charitable toward politicians' motives," Ellison said. In his first long political piece since he took on Irving Howe, Ellison disagreed with Zinn on several other counts. For all the myths and mysteries around it, the southern mystique *was* real. It worked its will through *"actions,* the goal of which is the manipulation of power." Southern politicians knew how to use the mystique, their inheritance from the past, to hold on to their power. Zinn paid too much attention to psychological theories that ignored the past, which had made the present culture what it was. The movement itself came out of the past. The *Brown* decision had not transformed Negroes from obsequious "Sambos" into political actors. Negroes had been preparing themselves for freedom all along.

Yet, unable as Zinn was still to see Negroes complexly, Ellison admired his willingness to go south to live in a Negro community and become part of the change that was happening there. In his effort to understand both what *was* happening and what *could* happen—"to forge, for himself at least, a fresh concept of man"—Zinn stood apart from other intellectuals. His was "an act of intellectual responsibility in an area that has been cast outside the range of intellectual scrutiny through our timidity of mind in the face of American cultural diversity." Ellison sympathized with Zinn's "attempt to do pragmatically what our best critical minds have failed even to recognize as important."

Zinn had stirred in Ellison a response that demonstrated how closely the novelist had observed what was happening in the years since the *Brown* decision, and how deeply he had thought about it. He used the occasion of this review to launch a bitter indictment of northern intellectuals. The same northern intellectuals who found French existentialists' idea of *engagement* so fascinating had failed to "involve themselves either by their writings or their activities . . . in our own great national struggle. . . . The events set in motion by the Supreme Court decision of 1954 and accelerated by the Civil Rights Act of 1964, and which are now transforming not only the South but the entire nation—events that are creating a revolution not only in our race relations but in our political morality—have found them ominously silent."

What C. Vann Woodward had wrongly called the Second Reconstruction was nearly over. As in the earlier Reconstruction, there had come a compromise—"the Compromise of 1964," Woodward termed it in an essay he was writing for Mississippian Willie Morris at *Harper's*. This new compromise took the form of *tokenism*, or "nominal compliance without fundamental change." Ten years after *Brown*, in the old Confederate states, only 2 percent of Negro children were attending school with white children. National sympathy with Negroes had risen during the Birmingham crisis but had quickly receded. As summer riots erupted in northern cities, the radical right gained strength. Woodward, prone to optimism, still believed that this Reconstruction was not likely to end with as little effect as the first. Negroes were more politically powerful now and could no longer be sold out so easily.

Sharing a draft of the article with his old friend Bill Carleton, a retired University of Florida professor who himself wrote for magazines, Woodward worried that he did not display in it enough feeling for the movement. Not to worry, Carleton said: "As to its lack of CARING, of ENGAGEMENT—forget that nonsense. It does not belong in a piece like this one." What did worry Carleton about the piece was its abstraction; he missed the concrete stories and details that would draw in the reader. Woodward had woven a "brilliantly clarifying pattern," but would the article lose the average reader? "This is the kind of writing which brings one to the top of the intelligentsia today," he wrote Woodward; "but socially it may be too bad, another trend widening the gulf between the intellectuals and the folk. If I were the editor of *Harper's* I would be grateful for it, knowing at the same time that I could not use many articles that abstract without losing my readers."[64]

Harper's ran that risk, and the article appeared in April 1965, in a special issue marking the hundredth anniversary of the Confederacy's defeat at Appomatox.[65] Shortly after it appeared on the stands, history cut in: on March 7, movement marchers from Selma, bound for Montgomery, fell beneath the blows of Alabama State Police on the Edmund Pettus Bridge. The day would be called Bloody Sunday. Television viewers watching *Judgment at Nuremberg*, a movie about the trials of Nazi war criminals, suddenly saw, as the news broke in,

American policemen beating American citizens. Across the country, demonstrators marched in protest, their numbers increasing after a white Unitarian minister from Boston, the Reverend James J. Reeb, died from a beating outside the Silver Moon bar in Selma. Stirred by all these events, President Lyndon Johnson appeared before Congress to ask for a voting rights bill. After a federal judge issued an order protecting the marchers, Johnson supplied federal troops to protect the marchers who again started out from Selma on March 21 to walk the fifty miles to the capital.[66]

It would take four days to reach the edge of Montgomery. On the next to the last full day of walking, Zinn, traveling in the South for the *Nation,* joined the three hundred marchers allowed by court order to walk down the two-lane stretch of the road. It had been raining and cold, and the ground where they camped was muddy. Fires ringed the field—the fires of their soldier-guards. At dawn of the next day, the fires burned low; the moon pushed the clouds aside. Marchers prepared to walk, some barefoot, to the accompaniment of an army helicopter. With every hour more marchers joined them. The sun would come out, then rain would flash hard, and the sun would come out again.[67] For the last night, the marchers camped at a Catholic compound, the City of St. Jude. Harry Belafonte had arranged a performance. He, Joan Baez, and Sammy Davis Jr. all sang, and James Baldwin spoke. When Martin Luther King asked the crowd, "What do you want?," twenty thousand voices answered, "Freedom now!"

The following day, the rain stopped but the sky remained overcast as the marchers trudged into Montgomery. Thousands of marchers from all over the country poured into the city. A contingent of historians had arrived—several dozen, marching near the front of the line under a hand-lettered sign, "U.S. Historians." The marchers passed first through a Negro neighborhood where young girls in their Sunday dresses joined thousands of others along the road, some crying out, "At last, at last!" while others wept. In the business district, those whites who had not fled the city or retreated indoors stood silent, as if, one historian said, "they were watching a funeral procession."[68]

John Hope Franklin, "scared to death," clutched the hand of the woman next to him.[69] James Baldwin strode alongside singer Joan Baez. Ralph Bunche walked at the head of the line with Martin Luther King. The marchers arrived at the gleaming white capitol, where King asked the crowd to listen carefully while he drew a history lesson from *The Strange Career of Jim Crow*. Woodward, present with the other historians, had no idea if King knew he was there, but he was proud to be mentioned at this hour.[70]

Speaking near the steps of the capitol, King told the thousands assembled before him: "We are on the move now. The bombing of our churches will not deter us. We are on the move now. The bombing of our homes will not dissuade us. We are on the move now. The beating and killing of our clergymen and young people will not divert us. We are on the move now."[71]

That night, a white woman from Detroit, Viola Liuzzo, driving another marcher back to Selma, was shot and killed on the lonely highway.

On May 26, Congress passed a voting rights bill that authorized federal officials to register voters turned down by local registrars.

In mid-August, in Los Angeles, across the continent from the former Confederate states, fire and violence swept through the large black section known as Watts. Property damage approached $225 million. Nearly nine hundred people suffered injuries. Thirty-four died.[72]

The movement for racial equality had not ended, but one stage of it had. The nation's attention would shift north and west, to the cities where riots blazed. While American planes bombed North Vietnam, military tanks lumbered through American streets. Kenneth Clark's *Dark Ghetto* would become the book of the hour. James Baldwin had told reporter Fern Eckman that he was writing a book on the FBI— he had "an *enormous* file" in his closet.[73] He never wrote the book. He would write other essays and novels, but *The Fire Next Time* would mark the height of his public influence, and he would often seem, in later life, troubled and small. Both Baldwin and Ralph Ellison would lose standing in the rush for Black Power. Ellison died without completing his second novel; a portion of it, titled *Juneteenth*, was released in 1999 after his death.

After an initial round of speeches, Jim Silver declined to become a fixture in public life, although later he told his Mississippi story in a memoir, *Running Scared*. In *Children of Crisis*, Robert Coles brought together experiences of young people involved in the movement. From there he went on to travel the world, studying the spiritual, cultural, and political life of children.

Howard Zinn wrote the first published history of SNCC, *SNCC: The New Abolitionists*, in which he presented SNCC as a group of "youngsters" fired up by "idealism." This movement was not like radical movements in the thirties, he asserted. SNCC workers "have not become followers of any dogma, have not pledged themselves to any rigid ideological system." True, they were "young radicals; the word 'revolution' occurs again and again in their speech. Yet they have no party, no ideology, no creed."[74]

Robert Penn Warren published *Who Speaks for the Negro?*—his account of in-depth interviews he conducted with movement leaders in the North and the South. The book's sales were slow, and Warren's greater contribution was the interviews themselves, preserved at Yale. Lawrence Reddick never wrote his history of the movement, though his many boxes of records were placed, after his death, at the Schomburg Center, a resource for other scholars.

Pauli Murray, critical of sexism within the civil rights movement, turned her energies to the women's movement. She eventually became an Episcopalian priest. Lorraine Hansberry died of cancer in 1965. Before Lillian Smith died in 1966, she not only turned against SNCC for coming under the influence of "intruders," but also resigned from the national advisory committee of CORE because CORE delegates had endorsed the right of self-defense.

In September 1966, C. Vann Woodward wrote to Robert Penn Warren, "The reaction is on us and strong, Northern liberals in full retreat and nothing in sight to run them back. Colored ranks in confusion or knifing each other."[75] In January 1967, in an essay in *Harper's*,

Woodward announced that a "great withdrawal" had set in. Distracted by Vietnam, put off by Black Power, the New Left and white liberals had withdrawn from the struggle for racial equality. "A great stillness descended upon quarters long noted for outspoken opinions." Thus ended, for the time being, what Woodward considered another of those periodic "love affairs with other classes" to which American intellectuals were prone.[76]

Kenneth Clark, too, saw a liberal retreat, and blamed it on the shift of the movement's center to the North. He also blamed the media for placing Black Power on center stage.[77] As the Black Power movement gathered strength, Harold Cruse brought out *The Crisis of the Negro Intellectual* in 1967. He attacked Lorraine Hansberry and other African American intellectuals for their support of integration, and he traced their corruption to the influence of the Communist Party.

The hope some African American intellectuals had placed in Africa proved an illusion. Africans had too many problems of their own to lend a hand to African Americans. Maya Angelou came home from Ghana. Julian Mayfield stayed longer, but he, too, eventually left Ghana. Fine novelist though he was, Mayfield, like Horace Cayton, would be soon nearly forgotten. Langston Hughes, John Killens, and Amiri Baraka would fare better. John Henrik Clarke would edit a 1968 book that poured out the long-standing resentment that black intellectuals felt toward white liberals: *William Styron's Nat Turner: Ten Black Writers Respond.*

Looking back from the early 1990s, Kenneth B. Clark, such a key figure in the movement for racial equality, wrote darkly,

My beloved wife is dead and my career is nearing an end. Reluctantly, I am forced to face the likely possibility that the United States will never rid itself of racism and reach true integration. I look back and I shudder at how naïve we all were in our belief in the steady progress racial minorities would make through programs of litigation and education, and while I very much hope for the emergence of a revived civil rights movement with innovative programs

and dedicated leaders, I am forced to recognize that my life has, in
fact, been a series of glorious defeats.[78]

John Hope Franklin was more optimistic. Named to head President Bill Clinton's initiative on race in the late 1990s, he traveled the country, holding hearings, meeting people, and being barraged by criticism from every side. Nearing the end of that work, he spoke one summer evening in 1998 to a small crowd at a Washington bookstore near DuPont Circle. His son was with him, standing by while Franklin—elegant, poised, and eighty-three—talked on his feet for more than an hour without any sign of fatigue.

His best-read work, *From Slavery to Freedom*, was still in print and undergoing revision for yet one more edition, and Franklin spoke about what writing that book had meant to him. It had been a powerful experience—the greatest intellectual experience of his life. As he wrote, all those years had passed before his eyes and through his mind: "I internalized that experience in a way that would last me a lifetime. I've seen it all—there's no room in my life to be shocked," he told the little group crowded between the bookstore's shelves.

Someone asked Franklin how he felt about the country's racial situation today after traveling far and wide. He was encouraged, he said—reassured by the evidence he saw that Americans in some communities were working together. He spoke of the changes he had seen in his own lifetime. There had been a time in this town when he could not have gone to the Indian restaurant down the street, or to the theater, or the symphony. "I have an aesthetic appreciation when I see a black man using a jackhammer," he said.[79]

When his commission made its report to the president soon after, however, the White House underlined, dryly, its bitter truth:

Race and ethnicity continue to be salient predictors of well-being
in American society. Non-Hispanic whites and Asians tend to expe-
rience advantages in health, education, and economic status relative
to blacks, Hispanics, and American Indians.

Over the second half of the 20th century, black Americans have made substantial progress relative to whites in many areas. But this progress generally slowed, or even reversed between the mid-1970s and early 1990s. Data from the 1990s show renewed gains, but in many cases large disparities persist.[80]

POSTSCRIPT

Traveling in the South for this book, I could not escape the contrast between the hopes of the past and the reality of the present: some communities that were a dramatic part of the southern movement are still mired in deep poverty. My young daughter, on the other hand, saw what I nearly missed. "They sure like campaigns," she said, pointing out the election signs in so many yards. Some things have, after all, changed. Not nearly enough has changed, though, and intellectuals bear as much responsibility for that as anyone else, and perhaps more. Despite all the talk about race—and the period I have described did mark a break in the silence—race remains, in many contexts, the great unmentionable. Eric Deggans, a television critic I know and an African American, has summed up our present state of affairs as well as anyone. Describing the PBS documentary series *Africans in America: America's Journey through Slavery*, he wrote in the *St. Petersburg Times*, "Three hundred years later, we're still tongue-tied on racial issues, struggling to reconcile a legacy of hate, prejudice and division that hobbles everyone involved."[1]

Since his days as a student at the university where I teach, Deggans and I have talked from time to time about race, and so, as I thought about why we still fall so short of facing our racial divisions squarely, I turned to him. "My only thought," he wrote to me,

> is that the main discomfort in discussing race seems to be the disconnect between the America that is and the America we'd like to believe in. America can't look in the mirror and admit its current success is built on the backs of minorities and poor white people. That's why intellectual discussions about race are always going to be hard. Because an honest dialogue will eventually lead to picking at the

bones of modern society. Intellectuals are as invested in the system as any middle class person in society. . . .

I think he has it right, and I would add to his analysis only this—that intellectuals' failure to confront the inequalities of American life is part of a larger failure. As a class, American intellectuals—who claim social resources in return for the time to think and reflect on the culture—have abandoned their responsibility for society even more completely than they had in the 1950s and 1960s. A statement made by a University of Mississippi professor after the 1962 crisis there applies still to those intellectuals who work in academe. "The problem is that many faculty members in America have come to shirk their moral responsibilities," Russell H. Barrett wrote. "As American universities have developed more and more into trade schools of various quality, teachers have changed accordingly. They do their teaching and research so they will be 'successful' and not get into trouble."[2]

The professors I have encountered in my life as a professor in six institutions of higher learning are mostly careerists (or, more modestly, jobholders) concerned about their own tenure and standing in their profession. Seldom do they reach out to the communities of which they are geographically a part, much less to the larger society. In most research universities, professors can earn tenure only through publication by academic journals and university presses—neither effective ways of sharing knowledge or ideas with the public. Professors who write for magazines for the general public earn dual punishment: they do not get credit for the scholarly journal articles they could be writing, and they may be looked down upon for dabbling in journalism. Fiction writers (who have at times offered profound critiques of American culture) now often earn their living teaching in universities, too, and although they may publish with trade publishers, like other professors, they must keep an eye on their public personas, lest they become too indecorous (or political) for the academy. Thus those in the ivory tower become more and more distant from the society they ostensibly serve. Do universities not owe society anything other than research for its industries and job training for its children? Might there be some responsibility for publicly raising basic questions, for everyone to consider, about what we as a society are up to? That question rarely arises. Like other wage earners in society, academic researchers by and large do what they are paid to do, and, as we all know, he who pays the piper calls the tune.

Meanwhile, the publishing industry has moved farther and farther from any sense of obligation for the social enterprise. Publishers in the 1950s and 1960s were not indifferent to profit, but they were more independent, financially, than most leading publishing companies today. Their chief motive was to keep on going: they made enough to survive, to give their top officers a pleasant income and their lower employees a lesser one. That has all changed, dramatically: magazines and books for the general public for the most part emerge now from vast corporate factories; their goal is to make money for the company and its shareholders, and they do that by offering celebrities and advice on how to spend money. If intellectual life has retreated behind the walls of universities, if scholars and serious writers write mostly for each other, then trade publishers and magazines bear some responsibility for that. If publishers were to offer more thoughtful fare, on the other hand, how many readers would they have? Even professors don't read much any more, except in their fields of specialty (although, they might say in self-defense, that is partly because there is so little worth reading).

I am not sure our intellectual systems today—our educational institutions, our publishing industry—are attending any better to reality than they did in the 1950s and 1960s. I see little evidence that we, today, are responding adequately to the challenges of our own time: racism, still; environmental destruction; violent conflicts around the globe; nuclear weapons still poised for apocalypse. Cold War attitudes still dominate our political thought—that there is *an* American way and that it is the best way; that America has a treasure to offer the world—though we talk a good deal less now about democracy than about capitalism and technology. The apparent triumph of capitalism may have closed our thoughts up more tightly. At a time of enormous change, we respond with clichés. Stale ideas float through our national media like cigarette smoke after a party.

Has intellectual life disappeared altogether from the public sphere? Not quite. I detect it rising in little magazines and newsletters, in Internet chat rooms, in gatherings of people devoted to social change, in the same kinds of political communities that helped build the civil rights movement, even in pockets of university life. Once Americans break through the dominant paradigm (buy, consume, and to hell with the future), they begin to grapple with basic questions about the damage we are inflicting on the world and each other.

This book, then, should not be taken only as an argument for more political engagement by an intellectual class, although surely intellectuals, like everyone else, ought to take responsibility for the society they live in, and this book tells the story of some who did. But the story I have told suggests, too, that people designated as intellectuals often fail, not only in courage and compassion, but also in vision. We all had better take responsibility for thinking things through and not leave the job to those who are paid to do it. We all need to attend to the patterns of what we do, and where they come from and where they are leading us. This is the work of intellectuals, but whether we consider ourselves intellectuals or not, we had better all try to do it, not as an afterthought or a sideline or an amusement for idle hours, but as an activity on which life depends. We are not likely to do it well if we stay inside our furnished rooms, talking with our friends. Action sometimes makes the best crucible for thought. We may find, as the movement did, that we think best in the open air, on our feet.

June 2, 2000
Bloomington, Indiana

NOTES

All author's interviews were conducted between spring 1996 and spring 2000. Locations of manuscript collections cited are listed on p. 280.

Prologue

1. Cayton, *Long Old Road* (New York: Trident Press, 1965), pp. 271, 311.
2. Ibid., pp. 368–69.
3. Coles, *Children of Crisis* (Boston: Little, Brown, 1967), pp. 4–7.
4. Myrdal, *An American Dilemma: The Negro Problem and Modern Democracy*, vol. 1 (New York: Pantheon Books, 1972), pp. 40–48.
5. Isaacs, "The American Negro and Africa: Some Notes" (address presented at the Second Annual Conference of the American Society of African Culture, New York, June 28, 1959), Massachusetts Institute of Technology Archives.
6. Hansberry, "A Challenge to Artists" (speech delivered at Rally to Abolish the House Un-American Activities Committee, Oct. 27, 1962), *Freedomways 3* (Winter 1963): 34. There's an irony here—a contradiction within her own position. The goal of the loyalty committees, she argued, had been creating an atmosphere that would make Americans fearful of saying no to their government. Yet that is exactly what resisting southern whites were saying to the Supreme Court, while she wanted the federal government to force resisting whites to obey the Court.

Chapter 1: "Go Slow"

1. For a description of the gathering, see "Talk of the Town: Off the Cuff," *New Yorker*, Feb. 7, 1953, pp. 21–22. Ellison, "Brave Words for a Startling Occasion," in *The Collected Essays of Ralph Ellison*, ed. John F. Callahan (New York: Modern Library, 1995), p. 153.
2. Ralph Ellison, William Styron, Robert Penn Warren, and C. Vann Woodward, "The Uses of History in Fiction," *Southern Literary Journal* 1 (Spring 1969): 64.
3. Faulkner, "Mississippi," *Holiday*, April 1954, p. 44.
4. Faulkner, "To the Editor of the Memphis Commercial Appeal" (March 20, 1995), in *Essays, Speeches and Public Letters* (New York: Random House, 1965), p. 216.
5. "Faulkner on Schools," *New Leader*, June 20, 1955, p. 4; Joe Steele, "Faulkner's Stand on Segregated Schools," *Masses & Mainstream*, July 1955, p. 57.
6. Joseph Blotner, *Faulkner: A Biography*, vol. 2 (New York: Random House, 1974), p. 1532.
7. Faulkner to Else Johnsson, June 12, 1955, in *Selected Letters of William Faulkner*, ed. Joseph Blotner (New York: Random House, 1977), p. 382.

8. I have drawn the details of this Japanese visit from Blotner, *Faulkner,* 2:1545–56.

9. Ibid., pp. 1569–70.

10. Faulkner, "Press Dispatch Written in Rome, Italy, for the United Press, on the Emmett Till Case," *New York Herald Tribune,* Sept. 9, 1955, in *Essays, Speeches and Public Letters,* p. 223; "American Voices: William Faulkner and Robert Hutchins," *Masses & Mainstream,* Oct. 1955, pp. 60–61.

11. Silver, "Faulkner and Civil Rights" (typescript), Silver Papers; unless otherwise specified, this is a source of other details of the Memphis meeting described in the next section.

12. Author's interview with Wall.

13. John Egerton, *Speak Now against the Day: The Generation before the Civil Rights Movement in the South* (New York: Alfred A. Knopf, 1994), p. 619.

14. Faulkner, Mays, and Cecil Sims, "Three Views of the Segregation Decisions: Papers Read at a Session of the Twenty-first Annual Meeting of the Southern Historical Association, Memphis, Tennessee, November 10, 1955," with a foreword by Bell I. Wiley (Atlanta: SRC, 1956), pp. 13–18; in Silver Papers.

15. Woodward to Virginia Durr, Dec. 9, 1956, Woodward Papers. "Novelist Attacks Segregation," *New York Times,* Nov. 12, 1955, p. 12.

16. "Three Views of the Segregation Decisions," p. 7.

17. Bell Wiley described these negotiations to C. Vann Woodward Aug. 7 and 15, 1956, Woodward Papers.

18. Faulkner to Harold Ober, [Jan. 18, 1956], in *Selected Letters of William Faulkner,* ed. Joseph Blotner (New York: Random House, 1977), p. 392.

19. Faulkner, "On Fear," *Harper's,* June 1956, pp. 29–34.

20. Faulkner to Bob Flautt, Dec. 8, 1955, in *Selected Letters of William Faulkner,* p. 389.

21. Copies of this correspondence between Faulkner and Neill are contained in the Warren Papers. Faulkner's letter quoted here is Jan. 23, [1956]. Neill's reference to Faulkner as the "prime literary figure" appears in a letter from Neill to his cousin Robert T. Neill, Jan. 21, 1956.

22. C. Vann Woodward, *The Strange Career of Jim Crow,* 2nd rev. ed. (New York: Oxford Univ. Press, 1966), pp. 153–55.

23. Leonard W. Levy, "Jim Crow Schools on Trial," *New Leader,* Nov. 30, 1953, p. 7.

24. For Faulkner's state of mind during the University of Alabama crisis, see Blotner, *Faulkner,* 2:1590–92; I have drawn some of the details for the following narrative of Faulkner's response to the crisis from Blotner's account.

25. Faulkner, "A Letter to the North," *Life,* March 5, 1956, pp. 51–52, republished as "Letter to a Northern Editor" (Faulkner's original title), in *Essays, Speeches and Public Letters,* pp. 86–91.

26. "South Worries over Miss Lucy," *Life,* Feb. 20, 1956, pp. 28–33.

27. Blotner, *Faulkner,* 2:1589–92.

28. Howe, "A Talk with William Faulkner," *Reporter,* March 22, 1956, pp. 18–20, the source of these quotations.

29. "Faulkner Believes South Would Fight," *New York Times,* March 15, 1956, p.

17; "The South: The Authentic Voice," *Time*, March 26, 1956, p. 26; "Letters," *Time*, April 23, 1956, p. 12.

30. Drake, "The Negro's Stake in Africa," *Negro Digest*, June 1964, p. 43.
31. Dwight Martin to Russell Warren Howe, Dec. 30, 1963, Ascoli Papers.
32. Howe to Philip C. Horton, n.d., stamped received July 2, 1963, Ascoli Papers.
33. *The Selected Letters of Ralph Ellison and Albert Murray*, ed. Albert Murray and John F. Callahan (New York: Modern Library, 2000), p. 127.
34. Republished in *Reader's Digest*, May 1956, pp. 75–78; "Letters to the Editors," *Life*, March 26, 1956, p. 19; King, "Our Struggle," *Liberation*, March 1956, p. 6; Barbara Giles, "Whose South? A Reply to William Faulkner," *Masses & Mainstream*, May 1956, pp. 38–43; "Faulkner Challenged," *New York Times*, April 16, 1956, p. 8; Faulkner turned him down: "Faulkner Bars Debate," ibid., April 18, 1956, p. 29; Faulkner to W. E. B. Du Bois, April 17, 1956, in *Selected Letters of William Faulkner*, p. 398.
35. Percy, "Stoicism in the South," *Commonweal*, July 6, 1956, pp. 342–44.
36. In the *Nation*, March 31, 1956, Roy Bongartz parodied Faulkner in "Give Them Time: Reflections on Faulkner," p. 259, and McWilliams wrote the editorial, "The Heart of the Matter," p. 249.
37. Baldwin, "Faulkner and Desegregation," in *Collected Essays* (New York: Library of America, 1998), pp. 209, 214, first published in *Partisan Review*, Winter 1956.
38. "A Letter to the Leaders in the Negro Race," in *Essays, Speeches and Public Letters*, pp. 107–12, first published as "If I Were a Negro," in *Ebony*, Sept. 1956.
39. Faulkner to Harold Ober, June 23, 1956, in *Selected Letters of William Faulkner*, p. 401.
40. Faulkner to Morrison, June 23, 1956, in *Selected Letters of William Faulkner*, pp. 400–401.
41. East, *The Magnolia Jungle: The Life, Times and Education of a Southern Editor* (New York: Simon & Schuster, 1960), pp. 187–89. The story that follows—on Faulkner and the *Southern Reposure*—is told on pp. 192–204.
42. Silver, *Running Scared: Silver in Mississippi* (Jackson: Univ. Press of Mississippi, 1984), p. 61; Gary Huey, *Rebel with a Cause: P. D. East, Southern Liberalism, and the Civil Rights Movement, 1953–1971* (Wilmington, Del.: Scholarly Resources, 1985), p. 122, nn. 13, 18; East, *Magnolia Jungle*, p. 204.
43. Faulkner, "A Word to Virginians" (address to the Raven, Jefferson, and ODK Societies of the Univ. of Virginia, Charlottesville, Feb. 20, 1958), in *Essays, Speeches and Public Letters*, pp. 154–59. An undated clip of the two-column AP story is attached to a letter from J. W. Clemons to Kenneth Clark, Feb. [n.d.] 1958, Clark Papers.
44. Fisher wrote Smith on March 5, 1956; Smith replied March 10. *How Am I to Be Heard? Letters of Lillian Smith*, ed. Margaret Rose Gladney (Chapel Hill: Univ. of North Carolina Press, 1993), pp. 196–99.
45. Smith to Carmelita Hinton, June 18, 1955, in *How Am I to Be Heard?*, p. 173.
46. Anne C. Loveland, *Lillian Smith: A Southerner Confronting the South* (Baton Rouge: Louisiana State Univ. Press, 1986), pp. 132–34.
47. Virginia Spencer Carr, *The Lonely Hunter: A Biography of Carson McCullers* (Garden City, N.Y.: Doubleday, 1975), p. 422.

48. Logan describes the meeting, held Aug. 28, 1957, in Logan Diaries, Library of Congress.

49. Brittin, "Non-Segregation, or Quality, in Schools of the Deep South?" *Antioch Review* 14 (Dec. 1954): 387–96. Loveland quotes Smith's letter to Paul Bixler in *Lillian Smith*, p. 119.

50. Waring, "The Southern Case against Desegregation," *Harper's*, Jan. 1956, pp. 39–45; the editors' explanation appeared in "Personal and Otherwise," pp. 22–23.

51. Jones, *The Cold Rebellion: The South's Oligarchy in Revolt* (London: Macgibbon & Kee, 1962), p. 93.

52. Smith, *How Am I to Be Heard?*, p. 200n.

53. Smith to Fisher, May 30, 1956, quoted ibid., p. 201n.

54. *Talking with Robert Penn Warren*, ed. Floyd C. Watkins, John T. Hiers, and Mary Louise Weaks (Athens: Univ. of Georgia Press, 1990), p. 392.

55. Tom Govan to Woodward, Nov. 25, 1951, Woodward Papers.

56. Murray, *South to a Very Old Place* (New York: Vintage Books, 1971), p. 26.

57. The quotations from his journey come from Warren, *Segregation: The Inner Conflict in the South* (New York: Random House, 1956), pp. 23, 58, 61. Two small notebooks containing notes from his trip are in the Warren Papers.

58. Ibid., pp. 51, 64–65.

59. *Christian Science Monitor*, Aug. 30, 1956, p. 7.

60. Reddick, "Whose Ordeal?," *New Republic*, Sept. 24, 1956, pp. 9–10.

61. For Woodward's biography, see his own *Thinking Back: The Perils of Writing History* (Baton Rouge: Louisiana State Univ. Press, 1986), and John Herbert Roper's biography, *C. Vann Woodward, Southerner* (Athens: Univ. of Georgia Press, 1987), which does not, however, draw on Woodward's own correspondence files at Yale.

62. Woodward, "The Irony of Southern History," in *The Burden of Southern History*, rev. ed. (Baton Rouge: Louisiana Univ. Press, 1968), p. 148.

63. The Woodward Papers contain correspondence documenting Woodward's contribution; Franklin describes his work with the Legal Defense Fund in "John Hope Franklin: A Life of Learning," *Race and History: Selected Essays, 1938–1988* (Baton Rouge: Louisiana State Univ. Press, 1989), pp. 287–88.

64. Woodward described the response in [Woodward] to Charlie, Nov. 6, 1954, Woodward Papers.

65. Robert [not legible] in Charlottesville, to Woodward, Oct. 1, 1954, and an accompanying clipping, Woodward Papers.

66. Woodward, *The Strange Career of Jim Crow* (New York: Oxford Univ. Press, 1955). Woodward mentioned the rush to publish in a letter to Miss Leona Capeless at Oxford Univ. Press, Jan. 28, 1955, Woodward Papers.

67. Author's interview with Woodward.

68. See, e.g., *C. Vann Woodward: A Southern Historian and His Critics*, ed. John Herbert Roper (Athens: Univ. of Georgia Press, 1997); Woodward, "Strange Career Critics: Long May They Persevere," in *The Future of the Past* (New York: Oxford Univ. Press, 1989), pp. 295–311.

69. Woodward, "The 'New Reconstruction' in the South," *Commentary*, June 1956, pp. 501, 506. This article became part of the revised edition of *Strange Career of Jim Crow* published in 1957.

70. Ibid., p. 508.
71. Fischer to W. Willard Wirtz, Feb. 21, 1956, Fischer Papers.
72. Richard P. Cecil to Woodward, May 15, 1957, Woodward Papers.
73. Raymond English to Woodward, Feb. 7, 1956, Woodward Papers.
74. Sass, "Mixed Schools and Mixed Blood," *Atlantic Monthly,* Nov. 1956, pp. 45–49; Handlin, "Where Equality Leads," ibid., pp. 50–54.
75. Woodward to Carol L. Thompson, Dec. 14, 1956, Woodward Papers.
76. Woodward, "The Disturbed Southerners," *Current History* 32 (May 1957): 280.
77. Woodward to Eric [no last name], Dec. 30, 1957, Woodward Papers.
78. Woodward to Howard [Quint], May 20, 1958, Woodward Papers.
79. Rubin to Woodward, Oct. 14, 1956, Woodward Papers.
80. Warren to Woodward, Dec. 9, 1958, Woodward Papers. Woodward's comment comes from author's interview.
81. Woodward, *Strange Career of Jim Crow,* rev. and enl. ed. (New York: Oxford Univ. Press Galaxy Book, 1957), pp. 160–61.
82. "Southern Moderation," clip sent to him by Anthony Harrigan, editorial writer at the *News and Courier,* Charleston, Sept. 19, 1958, Woodward Papers.
83. Woodward, "The Great Civil Rights Debate," *Commentary,* Oct. 1957, p. 291.
84. Woodward, "Report on Desegregation," review of *Go South to Sorrow,* in *Commentary,* Sept. 1957, pp. 271–72.
85. Author's interview with Franklin.
86. Hubert Pryor to Bill Arthur, Jan. 18, 1954, "Stories assigned to me," *Look* Papers, State Historical Society of Wisconsin Archives, Madison.
87. Smith, "No Easy Way, Now," *New Republic,* Dec. 16, 1957, p. 15.
88. Jones, *Cold Rebellion,* p. 93; Jones mentioned not being able to find an American publisher in a letter to Reddick, March 21, 1962, United Church Board for Homeland Ministries, Amistad Research Center.
89. Carter, "The Court's Decision and the South," *Reader's Digest,* Sept. 1954, pp. 51–56; Clark to executive editor, ibid., Sept. 15, 1954, Clark Papers.
90. Clark, "Memorandum on Southern Field Trip" (typescript), Clark Papers.
91. Clark to Richard K. Bennett, Phoebe Waterman Foundation, Dec. 16, 1957, Clark Papers.
92. Hill to Clark, March 21, 1956, Clark Papers.
93. Hopkins to Clark, Aug. 31, 1956, Clark Papers.

Chapter 2: Northern Reservations

1. *The Papers of Martin Luther King, Jr.,* ed. Clayborne Carson (Berkeley: Univ. of California Press, 1992–), 3:261.
2. "EDUCATION (REQUESTED)/ TO: GRACE BRYNOLSON, NYK/FM: BILL JOHNSON, BOSTON," May 3, 1956, enclosed with letter of explanation on *Time* letterhead from "Bob" to John Fischer, May 6, 1956, Fischer Papers.
3. Schlesinger, "Reinhold Niebuhr's Role in American Political Thought and Life," in *The Politics of Hope* (Boston: Houghton Mifflin, 1963), pp. 123–24, first published in *Reinhold Niebuhr: His Religious, Social and Political Thought,* ed. Charles Kegley and Robert Bretall (New York: Macmillan, 1956).

Biographical details come from Richard Wightman Fox, *Reinhold Niebuhr: A Biography* (New York: Pantheon Books, 1985).

4. Schlesinger, *The Politics of Hope*, pp. 124, 109.

5. Frances Stonor Saunders, *The Cultural Cold War: The CIA and the World of Arts and Letters* (New York: New Press, 1999), esp. pp. 201–5.

6. Schlesinger, *The Politics of Hope*, p. 120.

7. Niebuhr to Frankfurter, May 18, 1954, in *Remembering Reinhold Niebuhr: Letters of Reinhold and Ursula M. Niebuhr*, ed. Ursula M. Niebuhr (New York: HarperCollins, 1991), p. 308.

8. Niebuhr, "The Supreme Court on Segregation in the Schools," *Christianity and Crisis*, June 14, 1954, p. 75.

9. Niebuhr, "School, Church, and the Ordeals of Integration," *Christianity and Crisis*, Oct. 1, 1956, p. 121.

10. Niebuhr, "The Effect of the Supreme Court Decision," *Christianity and Crisis*, Feb. 4, 1957, p. 3.

11. Hook, "Democracy and Desegregation," *New Leader*, April 13, 1958, p. 3.

12. Clark, "Prospects for Desegregation in the Southern States" [1956 type-script], p. 14, Clark Papers.

13. C. Vann Woodward wrote, in *The Strange Career of Jim Crow*, 2nd rev. ed. (1966), "The country was clearly in no mood for radicalism. It was only beginning to emerge from a shattering crusade against radicals and a paranoid intolerance of any opinion to the left of Senator Joseph McCarthy" (p. 164).

14. Howe, *A Margin of Hope: An Intellectual Autobiography* (San Diego: Harcourt Brace Jovanovich, 1982), pp. 231, 173.

15. Niebuhr to Stevenson, Feb. 28, 1956, Niebuhr Papers.

16. Niebuhr to S. M. Levitas, June 21, 1956; the manuscript that accompanied the letter is also in the Niebuhr Papers.

17. Schlesinger, *Robert Kennedy and His Times* (Boston: Houghton Mifflin, 1978), p. 287.

18. Niebuhr, "A Theologian's Comments on the Negro in America," *Reporter*, Nov. 29, 1956, p. 24.

19. Niebuhr to Frankfurter, Feb. 8, 1957, in *Remembering Reinhold Niebuhr*, p. 311.

20. "We now face the fact that the very great step forward which the Supreme Court took in its decision abolishing segregated schools has unloosed passions and fears in the white minority in some states. . . ." Niebuhr, "The Race Problem in America," *Christianity and Crisis*, Dec. 26, 1955, p. 169.

21. Howe, "Reverberations in the North," *Dissent* 3 (Spring 1956): 121–23.

22. Podhoretz, "Norman Mailer: The Embattled Vision" (1959), in *Doings and Undoings: The Fifties and After in American Writing* (New York: Farrar, Straus, 1964), p. 179.

23. Hilary Mills, *Mailer: A Biography* (New York: Empire Books, 1982), pp. 153–57. For several episodes illustrating Mailer's provocative stance toward editors, see the index of the author's *It Wasn't Pretty, Folks, But Didn't We Have Fun? Esquire in the Sixties* (New York: W. W. Norton, 1995).

24. Mailer, *Advertisements for Myself* (New York: G. P. Putnam's Sons, 1959), p. 332. Other details of this episode, except as noted, come from *Advertisements*, pp. 332–34.

25. Du Bois, "Sex and Racism," reprinted from *Independent,* March 1957, p. 6, in *Writings by W. E. B. Du Bois in Periodicals Edited by Others,* comp. and ed. Herbert Aptheker, vol. 4, *1945–1961* (Millwood, N.Y.: Kraus-Thomson, 1982), p. 284.

26. *Advertisements for Myself,* p. 334.

27. Mailer, "The White Negro: Superficial Reflections on the Hipster," in *The Time of Our Time* (New York: Random House, 1998), p. 228, first published in *Dissent,* Summer 1957.

28. Baldwin, "The Black Boy Looks at the White Boy," in *Collected Essays,* pp. 276–77, first published in *Esquire,* May 1961. *To Be Young, Gifted, and Black: Lorraine Hansberry in Her Own Words,* adapted by Robert Nemiroff (New York: Vintage Books, 1995), p. 198.

29. Howe, *A Margin of Hope,* pp. 239–40; Mailer, "The White Negro," p. 220.

30. Mills, *Mailer,* p. 187.

31. This account of their conversation is based on the letters between them in the Arendt Papers, Library of Congress, and on Elisabeth Young-Bruehl's description of their relationship in *Hannah Arendt: For Love of the World* (New Haven: Yale Univ. Press, 1982), pp. 190–92.

32. Constance Webb, *Richard Wright: A Biography* (New York: G. P. Putnam's Sons, 1968), p. 216.

33. Kazin, *New York Jew* (New York: Alfred A. Knopf, 1978), p. 195.

34. *Hannah Arendt/Karl Jaspers Correspondence, 1926–1969,* ed. Lotte Kohler and Hans Saner (San Diego: Harvest Book/Harcourt Brace, 1993), pp. 211, 248. Arendt's close friend Mary McCarthy speaks of her tendency to see the potential for fascism everywhere "as though Nazism, once invented, were subject to eternal recurrence." "Hannah Arendt and Politics," in *Partisan Review: The 50th Anniversary Edition,* ed. William Phillips (New York: Stein & Day, 1984), p. 244.

35. Stephen E. Ambrose, *Rise to Globalism: American Foreign Policy, 1938–1980,* 2nd rev. ed. (Middlesex, Eng.: Penguin Books, 1980), pp. 223–24.

36. Arendt, "A Reply to Critics, *Dissent* 6 (Spring 1959): 179–81.

37. Young-Bruehl, *Hannah Arendt,* p. 311.

38. Handlin, "Civil Rights after Little Rock: The Failure of Moderation," *Commentary,* Nov. 1957, 396.

39. Arendt, "Reflections on Little Rock," *Dissent* 6 (Winter 1959): 45–56.

40. Author's interview with Stein.

41. The account that follows is based on Arendt's correspondence in the Library of Congress, author's interview with Podhoretz, and Podhoretz's *Ex-Friends: Falling Out with Allen Ginsberg, Lionel & Diana Trilling, Lillian Hellman, Hannah Arendt, and Norman Mailer* (New York: Free Press, 1999), pp. 139–52.

42. George [Lichtheim] to Hannah [Arendt], May 2, 1958, Nov. 21, 1957, Arendt Papers.

43. Victor Navasky, *Naming Names* (Middlesex, Eng.: Penguin Books, 1981), p. 43.

44. Arendt to Kurt Blumenfeld, Feb. 2, 1953, quoted by Young-Bruehl, *Hannah Arendt,* p. 288.

45. Hannah Arendt to George Lichtheim, Nov. 23, 1957, Arendt Papers.

46. Arendt to George [Lichtheim], Nov. 28, 1957; George [Lichtheim] to Arendt, Nov. 29, 1957, Arendt Papers.
47. George [Lichtheim] to Hannah [Arendt], March 2, 1958, Arendt Papers.
48. Hook, "Democracy and Desegregation," *New Leader*, April 13, 1958, pp. 3–16.
49. Howe to Arendt, Sept. 7, 1958, Arendt Papers.
50. Howe, *Margin of Hope*, p. 270.
51. Ibid., p. 236.
52. Irving [Howe] to Hannah [Arendt], Nov. 18 and Sept. 7, 1958, Arendt Papers; Stanley Plastrik to Richard Wright, Dec. 19, 1958, Wright Papers.
53. Melvin Tumin, "Pie in the Sky," *Dissent* 6 (Winter 1959): 65; Lichtheim to Arendt, Feb. 10, 1959, Arendt Papers.
54. Author's interview with Hill.
55. Young-Bruehl, *Hannah Arendt*, p. 315.
56. Warren, *Who Speaks for the Negro?* (New York: Vintage Books, 1966), pp. 343–44.
57. Arendt to Ellison, July 29, 1965, Arendt Papers.
58. "Desegregation: An Appraisal of the Evidence," *Journal of Social Issues* 9, no. 4 (1953). Clark's report occupied the entire issue.
59. Kenneth B. Clark to editor, Louisville *Courier-Journal*, Sept. 9, 1957; Clark sent a copy of the same letter to the *Washington Post*.
60. Smith, "To the Editors" (Oct. 1957), in *How Am I To Be Heard?: Letters of Lillian Smith*, ed. Margaret Rose Gladney (Chapel Hill: Univ. of North Carolina Press, 1993), p. 214.
61. Clark, "Observations on Little Rock," *New South*, June 1958, p. 5.
62. Handwritten notes of Harold Isaacs's interview with Ellison, Dec. 4, 1958, Isaacs Papers.
63. Typed notes of Harold Isaacs's interview with Clark, Oct. 20, 1958, Isaacs Papers.
64. Woodward to Hugh [Hawkins], Oct. 11, 1957, Woodward Papers.
65. Woodward to editor of *Commentary*, Dec. 8, 1957, original in Woodward Papers; published in *Commentary*, Jan. 1958, p. 76.
66. Niebuhr, "Bad Days at Little Rock," *Christianity and Crisis*, Oct. 14, 1957, p. 131.
67. Rauh to Ascoli, Sept. 6, 1957, Ascoli Papers.
68. King, *Stride toward Freedom*, in *A Testament of Hope: The Essential Writings and Speeches of Martin Luther King, Jr.*, ed. James Melvin Washington (New York: HarperCollins, 1986), p. 474.
69. Harold R. Isaacs's interview with Franklin, July 30, 1958, Isaacs Papers.
70. "Historians Tour Gettysburg Site: Columbia Professor Asserts Battle Helped Make U.S. an 'Organized Nation,' " *New York Times*, Nov. 18, 1957, p. 26.
71. Woodward, "Equality: America's Deferred Commitment," *American Scholar* 27 (Autumn 1958): 471–72.
72. Green to Woodward, Nov. 13, 1958, Woodward Papers.

Chapter 3: Missing Persons

1. Ellison's exile was temporary, and he would protest *Time*'s inclusion of him among the Negro exiles mentioned in "Amid the Alien Corn," *Time*, Nov. 17, 1958; see Ellison to *Time*, Nov. 27, 1958, in Isaacs Papers.

2. Cowley, *The Dream of the Golden Mountain: Remembering the 1930s* (New York: Viking Press, 1964), p. 40.

3. Diana Trilling, *The Beginning of the Journey: The Marriage of Diana and Lionel Trilling* (New York: Harcourt Brace, 1993), p. 195.

4. Ellison, "Remembering Richard Wright," in *The Collected Essays of Ralph Ellison,* ed. John F. Callahan (New York: Modern Library, 1995), p. 662.

5. Ellison to Wright, Nov. 3, 1941, Wright Papers.

6. Wright, Journal, Jan. 1, 1945, Wright Papers.

7. Wright, Journal, Jan. 10 and 22, 1945, Wright Papers.

8. Wright describes Ellison's efforts to avoid service in journal entries Jan. 22 and 28, 1945. He describes his own efforts to help Ellison get a psychiatric deferral in journal entries Jan. 22, 26, and 29, 1945; the boat story comes from a journal entry Jan. 7, 1945, Wright Papers.

9. Wilson Record, *The Negro and the Communist Party* (Chapel Hill: Univ. of North Carolina Press, 1951), pp. 229–31.

10. Fanny and Ralph Ellison to Langston Hughes, Aug. 20, 1945, Hughes Papers.

11. Ellison to Wright, Aug. 18, 1945, Wright Papers.

12. Ibid.

13. Ellison, "The Art of Fiction: An Interview," in *Collected Essays,* p. 218.

14. Ellison to Wright, Aug. 5, 1945, Wright Papers.

15. Ellison to Wright, Feb. 1, 1948, Wright Papers.

16. Ellison to Wright, Aug. 18, 1945, Wright Papers.

17. Killens's review was quoted by Harold Cruse in *The Crisis of the Negro Intellectual* (New York: William Morrow, 1967), p. 235.

18. Ibid., pp. 269–70. Julian Mayfield identifies himself and Cruse as former members of the party in Malaike Lumumba's Oral History interview, May 13, 1970, Manuscript Division, Moorland-Spingarn Research Center, Howard Univ.

19. Ellison, "Blues People," in *Collected Essays,* p. 286; "The Art of Fiction: An Interview," ibid., pp. 212, 224.

20. Ellison, "Twentieth-Century Fiction and the Black Mask of Humanity," in *Collected Essays,* pp. 81–99.

21. Ellison, "The Art of Fiction," pp. 223–24.

22. Ellison to Wright, Feb. 1, 1948, Wright Papers.

23. Fanny Ellison described life in Rome in a letter to Hughes, Dec. 5, 1955, Hughes Papers. The photograph appeared in "Haven of Art and Study: Americans Live and Work at Academy in Rome," *Life,* Dec. 23, 1957, p. 105.

24. Fanny Ellison recalled the visit in a letter to the Warrens, Dec. 7, 1985, Warren Papers; the description of their conversations and Ellison's comment are from Joseph Blotner, *Robert Penn Warren* (New York: Random House, 1997), p. 307.

25. Kristol to Warren, June 18, 1956, Warren Papers. Following reports by *Ramparts* and the *New York Times, Facts on File* (March 9–15, 1967, pp. 79–80) listed the Congress for Cultural Freedom as one of the organizations receiving support from the CIA.

26. Ellison told Albert Murray about working on the article for *Encounter* and about Warren's encouraging him to turn it into a book in *The Selected Letters*

of Ralph Ellison and Albert Murray, ed. Albert Murray and John F. Callahan (New York: Modern Library, 2000), pp. 142, 156. The essay published by the *Nation,* Sept. 20, 1965, appeared as "Tell It like It Is, Baby" in Ellison's *Collected Essays,* pp. 29–46, the source of the quotations that follow.

27. Ellison, "Introduction" to *Shadow and Act,* in *Collected Essays,* p. 58. A fuller story of Ellison's response to the civil rights movement can be told after his estate opens his correspondence at the Library of Congress. When I completed work on this book, part of the collection had been opened, but not his correspondence.

28. Smith, *Return to Black America* (Englewood Cliffs, N.J.: Prentice-Hall, 1970), p. 57.

29. Worthy submitted the statement to the Fellowship of Reconciliation and the National Council against Conscription; he sent it to Kenneth B. Clark in a letter dated Sept. 20, 1951, Clark Papers.

30. Logan, "Is the N.A.A.C.P. Communistic?," *Christian Century,* July 4, 1956, pp. 802–4.

31. Aug. 25 and 28, 1956, Logan Diaries, Library of Congress.

32. Feb. 19, March 30, and April 13, 1958, Logan Diaries, Library of Congress.

33. *The Autobiography of W. E. B. Du Bois,* ed. Herbert Aptheker (New York: International Publishers, 1968), p. 395.

34. Arnold Rampersad, *The Life of Langston Hughes* (New York: Oxford Univ. Press, 1986–88), vol. 2, esp. pp. 90–92, 140–44.

35. A summary of his statement appears as "Langston Hughes Speaks" in *Good Morning Revolution: Uncollected Social Protest Writings by Langston Hughes,* ed. by Faith Berry (New York: Lawrence Hill, 1973), pp. 143–45.

36. Hughes, "Where's the Horse for a Kid That's Black?" in *A Documentary History of the Negro People in the United States,* ed. Herbert Aptheker, vol. 6 (New York: Citadel Press, 1993), pp. 391–92.

37. Redding, foreword to *Good Morning Revolution,* ix–x.

38. White tells this story in *In Search of History: A Personal Adventure* (New York: Harper & Row, 1978), pp. 381–92.

39. Kenneth Robert Janken, *Rayford W. Logan and the Dilemma of the African American Intellectual* (Amherst: Univ. of Massachusetts Press, 1993), pp. 193–94.

40. July 21, 1954, Logan Diaries, Library of Congress.

41. Frazier, "Failure of the Negro Intellectual," in *On Race Relations: Selected Writings,* ed. G. Franklin Edwards (Chicago: Univ. of Chicago Press, 1968), p. 273.

42. Author's interview with Franklin.

43. Wright, Journal, Jan. 29, 1945, Wright Papers.

44. In an Aug. 8, 1964, symposium, Horace Cayton and Saunders Redding agreed that exile had not been good for Wright's work. "Reflections on Richard Wright: A Symposium on an Exiled Native Son," in *Anger and Beyond: The Negro Writer in the United States,* ed. Herbert Hill (New York: Harper & Row, 1966), pp. 196–212.

45. Burns, *Nitty Gritty: A White Editor in Black Journalism* (Jackson: Univ. Press of Mississippi, 1996), pp. 168–71.

46. Michel Fabre quotes the letter in *The Unfinished Quest of Richard Wright*, trans. Isabel Barzun (New York: William Morrow, 1973), pp. 363–64. *Ebony* editor Ben Burns wrote in "They're Not Uncle Tom's Children," *Reporter*, March 8, 1956, pp. 21–22, that *Ebony* actually rejected the piece, although in *Nitty Gritty*, he says he postponed writing the rejection letter in the hope that Johnson would change his mind and publish the piece; Burns also thought Johnson himself ought to write the rejection letter, since Johnson was the one who wanted to reject the piece. Finally, Wright, weary of waiting, withdrew the article (p. 171).

47. Seymour Lawrence, the editorial assistant, to Paul R. Reynolds, Nov. 21, 1952; Plimpton to Mrs. Richard Wright, Sept. 3, 1953, Wright Papers.

48. Himes to Wright, Oct. 19, 1952, Wright Papers.

49. Hoyt Fuller, "Interview with Chester Himes, May 15, 1969, Alicante, Spain" (typescript), Fuller Papers.

50. Reynolds to Wright, June 2, 1954, Wright Papers.

51. Reynolds to Wright, March 23 and April 12, 1954, Wright Papers.

52. Constance Webb, *Richard Wright* (New York: G. P. Putnam's Sons, 1968), pp. 336–37.

53. For reviews of *Black Power* and other books by Wright, see John M. Reilly, ed., *Richard Wright: The Critical Reception* ([New York:] Burt Franklin, 1978).

54. Richard Wright, *Black Power* (New York: HarperCollins, 1995), pp. xxxvii–xxxviii.

55. Frances Stonor Saunders quotes Sidney Hook's 1949 statement on Wright in *The Cultural Cold War: The CIA and the World of Letters* (New York: New Press, 1999), p. 69.

56. Gayle, *Richard Wright: Ordeal of a Native Son* (Garden City, N.Y.: Anchor Press/Doubleday, 1980), pp. 244, 250–54.

57. American Consulate General, Accra, to the Department of State, "Foreign Service Despatch No. 42," September 15, 1953 (State Department Decimal File 745.00/9–1553), Civilian Records, Textual Archives Services Division, National Archives.

58. Webb, *Richard Wright*, p. 381.

59. Gayle, *Richard Wright*, p. 258.

60. Frederick R. Karl, *William Faulkner: American Writer* (New York: Weidenfeld & Nicolson, 1989), p. 932; Faulkner to Harold Ober, received Jan. 30, 1956, in *Selected Letters of William Faulkner*, ed. by Joseph Blotner (New York: Random House, 1977), p. 393.

61. Burns speaks of his "years in the Communist Party" in *Nitty Gritty*, p. 56 and elsewhere; he describes his expulsion from the party on p. 107.

62. Burns wrote of working with Wright at the *Daily Worker* in *Nitty Gritty*, p. 168, and of the *Reporter* article on pp. 172–73. Burns's article " 'They're Not Uncle Tom's Children,' " appeared in the *Reporter*, March 8, 1956, pp. 21–22.

63. Myrdal made his comment in a letter to Wright, April 3, 1956, Wright Papers; lawyer's evaluation, Walter H. Liebman for Liebman, Eulau & Robinson, May 8, 1956, Wright Papers.

64. Boyle to Wright, Oct. 5, 1956, Wright Papers.

65. McCarthy, "Baldwin," in *James Baldwin: The Legacy*, ed. Quincy Troupe (New York: Simon & Schuster, 1989), pp. 47–48.

66. Baldwin, "The New Lost Generation," in *Collected Essays*, p. 659, first published in *Esquire*, July 1961; "Introduction," *The Price of the Ticket: Collected Nonfiction, 1948–1985* (New York: St. Martin's/Marek, 1985), pp. xii–xiii; "The Harlem Ghetto," in *Collected Essays*, p. 52, first published in *Commentary*, Feb. 1948.

67. Baldwin, *No Name in the Street*, in *Collected Essays*, p. 370, originally published in 1972 by Dial Press.

68. Baldwin, "Introduction," *The Price of the Ticket*, p. xiii.

69. Phillips, *A Partisan View: Five Decades of the Literary Life* (New York: Stein & Day, 1983), pp. 162, 275; Diana Trilling, *The Beginning of the Journey*, pp. 195, 287.

70. Saunders, *The Cultural Cold War*, pp. 162–64.

71. Baldwin, "Many Thousands Gone," in *Collected Essays*, pp. 19–34, first published in *Partisan Review*, Nov.–Dec. 1951.

72. *A Lifetime Burning in Every Moment: From the Journals of Alfred Kazin* (New York: HarperCollins, 1996), p. 131.

73. Baldwin, *No Name in the Street*, in *Collected Essays*, pp. 370–71.

74. Ibid., pp. 372–73.

75. Baldwin, "Equal in Paris," in *Collected Essays*, p. 116.

76. *New York Post* editor James Wechsler named Kempton as a former communist when he appeared before McCarthy's committee, according to Victor Navasky, *Naming Names* (Middlesex, Eng.: Penguin Books, 1981), p. 59; Kempton to Mike [Straight?], Feb. 23, 1955, *New Republic* Papers, MS Storage 304 Box 12, American Committee for Cultural Freedom folder, Houghton Library, Harvard Univ. Publication by permission of the Houghton Library.

77. Author's interviews with Hill and Stein.

78. Arnold's anti-communist activities are documented in the Melvin Arnold Papers, 1945–46, Rare Books and Manuscripts, Andover-Harvard Theological Library, Harvard Divinity School, Cambridge, Mass. See esp. Memorandum to: Jack Anderson; Subject: M.A. anti-Communist record, dated 6/30/52. He describes his evening with Philbrick in a Memo to Warren Walsh, May 14, 1952.

79. Author's interview with Hopkins. Michael Korda, an editor at Simon & Schuster, has said of publishers in the 1960s, "The civil rights crisis caught them not only unprepared but undecided and embarrassed. Book publishing, as an industry, was pretty much a white man's business." *Michael Korda: Another Life* (New York, Random House, 1999), p. 203.

80. Baldwin, "Princes and Powers," in *Collected Essays*, pp. 146–48.

81. Fern Marja Eckman, *The Furious Passage of James Baldwin* (New York: M. Evans, 1966), p. 123. David Leeming says they met at the Montana Bar and provides the date, in his *James Baldwin: A Biography* (New York: Henry Holt, 1994), p. 77.

82. The details of her life come from Leonard Silk, "Mary Painter Garin, 71, Innovator in Economic and Statistical Work," *New York Times*, Oct. 24, 1991, p. B-24. This substantial obituary, prominently placed, suggests Painter's professional standing.

83. Leeming, *James Baldwin*, p. 77.

84. This is only a hypothesis, mentioned as an avenue for future Baldwin biographers to explore; a former employee of the CIA who worked in Paris just a few years later confirms its credibility.
85. Leeming, *James Baldwin*, pp. 119–20.
86. Baldwin, *No Name in the Street*, in *Collected Essays*, p. 383.
87. Clark, introduction to *King, Malcolm, Baldwin: Three Interviews* (Middletown, Conn.: Wesleyan Univ. Press, 1985), p. 13.
88. My chief sources for biographical information on Clark are "Racial Progress and Retreat: A Personal Memoir," in *Race in America: The Struggle for Equality*, ed. Herbert Hill and James E. Jones Jr. (Madison: Univ. of Wisconsin Press, 1993), pp. 3–18; and "The Reminiscences of Kenneth B. Clark," interviews conducted in 1976 and 1985, by Ed Edwin (Oral History Research Office, Columbia Univ., 1989).
89. Numan V. Bartley quotes Eastland's remarks in *The Rise of Massive Resistance: Race and Politics in the South during the 1950's* (Baton Rouge: Louisiana State Univ. Press, 1969), pp. 119–20. After the *New York Law Review* published a critical article by Edmund Cahn, a member of the New York Univ. Law School faculty, Clark replied, but, he said in a letter to John P. Milligan, a New Jersey education official, the review "refused to print [his] answer unless [he] made certain deletions which they requested." Clark to Milligan, Dec. 16, 1957, Clark Papers.
90. Clark to Errold D. Collymore, July 25, 1956, Clark Papers.
91. W. J. Weatherby, *James Baldwin: Artist on Fire* (New York: Laurel, 1989), pp. 153–54; also Clark, introduction to *King, Malcolm, Baldwin*, p. 13.
92. Leeming, *James Baldwin*, p. 138.
93. The comment to his editor comes from ibid., p. 137; the nightmares are from Baldwin, *No Name in the Street*, in *Collected Essays*, p. 384.
94. Smith to Murray, June 4, 1954; Murray to Smith, June 11, 1954, Murray Papers.
95. I base my account of his journey on several essays in Baldwin's *Collected Essays*: "A Fly in the Buttermilk," pp. 187–96; "Nobody Knows My Name: A Letter from the South," pp. 197–208; *No Name in the Street*, pp. 383–03; "The Dangerous Road before Martin Luther King," pp. 638–45, and on Leeming, *James Baldwin*, pp. 137–47. A fuller story of Baldwin's role in the movement will be possible when the Baldwin estate makes his unpublished papers available to other scholars.
96. Baldwin to Cole, Oct. 1, 1957, Baldwin mss., Lilly Library, Indiana Univ., Bloomington.
97. "A Fly in the Buttermilk," in *Collected Essays*, pp. 194–96.
98. Fischer, *Why They Behave like Russians* (New York: Harper & Brothers, 1947), p. 233.
99. Webb, *Richard Wright*, pp. 355, 418, n. 11. Webb, wife of C. L. R. James, knew Wright personally.
100. Baldwin, "Nobody Knows My Name," in *Collected Essays*, p. 207.

Chapter 4: "To Be Transformed"
1. Wiley to Woodward, April 13, 1957, Woodward Papers.

2. Williamson to Woodward, March 4, 1958, Woodward Papers. On these events, see "Educators Score Gov. Timmerman," *New York Times,* Jan. 3, 1958, p. 14.

3. Howard [Quint] to Woodward, May 16, 1958, Woodward Papers.

4. Howard Quint, *Profile in Black and White: A Frank Portrait of South Carolina* (Washington, D.C.: Public Affairs Press, 1958), p. vii.

5. Oct. 16, 1957, Logan Diaries, Library of Congress.

6. Riesman, "Notes on trip to Atlanta, Georgia," Oct. 31, 1960, sent to C. Vann Woodward and in the Woodward Papers.

7. Dunbar, *A Republic of Equals* (Ann Arbor: Univ. of Michigan Press, 1966), pp. 17–18.

8. Reddick's colleague Norman Walton shared his memories of Reddick with me and is an important source of details about life at Alabama State. Reddick's Harlem activities are documented by items in the "Reddick" section of the Schomburg Center clipping file, 1925–74, microform (New York: New York Public Library; Alexandria, Va.: Chadwyck-Healey, distributor, 1985). Akwasi B. Assensoh mentions Reddick's acquaintance with African leaders in "Lawrence Dunbar Reddick," *OAH Newsletter,* Nov. 1995, p. 19.

9. David J. Garrow, *The FBI and Martin Luther King, Jr.* (New York: W. W. Norton, 1981), p. 116.

10. Author's interview with Norman Walton.

11. Walton, "The Walking City, a History of the Montgomery Boycott," *Negro History Bulletin* 20 (April 1957): 147–152, 166; Reddick, "The Boycott in Montgomery," *Dissent* 3 (Spring 1956): 107–17.

12. Reddick outlined the plan for the books in letters to St. Clair Drake, March 21 and May 2, 1957, Drake Papers; Taylor Branch discusses the motivation for King's book in *Parting the Waters: America in the King Years, 1954–1963* (New York: Simon & Schuster, 1988), p. 225.

13. Office Memorandum to Mr. Garrison, Mr. Kleinbard, and Mr. Zelenko, "Martin Luther King Book -#4515," Oct. 23, 1957, Murray Papers.

14. L. D. Reddick, *Crusader without Violence: A Biography of Martin Luther King, Jr.* (New York: Harper & Brothers, 1959), pp. 235–36.

15. Rodell wrote to King proposing one writer, Jan. 20, 1958; Saunders Redding told about Rustin's approach to him in a letter to Lewis Gannett, Jan. 13, 1958, Gannett Papers (bMS Am 1888.1), Saunders Redding file, Houghton Library, Harvard Univ. Publication by permission of the Houghton Library.

16. Levison to King, Jan. 24, 1958, King Papers, Boston Univ.

17. Ella Baker offered her comments on Reddick's possible authorship in an interview, Sept. 4, 1975, Durham, N.C., conducted by Eugene Walker for the Southern Oral History Program, Southern Historical Collection, #4007: G-7, p. 84. The King Papers in Boston contain numerous exchanges between editors and others involved in producing the book.

18. Frances Stonor Saunders, *The Cultural Cold War: The CIA and the World of Art and Letters* (New York: New Press, 1999), pp. 65, 136.

19. Arnold's request comes from Stephen B. Oates, *Let the Trumpet Sound: The Life of Martin Luther King, Jr.* (New York: New American Library, 1982), p. 131.

20. Reddick, *Crusader without Violence,* p. 22.
21. Reddick to Drake, Jan. 9, 1959, Drake Papers; Reddick to Wright, April 29, 1959, Wright Papers.
22. Reddick, "The Negro as Southerner and American," in *The Southerner as American,* ed. Charles Grier Sellers Jr. (Chapel Hill: Univ. of North Carolina Press, 1960), pp. 142, 145.
23. Ibid., p. 147.
24. August Meier, "The Successful Sit-ins in a Border City: A Study in Social Causation," *Journal of Intergroup Relations* 2 (Summer 1961): 230–37, reprinted in Meier, *A White Scholar and the Black Community, 1945–1965: Essays and Reflections* (Amherst: Univ. of Massachusetts Press, 1992), pp. 119–20.
25. *Arna Bontemps/Langston Hughes: Letters, 1925–1967,* sel. and ed. by Charles H. Nichols (New York: Paragon House, 1990), pp. 397–98.
26. Branch, *Parting the Waters,* pp. 291–92.
27. Dunbar, *A Republic of Equals,* p. 21.
28. This account of the Atlanta sit-ins, along with Zinn's biography, is based on Howard Zinn, *You Can't Be Neutral on a Moving Train: A Personal History of Our Times* (Boston: Beacon Press, 1994), pp. 15–45, 164–82; and Zinn, *The Southern Mystique* (New York: Alfred A. Knopf, 1964) pp. 42–53, 107–234; the advertisement and Vandiver's comments appear on pp. 110–11.
29. Author's interview with Zinn.
30. Zinn, "Fate Worse than Integration," *Harper's,* Aug. 1959, pp. 53–56.
31. "Southern Whites Prefer Race Mix" with overline "SAYS HISTORIAN" from the *State Times,* Aug. 16, 1959; MEMO TO: Director, State Sovereignty Commission FROM: Zack J. Van Landingham; SUBJECT: Segregation in the South, publicity; Aug. 19, 1959. Mississippi State Sovereignty Commission files.
32. "Finishing School for Pickets," in *The Zinn Reader: Writings on Disobedience and Democracy* (New York: Seven Stories Press, 1997), p. 41, first published in *Nation,* Aug. 6, 1960.
33. Branch, *Parting the Waters,* p. 176.
34. *Atlantic Monthly,* Dec. 1960, pp. 85–86.
35. Riesman, "Notes on trip to Atlanta, Georgia."
36. "Sitdown Staged in Alabama Shop; Courthouse at Montgomery Is Scene of First Protest in the Deep South," UPI, *New York Times,* Feb. 26, 1960, p. 8.
37. Reddick, "The State vs. the Student," *Dissent* 7 (Summer 1960): 219.
38. Board of Education Minutes, March 25, 1960, Governor Patterson's Papers, Alabama Department of Archives, Montgomery. Subsequent information about board meetings, along with the press release quoted, comes from this file except when other sources are cited.
39. Reddick is identified with an arrow on a photograph from Alabama Bureau of Investigation files, reproduced in Levi Watkins, *Fighting Hard: The Alabama State Experience* (Detroit: Harlo, 1987), p. 32. Watkins was Trenholm's second in command and became president of Alabama State College in 1962.
40. Watkins, *Fighting Hard,* pp. 35–36.
41. "Negro Teacher Linked to Reds, Ordered Fired," *Montgomery Advertiser,* June 15, 1960.

42. Ibid.
43. *New York Times*, June 16, 1960, p. 20; "Alabama State head faces possible firing," undated clipping, Schomburg Clipping File, 1925, 1974, microfiche, Reddick file. According to internal documents at the Schomburg Center for Research in Black Culture, Reddick left his post there because of what he perceived as the city's inadequate support of the Schomburg Center and his own inadequate salary. See "Summary of Events Preceding and Following Dr. Reddick's Resignation," Schomburg Center for Research in Black Culture Records.
44. "Threat of Integration Raised after Dismissal," *Montgomery Advertiser*, June 16, 1960.
45. C. Vann Woodward, "Crisis in Southern Colleges," *Harper's*, Oct. 1962, p. 86.
46. Watkins, *Fighting Hard*, pp. 37, 203, 213.
47. "Groups in North and South Protest Reddick Dismissal," newsclip from an unidentified newspaper, July 25, 1960, Schomburg Clipping File, 1925, 1974, microfiche, Reddick file.
48. "6 Negroes Upheld on Expulsion Plea," AP, *New York Times*, Aug. 5, 1961, p. 39; "Alabama Rebuffed in High Court Order," UPI, ibid., Dec. 5, 1961, p. 30.
49. "Civil War Fetes Decried by Negro," *New York Times*, April 23, 1961, p. 74.
50. Letters in King Papers, Martin Luther King Center, Atlanta, document Reddick's continued involvement with the Southern Christian Leadership Conference. Reddick to King, Aug. 2, 1963, King Papers, Martin Luther King Center.
51. I base my account of his Tallahassee visit on Baldwin, "They Can't Turn Back," in *Collected Essays* (New York: Library of America, 1998), pp. 622–37, first published in *Mademoiselle*, Aug. 1960.
52. Baldwin, "Notes for a Hypothetical Novel," in *Collected Essays*, pp. 230.

Chapter 5: "On the Stage of the World"

1. Cayton, *Long Old Road*, p. 372.
2. Amiri Baraka, *The Autobiography of LeRoi Jones* (Chicago: Lawrence Hill Books, 1997), p. 243.
3. Julian Mayfield identifies himself and Cruse as former members of the party in Malaike Lumumba's interview, May 13, 1970, Civil Rights Documentation Project, Manuscript Division, Moorland-Spingarn Research Center, Howard Univ.
4. Taber to Clarke, June 21 [1960], Clarke Papers.
5. Baraka, *The Autobiography of LeRoi Jones*, pp. 243–44.
6. Jones (Baraka), "cuba libre," in *Home: Social Essays* (Hopewell, N.J.: Ecco Press, 1998), pp. 11–62.
7. Cruse, *The Crisis of the Negro Intellectual* (New York: William Morrow, 1967), p. 357.
8. Mayfield, "The Cuban Challenge," *Freedomways* 1 (Summer 1961): 188–89.
9. James Forman, *The Making of Black Revolutionaries* (Seattle: Univ. of Washington Press, 1997), pp. 176–77.
10. Cruse, *The Crisis of the Negro Intellectual*, pp. 351–81.

11. Mayfield, "Challenge to Negro Leadership: The Case of Robert Williams," *Commentary*, April 1961, p. 305.
12. "Letters from Readers," *Commentary*, July 1961, pp. 72–75.
13. Podhoretz, *Breaking Ranks* (New York: Harper & Row, 1979), pp. 119–21.
14. Lumumba's interview with Mayfield.
15. Mayfield to Mrs. Jack Alloy, Aug. 18, 1961, Mayfield Papers.
16. Victor Navasky, *Naming Names* (Middlesex, Eng.: Penguin Books, 1981), pp. 58–65.
17. Forman, *The Making of Black Revolutionaries*, pp. 189–206.
18. Lumumba's interview with Mayfield.
19. Debate, Cambridge Union Society, Feb. 18, 1965, BBC library videotape.
20 . Harold R. Isaacs, *The New World of New Americans: A Study from the Center for International Studies, Massachusetts Institute of Technology* (New York: Viking Press, 1964), p. 228.
21. Murray, *Song in a Weary Throat: An American Pilgrimage* (New York: Harper & Row, 1987), pp. 295–97; this autobiography provides the biographical information for Murray's story.
22. *Proud Shoes: The Story of an American Family*, rev. ed. (New York: Harper & Row, 1978), vii–viii.
23. Murray, Journal, Sept. 3, 1960, Murray Papers.
24. Murray to Carl Braden, July 24, 1962, Murray Papers.
25. Murray, Journal, Aug. 31, 1960, Murray Papers.
26. Murray, Journal, Sept. 14, 1960, Murray Papers.
27. In the Murray Papers, to editor of *Washington Post*, Aug. 29, 1960; Murray, Journal, Sept. 12, 1960; Al Friendly at *Washington Post* to Murray, Sept. 9, 1960; Murray to Friendly, Sept. 30, 1960.
28. Although he called the 1963 book that resulted *The New World of Negro Americans*, it is clear from the files on his work in the MIT Archives that his focus from early on was the relation of Negro Americans to Africa, specifically. See, e.g., an appeal for funding from the Field Foundation, "An Informal Proposal for Research on the Changing Mutual Images of Americans and Africans," CIS/MIT: July 1958, CIS Papers, Institute Archives and Special Collections, MIT.
29. Isaacs, *The Tragedy of the Chinese Revolution* (London: Secker & Warburg, 1938; reprint, Stanford: Stanford Univ. Press, 1951), vii–xiii.
30. Author's interview with Franklin.
31. Isaacs's notes on his interviews with Hansberry and Du Bois, Isaacs Papers, and the published accounts of those interviews in *The New World of Negro Americans*, pp. 277–87, 225–30.
32. Murray to Isaacs, Nov. 5 and 21, 1960, and Jan. 2, 1961, Isaacs Papers; Murray mentions the *Saturday Evening Post* in a letter to Caroline Ware, Dec. 2, 1960, Murray Papers.
33. Isaacs to Murray, Nov. 30, 1960, Isaacs Papers.
34. Isaacs to Murray, March 2, 1961, Isaacs Papers.
35. Stephen E. Ambrose, *Rise to Globalism: American Foreign Policy, 1938–1980*, 2nd rev. ed. (Middlesex, Eng.: Penguin Books, 1980), pp. 376–77.
36. Angelou describes this episode in *The Heart of a Woman* (New York: Bantam

Books, 1997), pp. 170–200; Baraka describes his role in *The Autobiography of LeRoi Jones*, p. 267.

37. "Riot in Gallery Halts U.N. Debate," *New York Times*, Feb. 16, 1961, p. 10.

38. Clarke, "The New Afro-American Nationalism," *Freedomways* 1 (Fall 1961): 285.

39. Baldwin, "East River Downtown: Postscript to a Letter from Harlem," in *Collected Essays* (New York: Library of America, 1998), pp. 180–81, first published as "A Negro Assays the Negro Mood," *New York Times Magazine*, March 12, 1961.

40. "Letters," *New York Times*, March 26, 1961, sec. 6, p. 4.

41. Mayfield, "And Then Came Baldwin," *Freedomways* 3 (Spring 1963): 146–47.

42. Baldwin, "The Dangerous Road before Martin Luther King," in *Collected Essays*, pp. 638–58.

43. King to Baldwin, Sept. 26, 1961, King Papers, Boston Univ.

44. Baldwin to King, Nov. 15, 1961, King Papers, Boston Univ.

45. In a letter of April 10, 1961, Isaacs Papers, Isaacs told Murray the UN demonstrations prompted the article "A Reporter at Large: Back to Africa," *New Yorker*, May 13, 1961, pp. 105–42.

46. Isaacs to Murray, April 10, 1961, Isaacs Papers.

47. Murray to Isaacs, May 28, 1961, Isaacs Papers.

48. Ware to Isaacs, June 18, 1961; Isaacs to Ware, June 19, 1961, Isaacs Papers.

49. June 13, 1961, Isaacs to Peggy Brooks; Brooks responded, asking him how to get in touch with Murray, June 15, 1961; nothing came of it, although Isaacs apparently forwarded this correspondence to Murray; Murray Papers.

50. Murray, *Song in a Weary Throat*, pp. 328, 331–32. The complete manuscript is in the Pauli Murray Papers.

51. Isaacs's interview with Kenneth Clark, Jan. 5, 1962, Isaacs Papers, Clark; Drake's speech was published as "The Negro's Stake in Africa," *Negro Digest*, June 1964, pp. 33–48.

52. Isaacs, "The American Negro and Africa; Some Notes" (Second Annual Conference of the American Society of African Culture, New York, June 28, 1959), Isaacs file, CIS/MIT: CIS Papers, Institute Archives and Special Collections, MIT.

53. Howe, "Strangers in Africa," *Reporter*, June 22, 1961, pp. 34–35.

54. See Penny M. Von Eschen, *Race against Empire: Black Americans and Anticolonialism, 1937–1957* (Ithaca: Cornell Univ. Press, 1997), pp. 145–66; Brenda Gayle Plummer, *Rising Wind: Black Americans and U.S. Foreign Affairs, 1935–1960* (Chapel Hill: Univ. of North Carolina Press, 1996), pp. 167–216.

55. *Facts on File*, March 9–15, 1967, pp. 79–80.

56. Noam Chomsky mentioned CIA funding of CIS projects in *The Chomsky Reader* (New York: Pantheon Books, 1987), p. 47; Donald Blackmer, an MIT political science professor who monitored CIA support for the center during the time Isaacs was working on his study, rejected any suggestion that Isaacs' own study might have been supported by the CIA. Blackmer said (e-mail to author, April 13, 2000), "I knew about the funding sources of all the Center's projects, both those supported by various Foundations and those supported by government agencies, including the CIA. One of my jobs, in fact, was to

prepare regular reports for the CIA on the projects it supported, none of which had anything to do with American politics or society. I can state with absolute certainty that Harold Isaacs's work was never supported by the CIA." As Blackmer saw him—and he knew him from the mid-1950s until his death—Isaacs was simply not the kind of man who would have knowingly worked for the CIA. "He was indeed fiercely independent and could never have tolerated such a situation." Isaacs' file in the CIS papers at the MIT Institute Archives and Special Collections contains appeals for funding from several foundations.

57. Mary F. Corey describes *The New Yorker*'s reluctant swing into the Cold War orbit in *The World through a Monocle: The New Yorker at Midcentury* (Cambridge: Harvard Univ. Press, 1999), pp. 58–76.

58. Frances Stonor Saunders, *The Cultural Cold War: The CIA and the World of Arts and Letters* (New York: New Press, 1999), p. 309.

59. Horton to Howe, March 30, 1961, Ascoli Papers.

60. White, *In Search of History: A Personal Adventure* (New York: Harper & Row, 1978), p. 375.

61. Memo from Horton to Ascoli, May 4, 1961; Howe to Horton, n.d., stamped received July 2, 1963, Ascoli Papers.

62. Rostow, "The Freedom Riders and the Future," *Reporter*, June 22, 1961, pp. 18–21.

63. "Why Yale Chaplain Rode: Christians Can't Be Outside," *Life*, June 2, 1961, p. 54.

64. Riesman to Woodward, April 24, 1962; Riesman to Woodward, Dec. 28, 1961, Woodward Papers.

65. Carleton to Glen and Vann Woodward, n.d. [Dec. 1961], Woodward Papers.

66. Woodward to Franklin, Feb. 13, 1961; Riesman to Woodward, Dec. 28, 1961, Woodward Papers.

67. Woodward to Shapiro, March 14, 1962; Shapiro to Woodward, March 22, 1962, Woodward to Clifford Durr, May 13, 1962, Woodward Papers; the files include other letters documenting Woodward's effort to publish the piece.

68. Woodward, "The Unreported Crisis in the Southern Colleges," *Harper's*, Oct. 1962, pp. 82–89.

69. Silver to Woodward, Oct. 19, 1962, Woodward Papers.

70. Edmund Wilson, *The Sixties: The Last Journal, 1960–1972,* ed. Lewis M. Dabney (New York: Farrar Straus Giroux, 1993), p. 170.

71. Hansberry, "A Challenge to Artists" (speech delivered at Rally to Abolish the House Un-American Activities Committee, Oct. 27, 1962), *Freedomways* 3 (Winter 1963): 35.

72. Baldwin to King, Nov. 15, 1961, King Papers, Boston Univ.

73. Clark, "The Duty of the Intellectual," in *Pathos of Power* (New York: Harper & Row, 1974), p. 23. When Bertrand Russell submitted Clark's speech to *Encounter* magazine, English poet Stephen Spender, one of the editors, turned it down. "I have read it and do not really think it is very good," he said. "It implies that white intellectuals are finished, and that the only hope for the future lies in Negro ones, citing James Baldwin and Ralph Ellison as examples. Do you know the works of these writers? Would you really think they

are such isolated examples in America?" Spender to Russell, Sept. 20, 1961, Clark Papers.

74. Isaacs' interview with Baldwin, July 27, 1961, and with Franklin, Jan. 4, 1962, Isaacs Papers.

75. "The Reminiscences of Kenneth B. Clark," interviewed in 1976 by Ed Edwin, Oral History Research Office, Columbia Univ.

76. Isaacs, "#23 - Re-interview, January 5, 1962: KENNETH CLARK," Isaacs Papers.

77. Fuller told this story in "Another Angle of Feeling," which, according to correspondence in the Fuller Papers, he offered unsuccessfully to the *Nation* (Carey McWilliams to Fuller, Sept. 28, 1962) and to the *Village Voice* (Dan Wolf to Fuller, Oct. 7, 1962), before he placed it in the *Chicago Jewish Forum*, which published it in vol. 21 (Spring 1963), pp. 213–16. This account is based on the published version except where indicated.

78. This statement comes from the untitled typescript of the article in the Fuller Papers. The *Chicago Jewish Forum* removed the reference to Barry Goldwater: "He [Mailer] also said that President Eisenhower had found it necessary to send federal troops into Little Rock in order, figuratively, to keep the Russians out of the Congo."

Chapter 6: "And Then Came Baldwin"

1. Farmer to Baldwin, Nov. 30, 1962, Congress of Racial Equality Papers, MSS 160 (Western Administration), State Historical Society of Wisconsin Archives, Madison.

2. Hansberry, *To Be Young, Gifted and Black: Lorraine Hansberry in Her Own Words*, adapted by Robert Nemiroff (New York: Vintage Books, 1995), p. 198; Podhoretz, "My Negro Problem—and Ours," *Doings and Undoings: The Fifties and After in American Writing* (New York: Noonday Press, 1964), p. 368.

3. Ross to author, Aug. 2, 1999.

4. James Baldwin file, *New Yorker* Records, Manuscripts and Archives Division, New York Public Library; Astor, Lenox and Tilden Foundations.

5. Jay Edgerton, "Book News: Racism Is Blasted by Negro Novelist," Minneapolis Sunday *Tribune*, Feb. 24, 1963, p. 4.

6. Hentoff, *The New Equality* (New York: Viking Press, 1965), p. 47.

7. Mayfield, "And Then Came Baldwin," *Freedomways* 3 (Spring 1963): 143–55.

8. Baldwin, "Down at the Cross," in *Collected Essays* (New York: Library of America, 1998), pp. 296–347, also the source of quotations in the paragraphs that follow.

9. Baldwin's appearance on that panel was announced in "Nationalism, Colonialism and the United States" (an announcement), *Liberator*, May 1961, p. 1; "LCA First Anniversary Meeting a Tremendous Success," ibid., June 1961, p. 1.

10. Angelou, *The Heart of a Woman* (New York: Bantam Books, 1997), p. 309.

11. Herbert Hill described those nights in Baldwin's apartment to the author; see also Baldwin, "Sweet Lorraine," in *Collected Essays*, p. 757, first published in *Esquire*, Nov. 1969.

12. Eve Auchincloss, Nancy Lynch, interviewers, "Disturber of the Peace: James Baldwin," *Mademoiselle*, May 1963, p. 175.

13. "James Baldwin," undated clip from *Nugget*, in Fuller Papers. The comment about African freedom struggles comes from "Disturber of the Peace: James Baldwin," p. 202.

14. Mailer, "Evaluations—Quick and Expensive Comments on the Talent in the Room," in *Advertisements for Myself* (New York: G. P. Putnam's Sons, 1959), p. 471.

15. Baldwin, "The Black Boy Looks at the White Boy," in *Collected Essays*, pp. 269–85, first published in *Esquire*, May 1961; Schlesinger, *A Thousand Days: John F. Kennedy in the White House* (Boston: Houghton Mifflin, 1965), p. 961.

16. Smart to author, Feb. 7, 2000.

17. "A Letter to My Nephew" appeared in the *Progressive*'s issue commemorating the Emancipation Proclamation's centennial, vol. 26 (Dec. 1962): 19–20. Other contributors included John Hope Franklin, C. Vann Woodward, and Lillian Smith.

18. Rexroth, "Baldwin's Scare Story of Race Relations: The Battle in Black and White," *San Francisco Examiner*, Feb. 3, 1963, Books, p. 17.

19. Fuller, "On Solving the Racial Puzzle: A Matter of Volition," retitled (possibly by Irving Howe) "Rexroth, Mr. Baldwin and White Liberalism" (typescript), Fuller Papers.

20. Howe to Fuller, April 20, 1963, Fuller Papers.

21. Howe to Fuller, April 30, 1963, Fuller Papers.

22. Howe, "Black Boys and Native Sons," *Dissent* 10 (Autumn 1963): 353–68.

23. Author's interview with Hill; Howe discusses his political past in *A Margin of Hope: An Intellectual Autobiography* (New York: Harcourt Brace Jovanovich, 1982), pp. 80ff.

24. Both of Ellison's replies to Howe, quoted below, come from Ellison, "The World and the Jug," *Shadow and Act* (New York: Random House, 1964), pp. 107–43.

25. Dupee, "James Baldwin and the 'Man,'" *New York Review of Books* 1 (Special issue, 1963), p. 2.

26. Coles, "Baldwin's Burden," *Partisan Review* 31 (Summer 1964): 409–16.

27. Fischer, "What the Negro Needs Most: A First Class Citizens' Council," *Harper's*, July 1962, pp. 12–19. The Fischer Papers include an outpouring of reader response, pro and con, to this piece. The King Papers in Boston include a series of 1958 letters in which Fischer proposed that King himself write such an essay. King apparently took the suggestion seriously; he sought Bayard Rustin's advice about whether he should write it (King to Rustin, Nov. 5, 1958).

28. Mayfield, "And Then Came Baldwin," pp. 144–45.

29. Podhoretz, *Breaking Ranks* (New York: Harper & Row, 1979), p. 124.

30. Podhoretz, "My Negro Problem—And Ours," pp. 354–71.

31. Podhoretz to Clark, Jan. 4, 1963, Clark Papers.

32. "Letters from Readers: My Negro Problem—1," *Commentary*, April 1963, pp. 338–50.

33. For more on Worthy, see Carol Polsgrove, *It Wasn't Pretty, Folks, But Didn't We Have Fun? Esquire in the Sixties* (New York: W. W. Norton, 1995), pp. 162–63.

34. "Disturber of the Peace: James Baldwin," p. 174.

35. Turner, "The Black Man's Burden: The White Liberal," *Dissent* 10 (Summer 1963): 215–16.

36. "To James Baldwin," in *The Courage for Truth: The Letters of Thomas Merton to Writers*, ed. Christine M. Bochen (New York: Farrar Straus Giroux, 1993), pp. 244–46.

37. Merton, "The Black Revolution: Letters to a White Liberal," in *Passion for Peace: The Social Essays*, ed. William H. Shannon. (New York: Crossroad, 1995), pp. 154–88.

38. Franklin to Logan, Sept. 24, 1962; Franklin to Berl I. Bernhard, Staff Director, U.S. Commission on Civil Rights, Sept. 24, 1962, Logan Papers, Manuscript Division, Moorland-Spingarn Research Center, Howard Univ. Franklin was not fully aware of the role his friend C. Vann Woodward played in this episode. While Woodward told both Franklin and the commission what he thought was wrong with the draft, in his letter to the commission he voiced his criticism in harsher terms. He said that manuscript "fails to meet the requirement of the contract for a history of 'the development and progress of civil rights in the United States during the last 100 years.' As I wrote him, it is 'not balanced, well proportioned, or adequate in its coverage.'" Woodward had *not* written Franklin that. He had told Franklin his title let him "in for a criticism that [his] book is not balanced, well proportioned or adequate in its coverage," as if he were helping to protect Franklin, not attacking him himself. He told the commission the report was "unsatisfactory" on another ground: its emphasis on one race was "wholly disproportionate," although a subtitle Franklin had added at Woodward's suggestion would help solve that problem. Speaking in its favor, he said the report was "forceful, spirited, and forthright," but in conclusion he damned Franklin's work with faint praise: "I would not claim that this report is particularly distinguished or outstanding, but it does strike me as competent and readable." Woodward to Franklin, Aug. 15, Sept. 9, 1962, Woodward to Berl I. Bernhard, U.S. Commission on Civil Rights, Woodward Papers. The published report did not carry Franklin's byline, although his work on it (and Woodward's, as his consultant) was acknowledged.

39. James Forman, *The Making of Black Revolutionaries* (Seattle: Univ. of Washington Press, 1997), pp. 294–308.

40. Baldwin describes this experience in transcript, Kay Boyle interview with James Baldwin, for Channel 13; Oral History Collection, Columbia Univ.; and in "Disturber of the Peace: James Baldwin," p. 201.

Chapter 7: This "Terrifying Crisis"

1. This account of the scene in the motel and the subsequent march is based on Andrew Young's *An Easy Burden: The Civil Rights Movement and the Transformation of America* (New York: HarperCollins, 1996), pp. 212–14.

2. King, "Letter from Birmingham City Jail," in *A Testament of Hope: The Essential Writings and Speeches of Martin Luther King* (New York: HarperCollins, 1986), pp. 292–95; the quotation in the paragraph below appears on p. 299.

3. Young, *An Easy Burden*, p. 224.

4. Weeks to King, May 29, 1963, King Papers, Martin Luther King Center.

5. Young, *An Easy Burden*, p. 240.

6. "Bunche Sees Civil-Rights Fight of Negroes in Climactic Phase," *New York Times*, June 9, 1963, p. 57.

7. Charles P. Henry, *Ralph Bunche: Model Negro or American Other?* (New York: New York Univ. Press, 1999), p. 222.

8. Hughes, in *Liberator*, July 1963, p. 4.

9. The *Time* article, May 17, 1963, pp. 26–27, carried a long quotation as a title, "At the root of the Negro problem is the necessity of the white man to find a way of living with the Negro in order to live with himself." "At a Crucial Time a Negro Talks Tough: 'There's a bill due that has to be paid,' " appeared in *Life*, May 24, 1963, pp. 81–90, with an accompanying story by Jane Howard.

10. "Kennedy Blamed by Baldwin," *New York Times*, May 13, 1963, p. 25.

11. Taylor Branch, *Parting the Waters: America in the King Years, 1954–63* (New York: Simon & Schuster, 1988), pp. 807–9.

12. Schlesinger offers an account of this meeting in *A Thousand Days: John F. Kennedy in the White House* (Boston: Houghton Mifflin, 1965), pp. 362–63, but my narrative of the meeting largely follows the account Clark gave to Jean Stein, Jan. 30, 1970 (typescript), Clark Papers; portions of this interview appeared in Stein's *American Journey: The Times of Robert Kennedy*, ed. George Plimpton (New York: Harcourt Brace Jovanovich, 1970). Stein was married to William vanden Heuvel, who was active in the Democratic Party, but published the book under her maiden name. Clark included a briefer account in his *King, Malcolm, Baldwin: Three Interviews* (Middletown, Conn.: Wesleyan Univ. Press, 1985), pp. 14–16, first published as *The Negro Protest: James Baldwin, Malcolm X, Martin Luther King Talk with Kenneth Clark* (Boston: Beacon Press, 1963).

13. This comes from Burke Marshall's recollection, in Stein, *American Journey*, p. 118.

14. King, "Bold Design for a New South," in *A Testament of Hope*, pp. 112–16, reprinted from *Nation*, March 30, 1963, pp. 259–62.

15. Schlesinger, *A Thousand Days*, p. 963.

16. Baldwin's recollection in Stein's *American Journey*, p. 119.

17. Branch, *Parting the Waters*, pp. 788–89. The reference to King's kitchen cabinet comes from Young, *An Easy Burden*, p. 200.

18. All comments from Shagaloff are from author's interviews.

19. Clark, *King, Malcolm, Baldwin*, pp. 51–52.

20. *New York Times*, May 25, 1963, pp. 1, 8; ibid., May 26, 1963, pp. 1, 59.

21. "Robert Kennedy Confers Today with Theater Men on Race Issue," *New York Times*, May 27, 1963, pp. 1, 19; "Negro Violence in North Feared/City Rights Leader Sees It Unless Equality Is Given," ibid., May 27, 1963, p. 19.

22. Henry Morgenthau III, producer of the television interviews, mentioned the rescheduling in "A Note about the Interviews," in *King, Malcolm, Baldwin*, p. vii; Gould, "TV: Challenge on Racism: James Baldwin Puts Problem Squarely in the Laps of All Americans," *New York Times*, May 30, 1963, pp. 1, 19.

23. "James Baldwin Rejects Despair Despite Race 'Drift and Danger,' " *New York Times*, June 3, 1963, pp. 1, 19.

24. Reston, "Washington: The Nation and the Parties on the Racial Issue," *New York Times*, June 7, 1963, p. 30.

25. James Campbell, *Talking at the Gates: A Life of James Baldwin* (New York: Viking Press, 1991), p. 175.

26. Warren, *Who Speaks for the Negro?* (New York: Vintage Books, 1966), p. 160.

27. Baldwin compared himself to Jeremiah in his debate with William F. Buckley, Cambridge Union Society, Feb. 18, 1965, BBC library videotape.

28. "James Baldwin 'Tense, Angry Cat,' " *Omaha World*, June 30, 1963.

29. *Sunday Times Weekly Review*, June 30, 1963.

30. Baldwin, interviewed by Fern Marja Eckman, Oct. 9, 1963, Columbia Univ. Oral History Project.

31. Clark, interviewed by Stein.

32. Johnson, "Memorial Day Address, Gettysburg, Pennsylvania, May 30, 1963," in *A Time for Action: A Selection from the Speeches and Writings of Lyndon B. Johnson, 1953–1964* (New York: Atheneum, 1964), p. 125.

33. The first quotation is from Mark Stern, *Calculating Visions: Kennedy, Johnson, and Civil Rights* (New Brunswick: Rutgers Univ. Press, 1992), p. 85; the second is from Taylor Branch, *Pillar of Fire: America in the King Years* (New York: Simon & Schuster, 1998), pp. 94–95.

34. "Nation-Wide Radio and Television Address on Race Problem in the U.S. Made by President Kennedy from the White House," June 11, 1963, mimeographed typescript, distributed to American nationals in Ibadan, West Africa, in my possession.

35. Stern, *Calculating Visions*, pp. 85–88.

36. Woodward, "The Populist Heritage and the Intellectual," in *The Burden of Southern History*, rev. ed. (Baton Rouge: Louisiana State Univ. Press, 1968), p. 166.

37. Baldwin, *No Name in the Street* in *Collected Essays* (New York: Library of America, 1998), p. 447.

38. Ann Waldron, *Eudora: A Writer's Life* (New York: Anchor Books, 1999), p. 268; Welty, "Where Is the Voice Coming From?," in *The Collected Stories of Eudora Welty* (San Diego: Harcourt Brace Jovanovich, 1980), p. 603.

39. Murray, "The Law As It Affects Desegregation: Implications of the Supreme Court Decision," *Radcliffe Quarterly* 47 (Aug. 1963): 19–28.

40. Eckman, *The Furious Passage of James Baldwin* (New York: M. Evans, 1966), pp. 200, 211–12. Eckman's biography is particularly useful because it is largely based on interviews with Baldwin himself, as well as with other sources, and the interviews were conducted so close in time to the events described. The transcripts of her interviews with Baldwin, available at the Oral History Research Office, Columbia Univ., enhance the worth of the book.

41. Baldwin, "Nothing Personal," in *Collected Essays*, p. 704.

42. The secretary is a friend of the author. For reports of the Paris activities, see "Civil Rights March Planned by 50 Americans in Paris," *New York Times*, Aug. 18, 1963, p. 50; "Americans Abroad Give Support to Rights March," ibid., Aug. 22, 1963, p. 18.

43. Joseph Barry, "Dateline: Your World. Baldwin—II," *New York Post*, Aug. 23,

1963, p. 42; "What the Marchers Really Want," *New York Times*, Aug. 25, sec. 6, pp. 7ff.

44. King to Harry Belafonte, July 23, 1963, King Papers, Martin Luther King Center.

45. Boyle, "No Other Place to Be," *Liberation*, Sept. 1963, p. 9.

46. Angelou, *All God's Children Need Traveling Shoes* (New York: Random House, 1986), pp. 123–27.

47. "Statement by James Baldwin," Sept. 16, 1963, Bayard Rustin Papers.

48. Baldwin, "We Can Change the Country," *Liberation*, Oct. 1963, pp. 7–8.

49. Eckman, *The Furious Passage of James Baldwin*, p. 214.

50. "NEGROES OUTRAGED, DEMAND FEDERAL GOVERNMENT ACT BEFORE NEGRO COMMUNITY IS FORCED TO SELF-DEFENSE," Sept. 18, 1963, Rustin Papers.

51. Angelou, *The Heart of a Woman* (New York: Bantam Books, 1997), p. 36.

52. For the speeches, see *New York Times*, Sept. 21, 1963, p. 63. Gloria E. K. Smart, Baldwin's sister (who was often with him during these years), wrote the author, Feb. 7, 2000, that Baldwin and Killens were not close friends, though they did meet "from time to time."

53. Jones, "What Does Nonviolence Mean?," in *Home: Social Essays* (Hopewell, N.J.: Ecco Press, 1998), pp. 133–54.

54. Dee and Davis describe their political life in *With Ossie and Ruby: In This Life Together* (New York: William Morrow, 1998).

55. "Negro Group Urges Christmas Boycott," *New York Times*, Sept. 22, 1963, pp. 1, 72.

56. See, e.g., Niebuhr, "Prospects for the South," *New Leader*, June 19, 1961, pp. 3–4.

57. "The Meaning of the Tragedy in Birmingham," a transcript of their dialogue, Sept. 22, 1963, in Niebuhr Papers.

58. "Rally to Mourn 6 Slain Negroes," *New York Times*, Sept. 19, 1963, p. 16; "Rallies in Nation Protest Killing of 6 in Alabama," ibid., Sept. 23, 1963, pp. 1, 23.

59. Baldwin, "We Can Change the Country," pp. 7–8; this is the speech he gave at the press conference. Roszak, "On the Killing of Children," *Liberation*, Nov. 1963, pp. 20–21.

60. I have based my account of the activities surrounding Freedom Day at Selma on Zinn, *You Can't Be Neutral on a Moving Train: A Personal History of Our Time* (Boston: Beacon Press, 1994), pp. 56–64; idem, *SNCC: The New Abolitionists* (Boston: Beacon Press, 1964), pp. 147–66; Forman, *The Making of Black Revolutionaries*, with a foreword by Julian Bond (Seattle: Univ. of Washington Press, 1997), pp. 345–54; and Fern Marja Eckman's interview with Baldwin, Oct. 9, 1963, Columbia Univ. Oral History Project.

61. Author's interview with Amelia Boynton.

62. Zinn, Kempton, and Pettigrew to editor of *New York Times*, Sept. 19, 1963, unpublished, SNCC Papers.

63. Zinn, *You Can't Be Neutral on a Moving Train*, pp. 62–64. Zinn published an account of the day (omitting James Baldwin's presence), "Registration in Alabama," *New Republic*, Oct. 26, 1963, pp. 11–12.

64. Author's interview with J. L. Chestnut Jr., for this quotation and the ones that follow. Chestnut also mentions Baldwin's visits and describes the Selma campaign in J. L. Chestnut Jr. and Julia Cass, *Black in Selma: The Uncommon Life of J. L. Chestnut Jr.* (New York: Farrar Straus Giroux, 1990).

65. Baldwin, "Nothing Personal," in *Collected Essays*, pp. 700–701.

66. Eckman, *The Furious Passage of James Baldwin*, p. 215.

67. Ibid., p. 195.

68. Baraka, "LeRoi Jones Talking," in *Home: Social Essays*, pp. 179–88.

69. Elkoff describes the roundtable in "Everybody Knows His Name," *Esquire*, Aug. 1964, pp. 120–21.

70. "Liberalism and the Negro: A Round-Table Discussion: James Baldwin, Nathan Glazer, Sidney Hook, Gunnar Myrdal," *Commentary*, March 1964, pp. 25–42, the source of the roundtable statements subsequently quoted. Reprinted by permission of *Commentary*; all rights reserved.

71. Reddick to King, Nov. 27, 1963, King Papers, Atlanta.

72. David J. Garrow, *Bearing the Cross: Martin Luther King, Jr., and the Southern Christian Leadership Conference* (New York: Vintage Books, 1988), p. 311.

73. Indecipherable signature on Pantheon Books letterhead to Clark, Dec. 12, 1963.

74. This and the following quotations from Elkoff's article appear in "Everybody Knows His Name," pp. 120–21, 63, 59.

75. Typescript, speech "On Race," n.d. [1964], Hayes Papers, Z. Smith Reynolds Library, Wake Forest Univ.; this episode involving the Elkoff assignment is described in the author's *It Wasn't Pretty, Folks, But Didn't We Have Fun? Esquire in the Sixties* (New York: W. W. Norton, 1995), pp. 116–17, based in part on an interview with Elkoff.

76. Als, "The Enemy Within," *New Yorker*, Feb. 16, 1998, p. 78.

Chapter 8: Calling the Question

1. Silver, *Running Scared: Silver in Mississippi* (Jackson: Univ. Press of Mississippi, 1984), p. 76. Silver describes his political life in Mississippi at length in this book.

2. Silver to Edgar Shook, *Time* bureau chief, Nov. 5, 1962, in Silver, *Mississippi: The Closed Society*, new enl. ed. (New York: Harcourt, Brace & World, 1966), p. 187. The Silver Papers contain several letters to and from Meg Greenfield at the *Reporter*; Silver apparently thought the *Reporter* might publish the article under a pseudonym, and he was miffed that he was not paid for it. Silver lists the dates of his *Economist* articles on a sheet in the Silver Papers; the article on the riot "Where White is Black," appeared Jan. 12, 1963, p. 111.

3. Bennett H. Wall told the author the story about the doll.

4. Silver to George [Tindall?], March 14, 1963, Silver Papers.

5. Silver, *Running Scared*, p. 86.

6. Clark to Silver, June 17, 1963; Potter to Silver, June 27, 1963, Silver Papers.

7. Tindall to Silver, July 1, 1963, Silver Papers.

8. Wade to Silver, July 6, 1963; this and other letters responding to his question are in the Silver Papers.

9. Henry A. Fly to Silver, Sept. 25, 1963, Silver Papers.

10. William B. Goodman to Silver, Oct. 21, 1963, Silver Papers.
11. Silver to Dunbar, Oct. 25, 1963, Silver Papers.
12. Silver to Dunbar, Oct. 22, 1963, Silver Papers.
13. Dunbar argued for book publication in a letter to Silver, Oct. 24, 1963, Silver Papers. Silver mentioned Dunbar's intervention in a letter to Dunbar, Oct. 28, 1963.
14. Wall to Silver, Oct. 31, 1963, Silver Papers.
15. Silver, *Running Scared*, pp. 90–92.
16. Typescript, speech, from Silver Papers, which also includes a tape of the speech. Bennett Wall supplied the detail about only two or three walking out.
17. *New York Times*, Nov. 8, 1963, pp. 1, 19.
18. The Silver Papers contain a list of periodicals that carried articles on the speech; they included those mentioned here: *St. Louis Post-Dispatch*, Dec. 21, 1963; McGill, "Hate Knows No Direction," *Saturday Evening Post*, Dec. 14, 1963, p. 10.
19. Fleming to Silver, Nov. 12, 1963, Silver Papers.
20. Silver to Detweiler, Nov. 25, 1963, Silver Papers, which include the cable and other responses to his speech.
21. Silver to Dunbar, Dec. 17, 1963, Silver Papers.
22. Johnston to Thomas J. Tubb, Dec. 2, 1963, Mississippi State Sovereignty Commission files.
23. Tubb to Johnston, Dec. 6, 1963, Mississippi State Sovereignty Commission files; Johnston reported on the appointment of the subcommittee in a Memorandum to the "File," Dec. 9, 1963, and in the "Director's Report to Sovereignty Commission members–Dec. 1963," Mississippi State Sovereignty Commission files; Sillers to Tubb, Feb. 14, 1964.
24. Silver, *Running Scared*, pp. 97–98.
25. Ibid., p. 98.
26. Silver to Teller, Aug. 10, 1964, Silver Papers.
27. Popham to Bennett [H. Wall], [1963], Silver Papers.
28. Silver to Davis, Oct. 5, 1964, Silver Papers.
29. This statement was provided to the author by June Shagaloff Alexander from her personal files.
30. Zinn, *The Southern Mystique* (New York: Alfred A. Knopf, 1964), pp. 186–90.
31. Author's interview with Zinn.
32. Zinn described the SRC's reception of his report in an interview by Katherine Shannon, Boston, Mass., Nov. 28, 1967, the Civil Rights Documentation Project, Moorland-Spingarn Research Center, Manuscript Division, Howard Univ. Claude Sitton's story on the report appeared in the *New York Times*, Nov. 14, 1962, pp. 1. 33; Zinn restated his findings in an article for the *Nation*, "Kennedy: The Reluctant Emancipator" (Dec. 1, 1962), in *The Zinn Reader: Writings on Disobedience and Democracy* (New York: Seven Stories Press, 1997), pp. 67–74. August Meier told the author that a civil rights activist who was secretly acting as a liaison with the FBI told him in the early 1960s that Zinn was a communist; Meier said the FBI was advertising Zinn "as a bona fide communist."
33. Zinn to Lewis and Forman, Oct. 1, 1963, SNCC Papers.

34. Zinn, "Registration in Alabama," *New Republic*, Oct. 26, 1963, pp. 11–12; the editorial was titled "Enforcing Civil Rights," pp. 3–4; for Marshall's response, see "Correspondence: Enforcing Civil Rights," *New Republic*, Nov. 16, 1963, pp. 29–30.

35. Marshall, *Federalism and Civil Rights* (New York: Columbia Univ. Press, 1964), pp. 40–41.

36. Zinn, "Action Urged to Enforce Legislation Now on Books," *New York Times*, Feb. 19, 1964, p. 38.

37. Zinn, "Incident in Hattiesburg," *Nation*, May 18, 1964, pp. 501–4.

38. Brauer, *John F. Kennedy and the Second Reconstruction* (New York: Columbia Univ. Press, 1977), p. 176.

39. Summary of meeting of Advisory Committee, Feb. 9–10, 1964, Zinn Papers; his files also include notes of other meetings of SNCC staff.

40. Lynd to author, Dec. 14, 1999.

41. Anne C. Loveland, *Lillian Smith: A Southerner Confronting the South* (Baton Rouge: Louisiana State Univ. Press, 1986), pp. 236, 251. The quotations come from a 1966 letter published in the *Atlanta Constitution*.

42. Lynd to Zinn, June 12 [1964], Zinn Papers; Lynd to Woodward, n.d., Woodward Papers.

43. Author's interview with Zinn.

44. An Aug. 26 memorandum in the Mississippi Sovereignty Commission files would strike a sinister note (considering the fate that had befallen three of the summer workers), recording information provided by the Mississippi Highway Patrol: Lynd's leadership in the summer project, his address, and his license plate number. See A. L. Hopkins on Mississippi State Sovereignty Commission letterhead to Director Erle Johnston, Aug. 26, 1964, Mississippi State Sovereignty Commission files. The memorandum also reports the highway patrol's effort to identify citizen band radios "operated by *COFO* or other agitation groups." The investigator had marked locations of these radios on a Mississippi map.

45. Memo to Bob Moses from Howard Zinn, "PLAN TO PREVENT OR MINIMIZE VIOLENCE AND TO MAINTAIN CONSTITUTIONAL RIGHTS IN MISSISSIPPI IN THE SUMMER OF 1964" [Spring 1964], Zinn Papers.

46. Lynd to Waskow, March 29, 1964; Waskow to Lynd, April 13, 1964, Zinn Papers.

47. Waskow to Lynd, April 22, 1964, Zinn Papers.

48. [Zinn] to Bond, April 26, 1964, Zinn Papers, which also include an undated typescript of the letter to the president.

49. Brauer, *John F. Kennedy and the Second Reconstruction*, p. 156.

50. Zinn to Ferguson, May 4, 1964, Zinn Papers.

51. Bond kept Zinn updated in several notes in May, Zinn Papers.

52. Coles has described his involvement in the movement on many occasions, and would play a larger role in this narrative if his major work on the movement, *Children of Crisis*, had not been published after the period treated here. Several of his magazine and journal articles from these years appear in *Farewell to the South* (Boston: Atlantic Monthly Press, 1972).

53. Author's interview with Zinn.

54. *Congressional Record*, June 15–16, 1964, pp. 13857–60, 13996–14013; this account of the hearing is drawn from this transcript.

55. Routing sheet, July 6, 1964, Ascoli Papers. Agent Lyn Nesbit from Sterling Lord had sent around Zinn's "Lyndon Johnson and the Mississippi Summer," July 2, 1964, Ascoli Papers.

56. Seth Cagin and Philip Dray, *We Are Not Afraid* (New York: Macmillan, 1988), pp. 375, 451.

57. Lynd used the phrase "a good thing with a tragic flaw" in a letter to author, Nov. 28, 1999. He analyzed the effect of Freedom Summer in "Freedom Summer: A Tragedy, Not a Melodrama," in *Living inside Our Hope: A Steadfast Radical's Thoughts on Rebuilding the Movement* (Ithaca: Cornell Univ. Press, 1997), pp. 27–35, where he also wrote about his involvement in the movement.

58. Forman, *The Making of Black Revolutionaries* (Seattle: Univ. of Washington Press, 1997), p. 382.

59. Halberstam, *The Children* (New York: Random House, 1998).

60. Warren, *Who Speaks for the Negro?* (New York: Vintage Books, 1966), pp. 125–26.

61. Author's interview with Lynd. Woodward raised the question, too, in a letter to Lynd, April 19, 1965, Woodward Papers.

62. Zinn, *Southern Mystique*, pp. 13, 231, 228.

63. Ellison, "If the Twain Shall Meet," in *Collected Essays*, ed. John F. Callahan (New York: Modern Library, 1995), pp. 563–76, first published in *Book Week*, Nov. 8, 1964. C. Vann Woodward voiced criticisms similar to Ellison's in his review of Zinn's *Southern Mystique*, "Southern Mythology," *Commentary*, May 1965, pp. 60–63.

64. Carleton to Woodward, Feb. 5, 1965, Woodward Papers.

65. Woodward, "From the First Reconstruction to the Second," *Harper's*, April 1965, pp. 128–33.

66. John L. Lewis, *Walking with the Wind* (New York: Simon & Schuster, 1998), pp. 336–42, and Alton Hornsby Jr., *Milestones in 20th-Century African-American History* (Detroit: Visible Ink Press/Gale Research, 1993), p. 79.

67. Zinn, "The Selma to Montgomery March," *The Zinn Reader*, pp. 108–11.

68. Walter Johnson, organizer of the historians' group, drew on other participants' accounts for "Historians Join the March on Montgomery," *South Atlantic Quarterly* 79 (Spring 1980): 158–74.

69. Author's interview with Franklin; Franklin also tells about his fear during the march in *Race and History: Selected Essays, 1938–1988* (Baton Rouge: Louisiana State Univ. Press), pp. 287–88.

70. In his memoir, *Thinking Back: The Perils of Writing History* (Baton Rouge: Louisiana State Univ. Press, 1986), p. 92, Woodward said that King had been "quoted as calling *The Strange Career* 'the historical Bible of the civil rights movement,' " and that comment has often been requoted. I have not located the source of that comment (other than Woodward himself), and it seems unlikely that a Baptist minister would refer to any book as a "Bible." When I interviewed Woodward, he traced the comment to King's remarks

at the Montgomery capitol. In the videotape of the live coverage of the speech (available in the Museum of Television and Radio in Manhattan), King does talk about *Strange Career,* but he does *not* refer to it as the movement's "Bible."

71. King, "Our God Is Marching On!" in *A Testament of Hope: The Essential Writings and Speeches of Martin Luther King* (New York: HarperCollins, 1986), p. 229. This is a transcription of a recording of the speech.

72. Hornsby, *Milestones in 20th-Century African-American History,* p. 81.

73. Eckman's interview with Baldwin, Oral History Research Office, Columbia Univ.

74. Zinn, *SNCC: The New Abolitionists* (Boston: Beacon Press: 1964), p. 13.

75. Woodward to Warren, Sept. 22, 1966, Warren Papers.

76. Woodward, "What Happened to the Civil Rights Movement?," *Harper's,* Jan. 1967, pp. 33–34.

77. Introduction to *King, Malcolm, Baldwin: Three Interviews* (Middletown, Conn.: Wesleyan Univ. Press, 1985), p. 5.

78. Clark, "Racial Progress and Retreat: A Personal Memoir," in *Race in America: The Struggle for Equality,* ed. Herbert Hill and James E. Jones Jr. (Madison: Univ. of Wisconsin Press, 1993), p. 18.

79. The author was present for this talk.

80. U.S. Information Agency, *Summaries of CEA and Race Advisory Board Initiative Studies,"* http://www.usinfo.state.gov/usa/race/091803.htm.

Postscript

1. Deggans, "Humans as Property: Should You Turn Away?," *St. Petersburg Times,* Oct. 19, 1998, LEXIS-NEXIS Academic Universe, General News Topics, Major Papers.

2. Barrett, *Integration at Ole Miss* (Chicago: Quadrangle Books, 1965), p. 244.

SELECT BIBLIOGRAPHY

This list contains selected books by writers who figure in *Divided Minds*; historical and biographical works are cited in notes and not listed here.

Angelou, Maya. *The Heart of a Woman*. New York: Bantam Books, 1997.

Aptheker, Herbert, ed. *A Documentary History of the Negro People in the United States*. Vol. 6. New York: Citadel Press, 1993.

Baldwin, James. *Collected Essays*. New York: Library of America, 1998.

———. *The Price of the Ticket: Collected Nonfiction, 1948–1985*. New York: St. Martin's/Marek, 1985.

Baraka, Amiri. *The Autobiography of LeRoi Jones*. Chicago: Lawrence Hill Books, 1997.

———. *Home: Social Essays*. Hopewell, N.J.: Ecco Press, 1998.

Cayton, Horace. *Long Old Road*. New York: Trident Press, 1965.

Chestnut, J. L., Jr., and Julia Cass. *Black in Selma: The Uncommon Life of J. L. Chestnut, Jr.* New York: Farrar Straus Giroux, 1990.

Clark, Kenneth. *King, Malcolm, Baldwin: Three Interviews*. Middletown, Conn.: Wesleyan Univ. Press, 1985.

———. *Pathos of Power*. New York: Harper & Row, 1974.

———. *Prejudice and Your Child*. Boston: Beacon Press, 1955.

Cruse, Harold. *The Crisis of the Negro Intellectual*. New York: William Morrow, 1967.

Du Bois, W. E. B. *The Autobiography of W. E. B. Du Bois*. Edited by Herbert Aptheker. New York: International Publishers, 1968.

———. *Writings by W. E. B. Du Bois in Periodicals Edited by Others*. Edited by Herbert Aptheker. Vol. 4, *1945–1961*. Millwood, N.Y.: Kraus-Thomson, 1982.

Dunbar, Leslie. *A Republic of Equals*. Ann Arbor: Univ. of Michigan Press, 1966.

East, P. D. *The Magnolia Jungle: The Life, Times and Education of a Southern Editor*. New York: Simon & Schuster, 1960.

Ellison, Ralph. *The Collected Essays of Ralph Ellison*. Edited by John F. Callahan. New York: Modern Library, 1995.

———. *Shadow and Act*. New York: Random House, 1964.

Ellison, Ralph, and Albert Murray. *The Selected Letters of Ralph Ellison and Albert Murray*. Edited by Albert Murray and John F. Callahan. New York: Modern Library, 2000.

Faulkner, William. *Essays, Speeches and Public Letters*. New York: Random House, 1965.

————. *Selected Letters of William Faulkner.* Edited by Joseph Blotner. New York: Random House, 1977.

Forman, James. *The Making of Black Revolutionaries.* Seattle: Univ. of Washington Press, 1997.

Franklin, John Hope. *Race and History: Selected Essays, 1938–1988.* Baton Rouge: Louisiana State Univ. Press, 1989.

Franklin, John Hope, and Alfred A. Moss. From *Slavery to Freedom: A History of African Americans.* 8th ed. Boston: McGraw-Hill, 1999.

Frazier, E. Franklin. *On Race Relations: Selected Writings.* Edited by G. Franklin Edwards. Chicago: Univ. of Chicago Press, 1968.

Gladney, Margaret Rose, ed. *How Am I to Be Heard? Letters of Lillian Smith.* Chapel Hill: Univ. of North Carolina Press, 1993.

Hansberry, Lorraine. *To Be Young, Gifted, and Black: Lorraine Hansberry in Her Own Words.* Adapted by Robert Nemiroff. New York: Vintage Books, 1995.

Hill, Herbert, ed. *Anger and Beyond: The Negro Writer in the United States.* New York: Harper & Row, 1966.

Hill, Herbert, and James E. Jones, eds. *Race in America: The Struggle for Equality.* Madison: Univ. of Wisconsin Press, 1993.

Himes, Chester. *My Life of Absurdity: The Later Years.* New York: Paragon House, 1976.

Hook, Sidney. *Out of Step: An Unquiet Life in the 20th Century.* New York: Harper & Row, 1987.

Howe, Irving. *A Margin of Hope: An Intellectual Autobiography.* New York: Harcourt Brace Jovanovich, 1982.

Hughes, Langston. *Good Morning Revolution: Uncollected Social Protest Writings by Langston Hughes.* Edited by Faith Berry. New York: Lawrence Hill, 1973.

Isaacs, Harold R. *The New World of Negro Americans: A Study from the Center for International Studies, Massachusetts Institute of Technology.* New York: John Day, 1963.

Jones, Lewis W. *The Cold Rebellion: The South's Oligarchy in Revolt.* London: Macgibbon & Kee, 1962.

Kazin, Alfred. *A Lifetime Burning in Every Moment: From the Journals of Alfred Kazin.* New York: HarperCollins, 1996.

King, Martin Luther, Jr. *The Papers of Martin Luther King, Jr.* Edited by Clayborne Carson. 3 vols. to date. Berkeley: Univ. of California Press, 1992–.

————. *A Testament of Hope: The Essential Writings and Speeches of Martin Luther King, Jr.* Edited by James Melvin Washington. New York: HarperCollins, 1986.

Kohler, Lotte, and Hans Saner, ed. *Hannah Arendt/Karl Jaspers Correspondence, 1926–1969.* New York: Harcourt Brace, 1993.

Lynd, Staughton, *Living inside Our Hope: A Steadfast Radical's Thoughts on Rebuilding the Movement.* Ithaca: Cornell Univ. Press, 1997.

Mailer, Norman. *Advertisements for Myself.* New York: G. P. Putnam's Sons, 1959.

————. *The Time of Our Time.* New York: Random House, 1998.

Merton, Thomas. *The Courage for Truth: The Letters of Thomas Merton to Writers.* Edited by Christine M. Bochen. New York: Farrar Straus Giroux, 1993.

————. *Passion for Peace: The Social Essays.* Edited by William H. Shannon. New York: Crossroad, 1995.

Murray, Albert. *South to a Very Old Place.* New York: Vintage Books, 1971.

Murray, Pauli. *Proud Shoes: The Story of an American Family.* Rev. ed. New York: Harper & Row, 1978.

————. *Song in a Weary Throat: An American Pilgrimage.* New York: Harper & Row, 1987.

Nichols, Charles H., ed. *Arna Bontemps/Langston Hughes: Letters, 1925–1967.* New York: Paragon House, 1990.

Niebuhr, Ursula M., ed. *Remembering Reinhold Niebuhr: Letters of Reinhold and Ursula M. Niebuhr.* New York: HarperCollins, 1991.

Phillips, William. *A Partisan View: Five Decades of the Literary Life.* New York: Stein & Day, 1983.

Podhoretz, Norman. *Breaking Ranks.* New York: Harper & Row, 1979.

————. *Ex-Friends: Falling Out with Allen Ginsberg, Lionel & Diana Trilling, Lillian Hellman, Hannah Arendt, and Norman Mailer.* New York: Free Press, 1999.

Quint, Howard. *Profile in Black and White: A Frank Portrait of South Carolina.* Washington, D.C.: Public Affairs Press, 1958.

Reddick, L. D. *Crusader without Violence: A Biography of Martin Luther King, Jr.* New York: Harper & Brothers, 1959.

Schlesinger, Arthur M., Jr. *The Politics of Hope.* Boston: Houghton Mifflin, 1963.

————. *Robert Kennedy and His Times.* Boston: Houghton Mifflin, 1978.

————. *A Thousand Days: John F. Kennedy in the White House.* Boston: Houghton Mifflin, 1965.

Sellers, Charles Grier, Jr., ed. *The Southerner as American.* Chapel Hill: Univ. of North Carolina Press, 1960.

Silver, James W. *Mississippi: The Closed Society.* New enl. ed. New York: Harcourt, Brace & World, 1966.

————. *Running Scared: Silver in Mississippi.* Jackson: Univ. Press of Mississippi, 1984.

Smith, Lillian. *Killers of the Dream.* New York: W. W. Norton, 1949. Reprint, New York: W. W. Norton, 1994.

————. *Now Is the Time.* New York: Dell, 1965.

Smith, William Gardner. *Return to Black America* (Englewood Cliffs, N.J.: Prentice-Hall, 1970.

Trilling, Diana. *The Beginning of the Journey: The Marriage of Diana and Lionel Trilling.* New York: Harcourt Brace, 1993.

Warren, Robert Penn. *Segregation: The Inner Conflict in the South.* New York: Random House, 1956.

————. *Who Speaks for the Negro?* New York: Vintage Books, 1966.

Woodward, C. Vann. *The Future of the Past.* New York: Oxford Univ. Press, 1989.

————. *The Strange Career of Jim Crow.* New York: Oxford Univ. Press, 1955. Revised and enlarged, 1957. Revised, 1966.

————. *Thinking Back: The Perils of Writing History.* Baton Rouge: Louisiana State Univ. Press, 1986.

Zinn, Howard. *SNCC: The New Abolitionists.* Boston: Beacon Press: 1964.

————. *The Southern Mystique.* New York: Alfred A. Knopf, 1964.

————. *You Can't Be Neutral on a Moving Train: A Personal History of Our Times.* Boston: Beacon Press, 1994.

————. *The Zinn Reader: Writings on Disobedience and Democracy.* New York: Seven Stories Press, 1997.

Locations of Correspondence Cited

Only collections cited more than once are included in this list; locations of other collections are given in the notes.

Arendt, Hannah. Manuscript Division, Library of Congress, Washington, D.C.

Ascoli, Max. Department of Special Collections, Boston Univ. Library.

Clark, Kenneth B. Manuscript Division, Library of Congress, Washington, D.C.

Clarke, John Henrik. Schomburg Center for Research in Black Culture, New York Public Library.

Drake, St. Clair. Schomburg Center for Research in Black Culture, New York Public Library.

Fischer, John. State Historical Society of Wisconsin Archives, Madison.

Fuller, Hoyt W. Archives/Special Collections Department, Robert W. Woodruff Library, Atlanta Univ. Center.

Gannett, Lewis. Manuscript Department, Houghton Library, Harvard Univ., Cambridge, Mass.

Hughes, Langston. Manuscripts and Archives, Yale Univ. Library, New Haven, Conn.

Isaacs, Harold. Institute Archives and Special Collections, Massachusetts Institute of Technology, Cambridge, Mass.

King, Martin Luther, Jr. Department of Special Collections, Boston Univ. Library.

King, Martin Luther, Jr. King Library and Archives, Atlanta (location at time of this book's writing).

Logan, Rayford. Diaries. Manuscript Division, Library of Congress, Washington, D.C.

Logan, Rayford. Papers. Manuscript Division, Moorland-Spingarn Research Center, Howard Univ., Washington, D.C.

Mayfield, Julian. Schomburg Center for Research in Black Culture, New York Public Library.

Mississippi State Sovereignty Commission. Mississippi Department of Archives and History, Jackson.

Murray, Pauli. Schlesinger Library, Harvard Univ., Cambridge, Mass.

Niebuhr, Reinhold. Manuscript Division, Library of Congress, Washington, D.C.

Rustin, Bayard. Manuscript Division, Library of Congress (microfilm).

Silver, James. Archives and Special Collections, Library, Univ. of Mississippi, Oxford.

Student Nonviolent Coordinating Committee (microfilm). King Library and Archives, Atlanta.

Warren, Robert Penn. Manuscripts and Archives, Yale Univ. Library, New Haven, Conn.

Woodward, C. Vann. Manuscripts and Archives, Yale Univ. Library, New Haven, Conn.

Wright, Richard. Manuscripts and Archives, Yale Univ. Library, New Haven, Conn.

Zinn, Howard. State Historical Society of Wisconsin Archives, Madison (microfilm).

INDEX

ABOUT THE AUTHOR

Born in Kentucky, Carol Claxon Polsgrove lived in West Africa (in Ghana—then the Gold Coast—and Nigeria) in the late 1940s and 1950s as the daughter of white missionaries. Returning to the United States in 1960, she earned a B.A. from Wake Forest College in Winston-Salem, North Carolina. After a year in Europe, she worked at the Associated Press in Louisville in 1967–68, and earned M.A. and Ph.D. degrees from the University of Louisville. She taught at universities in Kentucky and California, wrote for national magazines, and was an editor at the *Progressive* and *Mother Jones* magazines before joining the faculty of the School of Journalism at Indiana University at Bloomington. She is the author of *It Wasn't Pretty, Folks, But Didn't We Have Fun? Esquire in the Sixties* (W. W. Norton, 1995).